naked

BY THE SAME AUTHOR
Barrel Fever

naked

david sedaris

LITTLE, BROWN AND COMPANY *Boston New York Toronto London*

Copyright © 1997 by David Sedaris

All rights reserved. No part of this book may be reproduced in any form or by any electronic or mechanical means, including information storage and retrieval systems, without permission in writing from the publisher, except by a reviewer who may quote brief passages in a review.

First Edition

Author's note: The events described in these stories are real. Other than the family members, the characters have fictitious names and identifying characteristics.

Library of Congress Cataloging-in-Publication Data

Sedaris, David.
    Naked / by David Sedaris. — 1st ed.
      p.   cm.
    ISBN 0-316-77949-0
    1. Sedaris, David — Biography. 2. Humorists, American — 20th century — Biography. 3. United States — Social life and customs — 20th century — Humor   I. Title.
    PS3569.E314Z469   1997
    818'.5402 — dc21
    [B]   96-44566

10   9   8   7   6   5   4

MV-NY

Book design by Caroline Hagen

Published simultaneously in Canada by Little, Brown & Company (Canada) Limited

Printed in the United States of America

For my sister Lisa

CONTENTS

contents

viii

naked

chipped beef

I'm thinking of asking the servants to wax my change before placing it in the Chinese tank I keep on my dresser. It's important to have clean money — not new, but well maintained. That's one of the tenets of my church. It's not mine *personally*, but the one I attend with my family: the Cathedral of the Sparkling Nature. It's that immense Gothic building with the towers and bells and statues of common people poised to leap from the spires. They offer tours and there's an open house the first Sunday of every October. You should come! Just don't bring your camera, because the flash tends to spook the horses, which is a terrible threat to me and my parents, seeing as the reverend insists that we occupy the first pew. He rang us up not long ago, tipsy — he's a tippler — saying that our faces brought him closer to God. And it's true, we're terribly good-looking people. They're using my mother's profile on the new monorail token, and as for my father and me, the people at NASA want to design a lunar module based on the shape of our skulls. Our cheekbones are aeronautic and the clefts of our chins can hold up to three dozen BBs at a time. When asked, most people say that my greatest asset is my skin, which glows — it really does! I have to tie a sock over my eyes in order to fall asleep at night. Others like my eyes or my perfect, gleaming teeth, my thick head of hair or my imposing stature, but if you want my opinion, I think my most outstanding feature is my ability to accept a compliment.

Because we are so smart, my parents and I are able to see through people as if they were made of hard, clear plastic. We know what they look like naked and can see the desperate inner workings of their hearts, souls, and intestines. Someone might say, "How's it hangin', big guy," and I can smell his envy, his fumbling desire to win my good graces with a casual and inappropriate folksiness that turns my stomach with pity. How's it hanging, indeed. They know nothing about me and my way of life; and the world, you see, is filled with people like this.

Take, for example, the reverend, with his trembling hands and waxy jacket of skin. He's no more complex than one of those five-piece wooden puzzles given to idiots and schoolchildren. He wants us to sit in the front row so we won't be a distraction to the other parishioners, who are always turning in their pews, craning their necks to admire our physical and spiritual beauty. They're enchanted by our breeding and want to see firsthand how we're coping with our tragedy. Everywhere we go, my parents and I are the center of attention. "It's them! Look, there's the son! Touch him, grab for his tie, a lock of his hair, anything!"

The reverend hoped that by delivering his sermon on horseback, he might regain a bit of attention for himself, but even with the lariat and his team of prancing Clydesdales, his plan has failed to work. At least with us seated in the front row, the congregation is finally facing forward, which is a step in the right direction. If it helps bring people closer to

naked

God, we'd be willing to perch on the pipe organ or lash ourselves to the original stainless-steel cross that hangs above the
altar. We'd do just about anything because, despite our recent
hardships, our first duty is to help others. The Inner City
Picnic Fund, our Annual Headache Drive, the Polo Injury
Wing at the local Memorial Hospital: we give unspeakable
amounts to charity, but you'll never hear us talk about it. We
give anonymously because the sackfuls of thank-you letters
break our hearts with their clumsy handwriting and hopeless
phonetic spelling. Word gets out that we're generous *and*
good-looking, and before you know it our front gate will become a campsite for fashion editors and crippled children,
who tend to ruin the grass with the pointy shanks of their
crutches. No, we do what we can but with as little fanfare as
possible. You won't find us waving from floats or marching
alongside the Grand Pooh-bah, because that would only
draw attention to ourselves. Oh, you see the hangers-on doing that sort of thing all the time, but it's cheap and foolish
and one day they'll face the consequences of their folly.
They're hungry for something they know nothing about, but
we, we know all too well that the price of fame is the loss of
privacy. Public displays of happiness only encourage the
many kidnappers who prowl the leafy estates of our better
neighborhoods.

When my sisters were taken, my father crumpled the ransom note and tossed it into the eternal flame that burns beside the mummified Pilgrim we keep in the dining hall of
our summer home in Olfactory. We don't negotiate with
criminals, because it's not in our character. Every now and
then we think about my sisters and hope they're doing well,
but we don't dwell upon the matter, as that only allows the
kidnappers to win. My sisters are gone for the time being
but, who knows, maybe they'll return someday, perhaps
when they're older and have families of their own. In the

chipped beef

3

meantime, I am left as the only child and heir to my parents' substantial fortune. Is it lonely? Sometimes. I've still got my mother and father and, of course, the servants, several of whom are extraordinarily clever despite their crooked teeth and lack of breeding. Why, just the other day I was in the stable with Duncan when . . .

"Oh, for God's sake," my mother said, tossing her wooden spoon into a cauldron of chipped-beef gravy. "Leave that goddamned cat alone before I claw you myself. It's bad enough you've got her tarted up like some two-dollar whore. Take that costume off her and turn her loose before she runs away just like the last one."

Adjusting my glasses with my one free hand, I reminded her that the last cat had been hit by a car.

"She did it on purpose," my mother said. "It was her only way out, and you drove her to it with your bullshit about eating prime rib with the Kennedys or whatever the hell it was you were yammering on about that day. Go on now, and let her loose. Then I want you to run out to the backyard and call your sisters out of that ditch. Find your father while you're at it. If he's not underneath his car, he's probably working on the septic tank. Tell them to get their asses to the table, or they'll be eating my goddamned fist for dinner."

It wasn't that we were poor. According to my parents, we were far from it, just not far enough from it to meet my needs. I wanted a home with a moat rather than a fence. In order to get a decent night's sleep, I needed an airport named in our honor.

"You're a snob," my mother would say. "That's your problem in a hard little nutshell. I grew up around people like you, and you know what? I couldn't stand them. Nobody could."

No matter what we had — the house, the cars, the vacations — it was never enough. Somewhere along the line a

naked

4

terrible mistake had been made. The life I'd been offered was completely unacceptable, but I never gave up hope that my real family might arrive at any moment, pressing the doorbell with their white-gloved fingers. "Oh, Lord Chisselchin," they'd cry, tossing their top hats in celebration, "thank God we've finally found you."

"It ain't going to happen," my mother said. "Believe me, if I was going to steal a baby, I would have taken one that didn't bust my ass every time I left my coat lying on the sofa. I don't know how it happened, but you're mine. If that's a big disappointment for you, just imagine what *I* must feel."

While my mother grocery-shopped, I would often loiter near the front of the store. It was my hope that some wealthy couple would stuff me into the trunk of their car. They might torture me for an hour or two, but after learning that I was good with an iron, surely they would remove my shackles and embrace me as one of their own.

"Any takers?" my mother would ask, wheeling her loaded grocery cart out into the parking lot.

"Don't you know any childless couples?" I'd ask. "Someone with a pool or a private jet?"

"If I did, you'd be the first one to know."

My displeasure intensified with the appearance of each new sister.

"You have *how many* children in your family?" the teachers would ask. "I'm guessing you must be Catholic, am I right?"

It seemed that every Christmas my mother was pregnant. The toilet was constantly filled with dirty diapers, and toddlers were forever padding into my bedroom, disturbing my seashell and wine-bottle collections.

I had no notion of the exact mechanics, but from overhearing the neighbors, I understood that our large family had something to do with my mother's lack of control. It was

chipped beef

her fault that we couldn't afford a summerhouse with bay windows and a cliffside tennis court. Rather than improve her social standing, she chose to spit out children, each one filthier than the last.

It wasn't until she announced her sixth pregnancy that I grasped the complexity of the situation. I caught her in the bedroom, crying in the middle of the afternoon.

"Are you sad because you haven't vacuumed the basement yet?" I asked. "I can do that for you if you want."

"I know you can," she said. "And I appreciate your offer. No, I'm sad because, shit, because I'm going to have a baby, but this is the last one, I swear. After this one I'll have the doctor tie my tubes and solder the knot just to make sure it'll never happen again."

I had no idea what she was talking about — a tube, a knot, a soldering gun — but I nodded my head as if she and I had just come to some sort of a private agreement that would later be finalized by a team of lawyers.

"I can do this one more time but I'm going to need your help." She was still crying in a desperate, sloppy kind of way, but it didn't embarrass me or make me afraid. Watching her slender hands positioned like a curtain over her face, I understood that she needed more than just a volunteer maid. And, oh, I would be that person. A listener, a financial advisor, even a friend: I swore to be all those things and more in exchange for twenty dollars and a written guarantee that I would always have my own private bedroom. That's how devoted I was. And knowing what a good deal she was getting, my mother dried her face and went off in search of her pocketbook.

a plague of tics

When the teacher asked if she might visit with my mother, I touched my nose eight times to the surface of my desk.

"May I take that as a 'yes'?" she asked.

According to her calculations, I had left my chair twenty-eight times that day. "You're up and down like a flea. I turn my back for two minutes and there you are with your tongue pressed against that light switch. Maybe they do that where you come from, but here in my classroom we don't leave our seats and lick things whenever we please. That is Miss Chestnut's light switch, and she likes to keep it dry. Would you like me to come over to your house and put my tongue on *your* light switches? Well, would you?"

I tried to picture her in action, but my shoe was calling. *Take me off,* it whispered. *Tap my heel against your forehead three times. Do it now, quick, no one will notice.*

"Well?" Miss Chestnut raised her faint, penciled eyebrows. "I'm asking you a question. Would you or would you not want me licking the light switches in your house?"

I slipped off my shoe, pretending to examine the imprint on the heel.

"You're going to hit yourself over the head with that shoe, aren't you?"

It wasn't "hitting," it was tapping; but still, how had she known what I was about to do?

"Heel marks all over your forehead," she said, answering my silent question.

"You should take a look in the mirror sometime. Shoes are dirty things. We wear them on our feet to protect ourselves against the soil. It's not healthy to hit ourselves over the head with shoes, is it?"

I guessed that it was not.

"Guess? This is not a game to be guessed at. I don't 'guess' that it's dangerous to run into traffic with a paper sack over my head. There's no guesswork involved. These things are facts, not riddles." She sat at her desk, continuing her lecture as she penned a brief letter. "I'd like to have a word with your mother. You do have one, don't you? I'm assuming you weren't raised by animals. Is she blind, your mother? Can she see the way you behave, or do you reserve your antics exclusively for Miss Chestnut?" She handed me the folded slip of paper. "You may go now, and on your way out the door I'm asking you please not to bathe my light switch with your germ-ridden tongue. It's had a long day; we both have."

It was a short distance from the school to our rented house, no more than six hundred and thirty-seven steps, and on a good day I could make the trip in an hour, pausing every few feet to tongue a mailbox or touch whichever single leaf or blade of grass demanded my attention. If I were to lose count of my steps, I'd have to return to the school and begin again. "Back so soon?" the janitor would ask. "You just can't get enough of this place, can you?"

He had it all wrong. I wanted to be at home more than

naked

anything, it was getting there that was the problem. I might touch the telephone pole at step three hundred and fourteen and then, fifteen paces later, worry that I hadn't touched it in exactly the right spot. It needed to be touched again. I'd let my mind wander for one brief moment and then doubt had set in, causing me to question not just the telephone pole but also the lawn ornament back at step two hundred and nineteen. I'd have to go back and lick that concrete mushroom one more time, hoping its guardian wouldn't once again rush from her house shouting, "Get your face out of my toadstool!" It might be raining or maybe I had to go to the bathroom, but running home was not an option. This was a long and complicated process that demanded an oppressive attention to detail. It wasn't that I enjoyed pressing my nose against the scalding hood of a parked car — pleasure had nothing to do with it. A person *had* to do these things because nothing was worse than the anguish of not doing them. Bypass that mailbox and my brain would never for one moment let me forget it. I might be sitting at the dinner table, daring myself not to think about it, and the thought would revisit my mind. *Don't think about it.* But it would already be too late and I knew then exactly what I had to do. Excusing myself to go to the bathroom, I'd walk out the front door and return to that mailbox, not just touching but jabbing, practically pounding on the thing because I thought I hated it so much. What I really hated, of course, was my mind. There must have been an off switch somewhere, but I was damned if I could find it.

I didn't remember things being this way back north. Our family had been transferred from Endicott, New York, to Raleigh, North Carolina. That was the word used by the people at IBM, *transferred.* A new home was under construction, but until it was finished we were confined to a rental property built to resemble a plantation house. The building

a plague of tics

9

sat in a treeless, balding yard, its white columns promising a majesty the interior failed to deliver. The front door opened onto a dark, narrow hallway lined with bedrooms not much larger than the mattresses that furnished them. Our kitchen was located on the second floor, alongside the living room, its picture window offering a view of the cinder-block wall built to hold back the tide of mud generated by the neighboring dirt mound.

"Our own little corner of hell," my mother said, fanning herself with one of the shingles littering the front yard.

Depressing as it was, arriving at the front stoop of the house meant that I had completed the first leg of that bitter-tasting journey to my bedroom. Once home I would touch the front door seven times with each elbow, a task made more difficult if there was someone else around. "Why don't you try the knob," my sister Lisa would say. "That's what the rest of us do, and it seems to work for us." Inside the house there were switches and doorstops to be acknowledged. My bedroom was right there off the hallway, but first I had business to tend to. After kissing the fourth, eighth, and twelfth carpeted stair, I wiped the cat hair off my lips and proceeded to the kitchen, where I was commanded to stroke the burners of the stove, press my nose against the refrigerator door, and arrange the percolator, toaster, and blender into a straight row. After making my rounds of the living room, it was time to kneel beside the banister and blindly jab a butter knife in the direction of my favorite electrical socket. There were bulbs to lick and bathroom faucets to test before finally I was free to enter my bedroom, where I would carefully align the objects on my dresser, lick the corners of my metal desk, and lie upon my bed, rocking back and forth and thinking of what an odd woman she was, my third-grade teacher, Miss Chestnut. Why come here and lick my switches when she never used the one she had? Maybe she was drunk.

naked

Her note had asked if she might visit our home in order to discuss what she referred to as my "special problems."

"Have you been leaving your seat to lick the light switch?" my mother asked. She placed the letter upon the table and lit a cigarette.

"Once or twice," I said.

"Once or twice what? Every half hour? Every ten minutes?"

"I don't know," I lied. "Who's counting?"

"Well, your goddamned math teacher, for one. That's her *job*, to count. What, do you think she's not going to notice?"

"Notice what?" It never failed to amaze me that people might notice these things. Because my actions were so intensely private, I had always assumed they were somehow invisible. When cornered, I demanded that the witness had been mistaken.

"What do you mean, 'notice what?' I got a phone call just this afternoon from that lady up the street, that Mrs. Keening, the one with the twins. She says she caught you in her front yard, down on your hands and knees kissing the evening edition of her newspaper."

"I wasn't kissing it. I was just trying to read the headline."

"And you had to get that close? Maybe we need to get you some stronger glasses."

"Well, maybe we do," I said.

"And I suppose this Miss . . ." My mother unfolded the letter and studied the signature. "This Miss Chestnut is mistaken, too? Is that what you're trying to tell me? Maybe she has you confused with the other boy who leaves his seat to lick the pencil sharpener or touch the flag or whatever the hell it is you do the moment her back is turned?"

"That's very likely," I said. "She's old. There are spots on her hands."

"How many?" my mother asked.

On the afternoon that Miss Chestnut arrived for her visit, I was in my bedroom, rocking. Unlike the obsessive counting and touching, rocking was not a mandatory duty but a voluntary and highly pleasurable exercise. It was my hobby, and there was nothing else I would rather do. The point was not to rock oneself to sleep: This was not a step toward some greater goal. It was the goal itself. The perpetual movement freed my mind, allowing me to mull things over and construct elaborately detailed fantasies. Toss in a radio, and I was content to rock until three or four o'clock in the morning, listening to the hit parade and discovering that each and every song was about me. I might have to listen two or three hundred times to the same song, but sooner or later its private message would reveal itself. Because it was pleasant and relaxing, my rocking was bound to be tripped up, most often by my brain, which refused to allow me more than ten consecutive minutes of happiness. At the opening chords of my current favorite song, a voice would whisper, *Shouldn't you be upstairs making sure there are really one hundred and fourteen peppercorns left in that small ceramic jar? And, hey, while you're up there, you might want to check the iron and make sure it's not setting fire to the baby's bedroom.* The list of demands would grow by the moment. *What about that television antenna? Is it still set into that perfect* V, *or has one of your sisters destroyed its integrity. You know, I was just wondering how tightly the lid is screwed onto that mayonnaise jar. Let's have a look, shall we?*

I would be just on the edge of truly enjoying myself, this close to breaking the song's complex code, when my thoughts would get in the way. The trick was to bide my time until the record was no longer my favorite, to wait until it had slipped from its number-one position on the charts and fool my mind into believing I no longer cared.

I was coming to terms with "The Shadow of Your Smile"

naked

when Miss Chestnut arrived. She rang the bell, and I cracked open my bedroom door, watching as my mother invited her in.

"You'll have to forgive me for these boxes." My mother flicked her cigarette out the door and into the littered yard. "They're filled with crap, every last one of them, but God forbid we throw anything away. Oh no, we can't do that! My husband's saved it all: every last Green Stamp and coupon, every outgrown bathing suit and scrap of linoleum, it's all right here along with the rocks and knotted sticks he swears look just like his old department head or associate district manager or some goddamned thing." She mopped at her forehead with a wadded paper towel. "Anyway, to hell with it. You look like I need a drink, scotch all right?"

Miss Chestnut's eyes brightened. "I really shouldn't but, oh, why not?" She followed my mother up the stairs. "Just a drop with ice, no water."

I tried rocking in bed, but the sound of laughter drew me to the top of the landing, where from my vantage point behind an oversized wardrobe box, I watched the two women discuss my behavior.

"Oh, you mean the touching," my mother said. She studied the ashtray that sat before her on the table, narrowing her eyes much like a cat catching sight of a squirrel. Her look of fixed concentration suggested that nothing else mattered. Time had stopped, and she was deaf to the sounds of the rattling fan and my sisters' squabbling out in the driveway. She opened her mouth just slightly, running her tongue over her upper lip, and then she inched forward, her index finger prodding the ashtray as though it were a sleeping thing she was trying to wake. I had never seen myself in action, but a sharp, stinging sense of recognition told me that my mother's impersonation had been accurate.

"Priceless!" Miss Chestnut laughed, clasping her hands in

a plague of tics

delight. "Oh, that's very good, you've captured him perfectly. Bravo, I give you an A-plus."

"God only knows where he gets it from," my mother said. "He's probably down in his room right this minute, counting his eyelashes or gnawing at the pulls on his dresser. One, two o'clock in the morning and he'll still be at it, rattling around the house to poke the laundry hamper or press his face against the refrigerator door. The kid's wound too tight, but he'll come out of it. So, what do you say, another scotch, Katherine?"

Now she was Katherine. Another few drinks and she'd probably be joining us for our summer vacation. How easy it was for adults to bond over a second round of cocktails. I returned to my bed, cranking up the radio so as not to be distracted by the sound of their cackling. Because Miss Chestnut was here in my home, I knew it was only a matter of time before the voices would order me to enter the kitchen and make a spectacle of myself. Maybe I'd have to suck on the broom handle or stand on the table to touch the overhead light fixture, but whatever was demanded of me, I had no choice but to do it. The song that played on the radio posed no challenge whatsoever, the lyric as clear as if I'd written it myself. "Well, I think I'm going out of my head," the man sang, "yes, I think I'm going out of my head."

Following Miss Chestnut's visit, my father attempted to cure me with a series of threats. "You touch your nose to that windshield one more time and I'll guarantee you'll wish you hadn't," he said driving home from the grocery store with a lapful of rejected, out-of-state coupons. It was virtually impossible for me to ride in the passenger seat of a car and not press my nose against the windshield, and now that the activity had been forbidden, I wanted it more than anything. I tried closing my eyes, hoping that might eliminate my desire, but found myself thinking that perhaps *he* was the one who should close his eyes. So what if I wanted to touch my nose to the windshield? Who was it hurting? Why was it that he could repeatedly worry his change and bite his lower lip without the threat of punishment? My mother smoked and Miss Chestnut massaged her waist twenty, thirty times a day — and here *I* couldn't press my nose against the windshield of a car? I opened my eyes, defiant, but when he caught me moving toward my target, my father slammed on the brakes.

"You like that, did you?" He handed me a golf towel to wipe the blood from my nose. "Did you like the feel of that?"

Like was too feeble for what I felt. I loved it. If mashed with the right amount of force, a blow to the nose can be positively narcotic. Touching objects satisfied a mental itch, but the task involved a great deal of movement: run upstairs, cross the room, remove a shoe. I soon found those same urges could be fulfilled within the confines of my own body. Punching myself in the nose was a good place to start, but the practice was dropped when I began rolling my eyes deep in their sockets, an exercise that produced quick jolts of dull, intoxicating pain.

"I know exactly what you're talking about," my mother said to Mrs. Shatz, my visiting fourth-grade teacher. "The eyes rolling every which way, it's like talking to a slot machine. Hopefully, one day he'll pay off, but until then, what do you say we have ourselves another glass of wine?"

"Hey, sport," my father said, "if you're trying to get a good look at the contents of your skull, I can tell you right now that you're wasting your time. There's nothing there to look at, and these report cards prove it."

He was right. I had my nose pressed to the door, the carpet, and the windshield but not, apparently, to the grindstone.

School held no interest whatsoever. I spent my days waiting to return to the dark bedroom of our new house, where I could roll my eyes, listen to the radio, and rock in peace.

I took to violently shaking my head, startled by the feel of my brain slamming against the confines of my skull. It felt so good and took so little time; just a few quick jerks and I was satisfied for up to forty-five seconds at a time.

"Have a seat and let me get you something cool to drink." My mother would leave my fifth- and then my sixth-grade teachers standing in the breakfast nook while she stepped into the kitchen to crack open a tray of ice. "I'm guessing you're here about the head-shaking, am I right?" she'd shout. "That's my boy, all right, no flies on him." She suggested my teachers interpret my jerking head as a nod of agreement. "That's what I do, and now I've got him washing the dishes for the next five years. I ask, he yanks his head, and it's settled. Do me a favor, though, and just don't hold him after five o'clock. I need him at home to straighten up and make the beds before his father gets home."

This was part of my mother's act. She played the ring-leader, blowing the whistle and charming the crowd with her jokes and exaggerated stories. When company came, she often pretended to forget the names of her six children. "Hey, George, or Agnes, whatever your name is, how about running into the bedroom and finding my cigarette lighter." She noticed my tics and habits but was never shamed or seriously bothered by any of them. Her observations would be collected and delivered as part of a routine that bore little resemblance to our lives.

"It's a real stretch, but I'm betting you're here about the tiny voices," she said, offering a glass of sherry to my visiting seventh-grade teacher. "I'm thinking of either taking him to

naked

16

an exorcist or buying him a doll so he can bring home some money as a ventriloquist."

It had come out of nowhere, my desperate urge to summon high-pitched noises from the back of my throat. These were not words, but sounds that satisfied an urge I'd never before realized. The sounds were delivered not in my voice but in that of a thimble-sized, temperamental diva clinging to the base of my uvula. "Eeeeeeee — ummmmmmmm-mmm — ahhhh — ahhh — meeeeeeee." I was a host to these wailings but lacked the ability to control them. When I cried out in class, the teachers would turn from their blackboards with increasingly troubled expressions. "Is someone rubbing a balloon? Who's making that noise?"

I tried making up excuses, but everything sounded implausible. "There's a bee living in my throat." Or "If I don't exercise my vocal cords every three minutes, there's a good chance I'll never swallow again." The noise-making didn't replace any of my earlier habits, it was just another addition to what had become a freakish collection of tics. Worse than the constant yelps and twitchings was the fear that tomorrow might bring something even worse, that I would wake up with the urge to jerk other people's heads. I might go for days without rolling my eyes, but it would all come back the moment my father said, "See, I knew you could quit if you just put your mind to it. Now, if you can just keep your head still and stop making those noises, you'll be set."

Set for what? I wondered. Often while rocking, I would imagine my career as a movie star. There I was attending the premiere beneath a floodlit sky, a satin scarf tied just so around my throat. I understood that most actors probably didn't interrupt a love scene to press their noses against the camera or wail a quick "Eeeeeee — ahhhhhhh" during a dramatic monologue, but in my case the world would be willing to make an exception. "This is a moving and touching film," the papers would report. "An electrifying, eye-popping performance that has audiences squealing and the critics nodding, 'Oscar, Oscar, Oscar.'"

I'd like to think that some of my nervous habits faded during high school, but my class pictures tell a different story. "Draw in the missing eyeballs and this one might not be so bad," my mother would say. In group shots I was easily identified as the blur in the back row. For a time I thought that if I accompanied my habits with an outlandish wardrobe, I might be viewed as eccentric rather than just plain retarded. I was wrong. Only a confirmed idiot would wander the halls of my high school dressed in a floor-length caftan; as for the countless medallions that hung from around my neck, I might as well have worn a cowbell. They clanged and jangled with every jerk of my head, calling attention when without them I might have passed unnoticed. My oversized glasses did nothing but provide a clearer view of my rolling, twitching eyes, and the clunky platform shoes left lumps when used to discreetly tap my forehead. I was a mess.

I could be wrong, but according to my calculations, I got exactly fourteen minutes of sleep during my entire first year of college. I'd always had my own bedroom, a meticulously clean and well-ordered place where I could practice my habits in private. Now I would have a roommate, some complete stranger spoiling my routine with his God-given right to exist. The idea was mortifying, and I arrived at the university in full tilt.

"The doctors tell me that if I knock it around hard enough, there's a good chance the brain tumor will shrink to the point where they won't have to operate," I said the first time my roommate caught me jerking my head. "Meanwhile, these other specialists have me doing these eye exercises to strengthen what they call the 'corneal fibers,'

naked

18

whatever that means. They've got me coming and going, but what can you do, right? Anyway, you go ahead and settle in. I think I'll just test this electrical socket with a butter knife and re-arrange a few of the items on my dresser. Eeeee-sy does it. That's what I always s-ahhhhhhh."

It was hard enough coming up with excuses, but the real agony came when I was forced to give up rocking.

"Gift it a rest, Romeo," my roommate moaned the first night he heard my bedsprings creak. He thought I was masturbating, and while I wanted to set the record straight, something told me I wouldn't score any points by telling him that I was simply rocking in bed, just like any other eighteen-year-old college student. It was torture to lie there doing nothing. Even with a portable radio and earphones, there was no point listening to music unless I could sway back and forth with my head on a pillow. Rocking is basically dancing in a horizontal position, and it allowed me to practice in private what I detested in public. With my jerking head, rolling eyes, and rapid stabbing gestures, I might have been a sensation if I'd left my bed and put my tics to work on the dance floor. I should have told my roommate that I was an epileptic and left it at that. He might have charged across the room every so often to ram a Popsicle stick down my throat, but so what? I was used to picking splinters out of my tongue. *What, I wondered, was an average person expected to do while stretched out in a darkened room?* It felt pointless to lie there motionless and imagine a brighter life. Squinting across the cramped, cinder-block cell, I realized that an entire lifetime of wishful thinking had gotten me no further than this. There would be no cheering crowds or esteemed movie directors shouting into their bullhorns. I might have to take this harsh reality lying down, but while attempting to do so, couldn't I rock back and forth just a little bit?

Having memorized my roommate's course schedule, I

took to rushing back to the room between classes, rocking in fitful spurts but never really enjoying it for fear he might return at any moment. Perhaps he might feel ill or decide to cut class at the last minute. I'd hear his key in the door and jump up from my bed, mashing down my wadded hair and grabbing one of the textbooks I kept on my prop table. "I'm just studying for that pottery test," I'd say. "That's all I've been up to, just sitting in this chair reading about the history of jugs." Hard as I tried, it always wound up sounding as if I were guilty of something secretive or perverse. *He* never acted in the least bit embarrassed when caught listening to one of his many heavy-metal albums, a practice far more shameful than anything I have yet to imagine. There was no other solution: I had to think of a way to get rid of this guy.

His biggest weakness appeared to be his girlfriend, whose photograph he had tacked in a place of honor above the stereo. They'd been dating since tenth grade, and while he had gone off to college, she'd stayed behind to attend a two-year nursing school in their hometown. A history of listening to Top 40 radio had left me with a ridiculous and clichéd notion of love. I had never entertained the feeling myself but knew that it meant never having to say you're sorry. It was a many-splendored thing. Love was a rose *and* a hammer. Both blind and all-seeing, it made the world go round.

My roommate thought that he and his girlfriend were strong enough to make it through the month without seeing each other, but I wasn't so sure. "I don't know that I'd trust her around all those doctors," I said. "Love fades when left untended, especially in a hospital environment. Absence might make the heart grow fonder, but love is a two-way street. Think about it."

When my roommate went out of town, I would spend the entire weekend rocking in bed and fantasizing about his tragic car accident. I envisioned him wrapped tight as a

naked

mummy, his arms and legs suspended by pulleys. "Time is a great healer," his mother would say, packing the last of his albums into a milk crate. "Two years of bed rest and he'll be as good as new. Once he gets out of the hospital, I figure I'll set him up in the living room. He likes it there."

Sometimes I would allow him to leave in one piece, imagining his joining the army or marrying his girlfriend and moving someplace warm and sunny, like Peru or Ethiopia. The important thing was that he leave this room and never come back. I'd get rid of him and then move on to the next person, and the one after that, until it was just me, rocking and jerking in private.

Two months into the semester, my roommate broke up with his girlfriend. "And I'm going to spend every day and night sitting right here in this room until I figure out where I went wrong." He dabbed his moist eyes with the sleeve of his flannel shirt. "You and me, little buddy. It's just you and me and Jethro Tull from here on out. Say, what's with your head? The old tumor acting up again?"

"College is the best thing that can ever happen to you," my father used to say, and he was right, for it was there that I discovered drugs, drinking, and smoking. I'm unsure of the scientific aspects, but for some reason, my nervous habits faded about the same time I took up with cigarettes. Maybe it was coincidental or perhaps the tics retreated in the face of an adversary that, despite its health risks, is much more socially acceptable than crying out in tiny voices. Were I not smoking, I'd probably be on some sort of medication that would cost the same amount of money but deny me the accoutrements: the lighters I can thoughtlessly open and close, the ashtrays that provide me with a legitimate reason to leave my chair, and the cigarettes that calm me down while giving me something to do with my hands and mouth. It's as if I

a plague of tics

had been born to smoke, and until I realized it, my limbs were left to search for some alternative. Everything's fine as long as I know there's a cigarette in my immediate future. The people who ask me not to smoke in their cars have no idea what they're in for.

"Remember when you used to roll your eyes?" my sisters ask. "Remember the time you shook your head so hard, your glasses fell into the barbeque pit?"

At their mention I sometimes attempt to revisit my former tics and habits. Returning to my apartment late at night, I'll dare myself to press my nose against the doorknob or roll my eyes to achieve that once-satisfying ache. Maybe I'll start counting the napkins sandwiched in their plastic holder, but the exercise lacks its old urgency and I soon lose interest. I would no sooner rock in bed than play "Up, Up, and Away" sixty times straight on my record player. I could easily listen to something else an equal number of times while seated in a rocking chair, but the earlier, bedridden method fails to comfort me, as I've forgotten the code, the twitching trick needed to decipher the lyrics to that particular song. I remember only that at one time the story involved the citizens of Raleigh, North Carolina, being herded into a test balloon of my own design and making. It was rigged to explode once it reached the city limits, but the passengers were unaware of that fact. The sun shone on their faces as they lifted their heads toward the bright blue sky, giddy with excitement.

"Beautiful balloon!" they all said, gripping the handrails and climbing the staircase to their fiery destiny. "Wouldn't you like to ride?"

"Sorry, folks," I'd say, pressing my nose against the surface of my ticket booth. "But I've got other duties."

naked

get your ya-ya's out!

It was for many years my family's habit to drive from North Carolina to western New York State to visit the relatives we had left behind. After spending ten days with my mother's family in Binghamton, we would drive the half hour to Cortland and spend an afternoon with my father's mother, the woman we adressed as Ya Ya.

Ya Ya owned a newsstand/candy store, a long narrow room fitted with magazine racks and the high, wall-mounted chairs the townspeople occupied while receiving their shoe-shines. She lived above the store in the apartment my father had grown up in.

"A shithole," my mother said, and even at the age of seven, I thought, *Yes, she's right. This is a shithole.*

My mother's parents also lived in an apartment, but theirs had been arranged with an eye toward comfort, complete with a bathroom door and two television sets. I spent my time at Ya Ya's wondering what this place might have been before someone got the cruel idea to rent it out as an apartment. The dark, stifling hallway had been miscast in the role of a kitchen, and the bathroom looked suspiciously like a closet. Clothespinned bedspreads separated the bedroom from the living room, where the dining table was tightly wedged between the sofa and refrigerator. Surely, there were other places to live, perhaps a tent or maybe an abandoned muffler shop, someplace, *anyplace*, cheerier than this.

I recall one visit when she carried on about her recently deceased pet, a common goldfish she kept in a murky jar up on the apartment's only window ledge. Ya Ya had returned from work and, finding the jar empty, decided that the fish had consciously thrown itself out the window.

"He no happy no more and think to have a suicide," she said.

"Commit," my mother said. "He *committed* suicide." She threw her cigarette butt out the window and stared down into the littered alley below. "You don't *have* a suicide, it has you."

"Okay," Ya Ya said. "But why he have the suicide? Is pretty, the fish. Why he want to take he life away?"

"You're asking *why?*" My mother lowered her sunglasses. "Open your eyes and take a lucky guess." She emptied the jar into the sink. "This place is a dump."

"What Sharon means," my father said, "is that a fish is incapable of thinking in those terms. They have tiny little *kaphalis* and don't get depressed."

When speaking to his mother, my father used his loudest voice, drifting in and out of pidgin Greek. "The *psari* didn't know any better. It wasn't your fault, *Matera*, it was a *lathos.*"

"He have the suicide and now I sad sometime." Ya Ya stared into the distance and sighed. I imagine she had spoken to the fish, had loved it the best she knew how, but her affection, like her cooking, was devoid of anything one might think of as normal. She regarded her grandchildren as if we were savings bonds, something certain to multiply in value

naked

through the majesty of arithmetic. Ya Ya and her husband had produced one child, who in turn had yielded five, a wealth of hearty field hands destined to return to the village, where we might crush olives or stucco windmills or whatever it was they did in her hometown. She was always pushing up our sleeves to examine our muscles, frowning at the sight of our girlish, uncalloused hands. Whereas our other grandparents asked what grade we were in or which was our favorite ashtray, Ya Ya never expressed any interest in that sort of thing. Childhood was something you endured until you were old enough to work, and money was the only thing that mattered. She would sooner iron a stack of dollar bills than open any of the magazines or newspapers that lined the walls of her store. She didn't know who the president was, much less the central characters in any of her bestselling comic books.

"I no know the jug head," she'd say, spit shining the keys on her cash register.

"Maybe he come here one day, but I no know it."

It was difficult to imagine her raising a child of her own, and chilling to realize that she had. As a baby my father had been confined to a grim corner of the newsstand, where he crawled on a carpet of newspapers, teething on nickels. He never had a bed, much less his own room, and considered himself lucky when the visitors left and he had the couch to himself. Our dog had it better than that.

"Louie," she would say, patting the hair on my father's knuckles, "Louie and the girl."

"The girl" was what she called my mother. My parents had been married twelve years, and Ya Ya still couldn't bring herself to call her daughter-in-law by name. My father had made the mistake of marrying an outsider, and it was my mother's lot to suffer the consequences. She had somehow tricked him, sunk in her claws, and dragged him away from his people. It would have been all right for him to remain at home for the rest of his life, massaging worry beads and drinking bitter coffee, but to marry a woman with two distinct eyebrows was unpardonable.

"Tell the girl she can sit down now," Ya Ya would say to my father, pointing to a stool on the far side of the room.

"Tell the gnome I won't be staying that long," my mother would respond. "Her cave's a little on the dingy side, and I think I might have an allergy to her mustache."

We would pass the afternoon at Ya Ya's table, eating stringy boiled meat served with spinach pie. The food tasted as though it had been cooked weeks beforehand and left to age in a musty trunk. Her meals had been marinated in something dank and foreign and were cooked not in pots and pans, but in the same blackened kettles used by witches. Once we'd been served, she performed an epic version of grace. Delivered in both Greek and broken English, it involved tears and excessive hand-wringing and came off sounding less like a prayer than a spell.

"Enough of the chanting," my mother would say, pushing away her plate. "Tell her I'll disappear as soon as my kids are fed." More often than not, my mother left the table and waited outside in the car until we had finished our meal.

"The girl go away now," Ya Ya would say, raising her glass of ginger ale. "Okay then, we eat."

Our visits concluded with an all-you-could-grab assault on the store. "You can each take *one* thing," my father said. My sisters and I carried bags and pillowcases, clearing the shelves of comic books. We stuffed our socks and pockets with candy and popcorn for the twelve-hour ride back home, overpowering the car with the scent of newsprint and Ya Ya's spooky love.

My mother was pregnant with her sixth child when we received the news that Ya Ya had been hit by a truck. She'd

naked

stood wide-eyed in the center of the street, staring down an advancing eighteen-wheeler driven by someone bearing a remarkable resemblance to my mother. That was the way I pictured it. The truth was considerably less dramatic. It seems she had been bumped by a pickup as it backed into a parking space. The impact was next to nothing, but she'd broken her hip in the fall.

"That's a shame," my mother said, admiring her newly frosted hair in the bathroom mirror. "I guess now they'll have to shoot her."

My father flew to Cortland and returned announcing that once she recovered, Ya Ya would be moving in with us. "We'll move a few of the girls downstairs to the basement, and Ya Ya can take the bedroom across the hall from your mother and me, won't that be fun!" He tried his best to make it sound madcap and adventurous, but the poor man wasn't fooling anybody, least of all my mother.

"What's wrong with a nursing home?" she asked. "That's what normal people do. Better yet, you could lease her out to a petting zoo. Smuggle her aboard a tanker and ship her back to the old country, why don't you. Hire her a full-time baby-sitter, enlist her in the goddamned Peace Corps, buy her a camper and teach her to drive — all I know is that she's not moving in here, do you understand me? There's no way I'll have her moping around *my* house, buddy, no way in hell."

We had lived in our house for two years and it still smelled new until Ya Ya moved in with her blankets and trunks and mildewed, overstuffed chairs that carried the unmistakable scent of her old apartment. Overnight our home smelled like the cloakroom at the Greek Orthodox church.

"It's the incense," my mother said. "Tell her she's not allowed to burn any more of that stinking myrrh in her bedroom."

"Tell the girl to give me back the matches," Ya Ya said.

get your ya-ya's out!

27

For a town its size, Raleigh was home to a surprising number of Greeks whose social life revolved around the Holy Trinity Orthodox Church. Our father dropped us off each Sunday on his way to the putting green and picked us up an hour or two after the service had ended. "She'll make friends there," he predicted. "They'll love her down at the church."

There were quite a few oldsters at the Holy Trinity, widows like Ya Ya who dressed in black and supported themselves on canes and walkers. Still, it was difficult to imagine Ya Ya's having friends. She didn't drive, didn't write letters or use the telephone, and never mentioned anyone back in Cortland, where she'd had umpteen years to make friends. What made my father think she might change all of a sudden?

"She could, I don't know, go to the movies with Mrs. Dombalis," he said.

"Right," my mother agreed. "Then they can wolf down a few steaks at the Peddler before heading over to the discotheque. Face it, baby, it's just not going to happen."

Her first Sunday in our church, Ya Ya stopped the service when she tossed aside her cane and crawled up the aisle on her hands and knees. The priest saw her coming, and we watched as he nervously shifted his eyes, taking one step back, then another and another. The man was pinned against the altar when Ya Ya finally caught up with him, caressing and ultimately kissing his shoes.

Someone needed to step forward and take charge of the situation, but my mother was at home asleep and my father was at the golf course. That left my sisters and me, and we wanted no part of it. Members of the congregation turned their heads, searching for the next of kin, and we followed suit.

"Beats me," we said. "I've never seen her before in my life. Maybe she's with the Stravides."

naked

Over time we learned to anticipate this kind of behavior. My mother would take Ya Ya to the department store for new underwear, and we'd watch from behind the racks as she wandered out of the dressing room in her bra and knee-length bloomers. Once in the parking lot she would stoop to collect empty cans and Styrofoam cups, stray bits of cardboard, and scraps of paper, happily tossing it all out the window once the car reached a manicured residential street. She wasn't senile or vindictive, she just had her own way of doing things and couldn't understand what all the fuss was about. What was wrong with kneading bread dough on the kitchen floor? Who says a newborn baby shouldn't sleep with a colossal wooden cross wedged inside the crib? Why not treat your waist-length hair with olive oil? What stains on the sofa? I don't know what you're talking about.

"That might play back on Mount Olympus," my mother would say. "But in *my* house we don't wash our stockings in the toilet."

Ya Ya accepted the women in my family as another of life's little disappointments. Girls were to be tolerated, but every boy was a king, meant to be pampered and stuffed full of sour balls. She was overcome with joy when my mother gave birth to her final child, a boy Ya Ya wanted to name Hercules.

"*Poulaki mu,*" she would say, pressing a fifty-cent piece in my hand. "*Poulaki mu krisom.*" This was her standard pet name, which roughly translates to "my dearest little golden bird in a nest." "You go get the baby now and we feed him some candy."

My brother and I came to view our Ya Ya as a primitive version of an ATM machine. She was always good for a dollar or two, and because we were boys, all we had to do was open her car door or inform her the incense had just set fire to one of her embroidered cushions. I'd learned never to accompany her in public, but aside from that, Ya Ya and I had no problem. I saw her as a benign ghost, silent and invisible until you needed a little spending money. One could always change the channel while Ya Ya was watching TV; there was no need to even ask. She could go from the State of the Union Address to a Bullwinkle cartoon without ever noticing the difference. You might sit with her in the living room, but never were you forced to fetch her snacks or acknowledge her in any way. That was our mother's job, not ours. Every now and then she'd leave the yard and the neighbors would call saying, "Did you know your grandmother is over here picking things out of our front lawn?"

We'd hand the phone to our mother. "They're probably just dandelions," she'd sigh, drying her hands on her skirt. "Don't worry, we won't charge you for the labor."

"You'd think we never fed her," my mother would complain once my father returned from work. "She's out there gathering nuts and eating sunflower seeds out of the Shirks' bird feeder. It's embarrassing."

Ya Ya would wander off and return with an apronful of greens, which she would boil to a paste. "That's all right," we'd say, covering our plates at the sight of her advancing kettle. "I'm sure they're delicious but I'm saving room for those toadstools you found beneath the Steigerwalds' doghouse."

The longer she lived with us, the more distant my mother became. As children we had worshiped her as a great beauty, but the strain of six children and a mother-in-law had begun to take its toll. The glass of wine with dinner was now preceded and followed by a series of cocktails that tended to fortify her rage. Rather than joining us at the table, she took to eating perched on a stool in the breakfast nook, wearing dark glasses and grinding out her cigarettes on the edge of her plate. Ya Ya had been diagnosed with diabetes, and it was my

naked

mother's thankless job to prepare a special diet and cart her around town for her numerous doctor's appointments. It was my mother who practiced injecting insulin into oranges and doled out the pills. She was the one forced to hide the peanut butter and confiscate the candy hidden in Ya Ya's dresser drawers — all this for a woman who still refused to call her by name. My father would return home at the end of the day and listen to bitter complaints delivered in two harsh languages. My mother offered to sell the baby, to take a part-time job picking tobacco — anything to raise enough money for a nursing home — but even the cat understood that my father could not place his mother in an institution.

It was against his religion. Greeks just didn't *do* things like that. They were too cheap — that's what has always kept their families together. The whole notion of the nursing home was something dreamed up by people like my mother; American women with sunglasses, always searching for their tanning lotion or cigarette lighters. He couldn't evict his mother, but neither could he care for her. The conflict divided our family into two distinct camps. My mother and sisters scraped bread dough off their heels in one corner, while my brother, father, and I jangled our change in the other. The children formed a committee, meeting in the driveway to discuss our parents' certain divorce. It was reported by scouts positioned outside the bedroom that my mother had thrown what sounded like an ashtray. A reconnaissance unit was sent and returned carrying a battered clock radio and the real estate section of the newspaper, the margins penciled with our mother's trademark series of stars and checks. How many bedrooms did the apartment have? Who would she take with her when she left? If we went with our father and Ya Ya, we could be assured of our privacy — but what did it matter, when our mother's attention was what we lived for?

"Tell that cow of yours to tone it down a little," my

mother would shout from her stool in the breakfast nook. "They can hear her chewing her goddamned cud all the way to the state line."

"Oh, Sharon," my father would sigh.

"Oh, Sharon, my fat ass," my mother would shout, dashing her plate across the counter and onto the floor. Moments later she would rethink her exact wording, adding, "It's fat, my ass, but not as big as the can on that prize heifer you've got shoveling down three sacks of clover she harvested from the Kazmerzacks' front yard, mama's boy."

My mother had a wealthy aunt, a calculating and ambitious woman who had married the founders of two Cleveland department stores. The woman died paranoid and childless, leaving the bulk of her estate to my mother, her sister, and a handful of nieces. Having money of her own provided my mother with a newfound leverage. She took to wandering the house in a white mink cape, reading aloud from the various real estate brochures provided by a man who arrived late one afternoon introducing himself as her broker.

"This one's got a full-sized redwood sauna, separate bedrooms for each of my children, *and* a view of the distant volcanoes. It reads 'Divorcées welcome, no Greeks allowed.' Oh, it sounds *perfect!* Don't you think?"

The money made her formidable, and within a month, it was decided that Ya Ya would be sent to a nursing home. My father packed her belongings into the station wagon, and we followed behind in my great aunt's Cadillac, fighting over who would use the fake-fur throw.

She went first to a private facility where she shared a room with a spritely, white-haired lunatic named Mrs. Denardo, who crept out of bed late at night to shit in the hamper and hide Ya Ya's dentures in the chilly tank of the toilet.

"I'm the stepsister of Jesus Christ sent back to earth to

naked

round up all the lazy, goddamned niggers and teach them to cook ribs the way they was meant to be cooked, goddamnit."

We were enchanted and took to giving her the gifts meant for Ya Ya.

"What's this? A sack of almonds, you say? You can take these and shove them right up your puckered pooholes for all I care. I don't want nuts, motherfucker, I want drapes and shoes to match."

Ya Ya complained strenuously, but lost in the energetic saga of her roommate, my siblings and I never paid any attention. We organized a variety show tailored to Mrs. Denardo's exotic tastes and practiced for weeks, moving from the song "Getting to Know You" to a dramatic re-enactment of the Saint Valentine's Day massacre.

"Your show was a piece of stinking shit," she yelled, surrounded by an audience of beaming senior citizens. "You don't know fuck about shit, niggers."

The private hospital had seven circles of hell, and when Mrs. Denardo was sent upstairs to its steaming core, my brother, my sisters, and I lost interest in visiting.

Once the construction was completed, Ya Ya moved into a spanking new building reserved exclusively for senior citizens, a high-rise development called Capitol Towers. The apartments featured metallic wallpaper and modish asymmetrical rooms, the wall-to-wall windows offering a view of the local mall. No one in Raleigh lived in a high-rise, and we found ourselves briefly captivated by the glamour. My sisters and I fought for the opportunity to spend the night in Ya Ya's swinging clubhouse, and one by one, we took our turns, standing at the darkened window swirling a mocktail and pretending to be mesmerized by the glittering lights of North Hills.

I enjoyed pretending that this was my apartment and that Ya Ya was just visiting.

get your ya-ya's out!

"This is where I'll be putting the wet bar," I'd say, pointing to her shabby dinette set. "The movie projector will go in the corner beside the shrine, and we'll knock down this dividing wall to build a conversation pit."

"Okay," Ya Ya would say, staring at her folded hands. "You make a pit."

Again my father hoped Ya Ya might make some friends, but the women of Capitol Towers tended to be short-haired modern grandmothers with compact cars and stylish denim pantsuits. They kept themselves busy with volunteer work and organized bus trips to Ocracoke and Colonial Williamsburg.

"That is so cute!" they'd say, fawning over the tissue-paper Santa decorating the lobby. "Isn't it cute? I told Hassie Singleton just the other day, I said, 'That Saint Nicholas is just about the cutest thing I've ever seen in my life!' And speaking of cute, where did you buy that sweatsuit? My goodness, it's cute!"

The word *cute* perfectly illustrated the gap between Ya Ya and her new neighbors. Stretched to its most ridiculous limit, their community password had no practical application to her life. She owned no makeup or jewelry, wore no breezy spangled sweatshirts or smart, tailored slacks. Her door was free of seasonal cutouts, and she would no sooner square-dance than join the Baptist ladies for a tour of the historic pantyhose factories of Winston-Salem. She left her apartment only to ransack the community garden or sit quietly sobbing in the lobby, drying her tears with the tissues used to sculpt the latest holiday display. This was not the picture Capitol Towers wished to present. These were robust seniors hoping to make the most of their retirement, and the sight of our grieving, black-clad Ya Ya deflated their spirits. It was suggested by the management that perhaps she might be more comfortable somewhere else. Legally she met their res-

naked

idency requirements, but spiritually she was just too dark. They began keeping tabs on her, looking for some technicality, and were overjoyed when she fell asleep late one afternoon and set a small fire with her neglected iron. Forced to leave Capitol Towers, Ya Ya took up residence at Mayview, a low brick nursing home located next door to the old county poorhouse. This was an older, considerably less mobile crowd than she'd known at Capitol Towers. Many of the residents were confined to wheelchairs, their spotted scalps visible through tufts of unkempt hair. They peed themselves and sat farting in the lobby, chuckling at the trumpeting sounds that issued from their nightgowns. Unlike her former home, Mayview made no attempt to disguise the inevitable. There was no talk of one's well-deserved golden years, no rented buses or craft carnivals. This was it, the end of the line, all passengers please double-check the overhead storage bin before disembarking.

It was a sad place to spend the afternoon, so rather than endure the death rattle of her roommate, my father often brought Ya Ya to the house, where she sat in the carport, staring off into space until it got dark enough to catch a few moths.

She was joining us for dinner one night in the backyard when my father, trying to engage her in conversation, said, "Talk about your shockers, did I ever tell you that Ya Ya found her own brother dead in the middle of the road? The guy was slit from his chin to the crotch, murdered by rebels just for the hell of it. Her own brother! Can you imagine a thing like that?"

"I imagine it every day of my life," my sister Lisa said, tossing an olive pit onto my plate. "How come *she* has all the luck?"

"Was there a lot of blood?" I asked. "Did he crap in his pants? I hear that's what happens when you die. Were his organs soft to the touch, or had they been hardened by the sun? How old was he? What was his name? Was he cute?"

Ya Ya cast her eyes toward the neighbors' basketball court. "In Jesus' blessy name," she said, crossing herself with a barbequed chicken leg.

It was maddening, trying to get information out of her. Here she had a captive audience *and* a truly gruesome story but was unwilling to share it. My father had told us on several occasions that Ya Ya's marriage had been arranged. She had been sent as a young woman from her village in Greece to New York City, where she was forced to marry a complete stranger, sight unseen.

"Did you have a plan B in case he was deformed?" we asked. "When you finally met, did you kiss him or just shake his hand? How did you know he wasn't related to you? Did you ever date other guys?"

Each time we asked, our questions went unanswered. What we considered newsworthy was just another mundane detail of her life. Her husband, the man we addressed as Papou, had been just as morose as she was. We had to turn their photographs upside down in order to catch them smiling. The fact that they had only one child told us everything we needed to know about their erotic life. He worked, she worked, their child worked; they never expected anything more out of life. Papou had died when I was six years old. He had been in the newsstand late one night when intruders hit him over the head with a lead pipe, rupturing a vein in his head. He was carried to the hospital and died on Christmas Day.

"Did you still open presents?" we asked. "After he died, did he crap in his pants? Did the thieves concentrate only on money or did they take magazines and candy bars while they were at it? Did they catch them? Did they go to the electric chair? After they were electrocuted, did they crap in their pants?"

"He go to Jesus now," Ya Ya would say. End of story. We asked our dad, who said only, "He was my father and I loved him."

That was not the information we were looking for, but to this day it is the only response he provides. Is it loyalty that keeps him from telling secrets about the dead, or is there simply nothing to report? How could you spend that many years sleeping at someone's feet and not remember a single detail?

"Of course you love Ya Ya," he would say. "She's your grandmother." He stated it as a natural consequence, when to our mind, that was hardly the case. Someone might be your blood relative, but it didn't mean you had to love her. Our magazine articles and afternoon talk shows were teaching us that people had to earn their love from one day to the next. My father's family relied on a set of rules that no longer applied. It wasn't enough to provide your children with a home and hand over all your loose change, a person had to be *fun* while doing it. For Ya Ya it was too late, but there was still time for my father, who over the next few years grew increasingly nervous. He observed my mother holding court in the bedroom, wondering how she did it. She might occasionally snap, but once the smoke cleared we were back at her feet, fighting for her attention.

I was in my second year of college when I received the news that Ya Ya had died. My mother called to tell me. I cradled the phone beneath my chin, a joint in one hand and a beer in the other, and noticed the time, 11:22 A.M. My roommate was listening in, and because I wanted to impress him as a sensitive and complex individual, I threw myself onto the bed and made the most of my grief. "It can't be true," I cried. "It can't be true-hu-hu-hu-hu." My sobs sounded as if I were reading them off a page. "A-ha-ha-ha-ha-ha. A-hu-hu-haw-haw-haw-haw-haw." I had just finished reading Truman Capote's *A Christmas Memory* and tried to pass it off as my own. "I feel like a piece of my soul has been ripped away and now I'm just a kite," I said rubbing my eyes in an effort to provoke tears.

"I'll walk across the campus later this afternoon and search the sky, expecting to find two clouds shaped like hearts."

"I've got just the thing for you, bud," my roommate said. "Just the thing for you and me both because, I don't know if I told you this, my own grandmother died just a few months ago. My brother dropped by to do his laundry and there she was, stretched out dead in front of her trophy case. That shit is harsh, my friend. You and me have got some grieving to do, and I've got just the thing to set free the spirit."

His remedy involved two hits of acid, a bag of ice cubes, and a needle. We split a pair of gold posts and sat hallucinating in the dormitory kitchen as a criminal-justice major pierced our ears.

I flew home to Raleigh the next day, where my father said, "There's no way you're coming into my house with an earring. No sir, no way."

I spent the next several hours in the carport, threatening to sleep in the station wagon, unwilling to compromise myself for the likes of him. "Asshole!" I yelled. "Nazi!"

"Listen," my mother said, stepping out the door with a tray of marble-sized meatballs. "You take the earring out, we go to the funeral, you stick it back in before you catch your plane. The hole won't close up that quickly, take my word for it. This is something I want you to do for your father, all right?" She set the tray upon the hood of the car and picked

naked

up a meatball, studying it for a moment. "Besides that, an earring looks really stupid combined with glasses. It sends a mixed message, and the effect is, well, it's troubling. Give me the earring and I'll put it away for you. Then I want you to come inside and help me straighten up the house. The Greeks will be here tomorrow afternoon, and we need to hide the booze."

I removed the earring and never put it back in. Looking back, it shames me that I chose that particular moment to make a stand. My father had just lost his only mother, and I assumed that, like the rest of us, he felt nothing but relief. He'd been cut loose from his Greek anchor and could now drift freely through our invigorating American waters. Ya Ya left behind no money or real estate, no priceless recipes or valuable keepsakes, nothing but a sense of release; and what sort of legacy is that? I can't help but imagine she had started off with loftier goals. As a young girl in Greece, she must have laughed at private jokes and entertained crushes on young stonemasons named Xerxes or Prometheus. When told she would be sent to a new world, I hope she took a few hours to imagine a life of cakes and servants, where someone else would shine her shoes and iron the money. Life had sentenced her to die among strangers. Set out to pasture, she spent her final years brooding and stamping her feet within the narrow confines of her fragrant stall.

"When I get like that, I want you to shoot me, no questions asked," my mother whispered. "Disconnect the feeding tubes and shut off the monitors, but under no circumstances do I want you to move me into your basement."

We nodded at the casket — my brother, my sisters, and I — knowing that with her, it would never come to that. Our father, on the other hand, the man weeping in the front row, he would prove to be more difficult.

next of kin

I found the book hidden in the woods beneath a sheet of ply-wood, its cover torn away and the pages damp with mildew.

Brock and Bonnie Rivers stood in their driveway waving good-bye to the Reverend Hassleback.

"Good-bye," they said, waving.

"Good-bye," the reverend responded. "Tell those two teens of yours, Josh and Sandi, that they'll make an excellent addition to our young persons' ministry. They're fine kids," he said with a wink. "Almost as fine and foxy as their parents!"

The Rivers chuckled, raising their hands in another wave. When the reverend's car finally left the driveway, they stood for a moment in the bright sunshine before descending into the basement dungeon to unshackle the children.

The theme of the book was that people are not always what they seem. Highly respected in their upper-middle-class community, the Rivers family practiced a literal interpretation of the phrase "Love thy neighbor." Limber as gymnasts, these people were both shameless and insatiable. Father and daughter, brother and sister, mother and son: after exhausting every possible combination, they widened their circle to include horny sea captains and door-to-door knife salesmen. They did it in caves with their Doberman pinscher and on their slanted roof with the construction crew hired to replace the shingles. The first two times I read the book, I found myself aching with pleasure. Yes, these people were naughty, but at the age of thirteen, I couldn't help but admire their infectious energy and spirited enjoyment of life. The third time I came away shocked, not by the characters' behavior but by the innumerable typos. Had nobody bothered to proofread this book before sending it to print? In the opening chapter the daughter is caught with her brother's *ceck* in her *pissy*, calling out, "*Feck* me hard, *hardir*." When on page thirty-three the son has sex with his mother, he leaves the woman's "*tots* glistening with *jasm*."

I showed the book to my sister Lisa, who tore it from my hands saying, "Let me hold onto this for a while." She and I often swapped baby-sitting jobs and considered ourselves fairly well read in the field of literary pornography.

"Look in the parents' bedroom beneath the sweaters in the second drawer of the white dresser," she'd say. We'd each read *The Story of O* and the collected writings of the Marquis de Sade with one eye on the front door, fearful that the homeowners might walk in and torture us with barbed whips and hot oils. "I know you" our looks would say as the parents checked on their sleeping children. "I know all about you."

The book went from Lisa to our eleven-year-old sister, Gretchen, who interpreted it as a startling, nonfiction exposé of the American middle class. "I'm pretty sure this exact

next of kin

same thing is going on right here in North Hills," she whispered, tucking the book beneath the artificial grass of her Easter basket. "Take the Sherman family, for instance. Just last week I saw Heidi sticking her hands down Steve Junior's pants."

"The guy has two broken arms," I said. "She was probably just tucking in his shirt."

"Would you ask one of *us* to tuck in *your* shirt?" she asked.

She had a point. A careful study suggested that the Shermans were not the people they pretended to be. The father was often seen tugging at his crotch, and his wife had a disturbing habit of looking you straight in the eye while sniffing her fingers. A veil had been lifted, especially for Gretchen, who now saw the world as a steaming pit of unbridled sexuality. Seated on a lounge chair at the country club, she would narrow her eyes, speculating on the children crowding the shallow end of the pool. "I have a sneaking suspicion Christina Youngblood might be our half sister. She's got her father's chin, but the eyes and mouth are pure Mom."

I felt uneasy implicating our parents, but Gretchen provided a wealth of frightening evidence. She noted the way our mother applied lipstick at the approach of the potato chip delivery man, whom she addressed by first name and often invited to use our bathroom. Our father referred to the bank tellers as "doll" or "sweetheart," and their responses suggested that he had taken advantage of them one time too many. The Greek Orthodox church, the gaily dressed couples at the country club, even our elderly collie, Duchess: they were all in on it according to Gretchen, who took to piling furniture against her bedroom door before going to sleep each night.

The book wound up in the hands of our ten-year-old sister, Amy, who used it as a textbook in the make-believe class she

naked

held after school each day. Dressed in a wig and high heels, she passed her late afternoons standing before a blackboard and imitating her teachers. "I'm very sorry, Candice, but I'm going to have to fail you," she'd say, addressing one of the empty folding chairs arranged before her. "The problem is not that you don't try. The problem is that you're stupid. Very, very stupid. Isn't Candice stupid, class? She's ugly, too, am I wrong? Very well, Candice, you can sit back down now and, for God's sake, stop crying. All right, class, now I'm going to read to you from this week's new book. It's a story about a California family and it's called *Next of Kin*.

If Amy had read the book, then surely it had been seen by eight-year-old Tiffany, who shared her bedroom, and possibly by our brother, Paul, who at the age of two might have sucked on the binding, which was even more dangerous than reading it. Clearly this had to stop before it got out of hand. The phrase "Tight willin' *gasshole*" was growing more popular by the day, and even our ancient Greek grandmother was arriving at the breakfast table with suspicious-looking circles beneath her eyes.

Gretchen took the book and hid it under the carpet of her bedroom, where it was discovered by our housekeeper, Lena, who eventually handed it over to our mother.

"I'll make sure this is properly disposed of," my mother said, hurrying down the hallway to her bedroom. "*Fecking,*" she laughed, reading aloud from a randomly selected page. "Oh, this ought to be good."

Weeks later Gretchen and I found the book hidden between the mattress and box spring of my parents' bed, the pages stained with coffee rings and cigarette ash. The discovery seemed to validate all of Gretchen's suspicions. "They'll be coming for us any day now," she warned. "Be prepared, my friend, because this time they'll be playing for keeps."

She was undoubtedly referring to the episode in chapter eight where Mr. and Mrs. Rivers offer their children to a band of crusty gold miners with foul breath and rough, calloused hands. The Rivers children seemed to enjoy it, but then again, they'd been raised that way.

We waited. I'd always made it a point to kiss my mother before going to bed, but not anymore. The feel of her hand on my shoulder now made my flesh crawl. She was hemming a pair of my pants one afternoon when, standing before her on a kitchen chair, I felt her hand graze my butt.

"I just want to be friends," I stammered. "Nothing more, nothing less."

She took the pins out of her mouth and studied me for a moment before sighing, "Damn, and here you've been leading me on all this time."

I read the book once more, trying to recapture my earlier pleasure, but it was too late now. I couldn't read the phrase "He paunched his daughter's rock-hard nopples" without thinking of Gretchen barricading herself in her room.

I thought I might throw the book away or maybe even burn it, but like a perfectly good outgrown sweater, it seemed a shame to destroy it when the world was full of people who might get some use out of it. With this in mind, I carried the book to the grocery-store parking lot and tossed it into the bed of a shining new pickup truck. Whistling out of apprehension and nervous relief, I took up my post beside the store's outdoor vending machine, waiting until the truck's owner returned pushing a cart full of groceries. He was a wiry man with fashionable mutton-chop sideburns and a half cast on his arm. As he placed his bags in the back of the truck, his eyes narrowed upon the book. I watched as he picked it up and leafed through the first few pages before raising his head to search the parking lot, combing the area as if he might spot either a surveillance camera or, prefer-

naked

44

ably, a vanload of naked swingers pressing their bare breasts against the windows and inviting him to join the fun. He took a cigarette from his pocket and tapped it against the roof of the truck before lighting it. Then he slipped the book into his back pocket and drove away.

cyclops

When he was young my father shot out his best friend's eye with a BB gun. That is what he told us. "One foolish moment and, Jesus, if I could take it back, I would." He winced, shaking his fist as if it held a rattle. "It eats me alive," he said. "I mean to tell you that it absolutely tears me apart."

On one of our summer visits to his hometown, my father took us to meet this guy, a shoe salesman whose milky pupil hugged the corner of his mangled socket. I watched the two men shake hands and turned away, sickened and ashamed by what my father had done.

Our next-door neighbor received a BB gun for his twelfth birthday and accepted it as a personal challenge to stalk and maim any living creature: sunbathing cats, sparrows, slugs, and squirrels — if it moved, he shot it. I thought this was an excellent idea, but every time I raised the gun to my shoulder, I saw my father's half-blind friend stumbling forth with an armload of Capezios. What would it be like to live with that sort of guilt? How could my father look himself in the mirror without throwing up?

While watching television one afternoon my sister Tiffany stabbed me in the eye with a freshly sharpened pencil. The blood was copious, and I rode to the hospital knowing that if I was blinded, my sister would be my slave for the rest of her life. Never for one moment would I let her forget what she'd done to me. There would be no swinging cocktail parties in her future, no poolside barbeques or episodes of carefree laughter, not one moment of joy — I would make sure of that. I'd planned my vengeance so thoroughly that I was almost disappointed when the doctor announced that this was nothing but a minor puncture wound, located not on but beneath the eye.

"Take a look at your brother's face," my father said, pointing to my Band-Aid. "You could have blinded him for life! Your own brother, a Cyclops, is that what you want?" Tiffany's suffering eased my pain for an hour or two, but then I began to feel sorry for her. "Every time you reach for a pencil, I want you to think about what you've done to your brother," my father said. "I want you to get on your knees and beg him to forgive you."

There are only so many times a person can apologize before it becomes annoying. I lost interest long before the bandage was removed, but not my father. By the time he was finished, Tiffany couldn't lift a dull crayon without breaking into tears. Her pretty, suntanned face assumed the characteristics of a wrinkled, grease-stained bag. Six years old and the girl was broken.

Danger was everywhere and it was our father's lifelong duty to warn us. Attending the country club's Fourth of July celebration, we were told how one of his Navy buddies had been disfigured for life when a cherry bomb exploded in his lap. "Blew his balls right off the map," he said. "Take a second and imagine what that must have felt like!" Racing to the farthest edge of the golf course, I watched the remainder of the display with my hands between my legs.

Fireworks were hazardous, but thunderstorms were even worse. "I had a friend, used to be a very bright, good-looking guy. He was on top of the world until the day he got struck by lightning. It caught him right between the eyes while he was trout fishing and cooked his brain just like you'd roast a chicken. Now he's got a metal plate in his forehead and can't even chew his own food; everything has to be put in a blender and taken through a straw."

If the lightning was going to get me, it would have to penetrate walls. At the first hint of a storm I ran to the basement, crouching beneath a table and covering my head with a blanket. Those who watched from their front porches were fools. "The lightning can be attracted by a wedding ring or even the fillings in your teeth," my father said. "The moment you let down your guard is guaranteed to be the day it strikes."

In junior high I signed up for shop class, and our first assignment was to build a napkin holder. "You're not going to be using a table saw, are you?" my father asked. "I knew a guy, a kid about your size, who was using a table saw when the blade came loose, flew out of the machine, and sliced his face right in half." Using his index finger, my father drew an imaginary line from his forehead to his chin. "The guy survived, but nobody wanted anything to do with him. He turned into an alcoholic and wound up marrying a Chinese woman he'd ordered through a catalog. Think about it." I did.

My napkin holder was made from found boards and, once finished, weighed in at close to seven pounds. My bookshelves were even worse. "The problem with a hammer," I

naked

was told, "is that the head can fly off at any moment and, boy, let me tell you, you've never imagined pain like that."

After a while we began to wonder if my father had any friends who could still tie their own shoes or breathe without the aid of a respirator. With the exception of the shoe salesman, we'd never seen any of these people, only heard about them whenever one of us attempted to deep-fry chicken or operate the garbage disposal. "I've got a friend who buys a set of gloves and throws one of them away. He lost his right hand doing the exact same thing you're doing. He had his arm down the drain when the cat rubbed against the switch to the garbage disposal. Now he's wearing clip-on ties and having the restaurant waiters cut up his steak. Is that the kind of life you want for yourself?"

He allowed me to mow the lawn only because he was too cheap to pay a landscaper and didn't want to do it himself. "What happened," he said, "is that the guy slipped, probably on a pile of crap, and his leg got caught up in the blade. He found his foot, carried it to the hospital, but it was too late to sew it back on. Can you imagine that? The guy drove fifteen, twenty miles with his foot in his lap."

Regardless of the heat, I mowed the lawn wearing long pants, knee-high boots, a football helmet, and a pair of goggles. Before starting, I scouted the lawn for rocks and dog feces, slowly combing the area as if it were mined. Even then I pushed the mower haltingly, aways fearing that this next step might be my last.

Nothing bad ever happened, and within a few years I was mowing in shorts and sneakers, thinking of the supposed friend my father had used to illustrate his warning. I imagined this man jumping into his car and pressing on the accelerator with his bloody stump, a warm foot settled in his lap like a sleeping puppy. Why hadn't he just called an ambulance to come pick him up? How, in his shock, had he

cyclops

49

thought to search the weeds for his missing foot? It didn't add up.

I waited until my junior year of high school to sign up for driver's education. Before taking to the road, we sat in the darkened classroom, watching films that might have been written and directed by my father. *Don't do it*, I thought watching the prom couple attempt to pass a lumbering dump truck. Every excursion ended with the young driver wrapped around a telephone pole or burned beyond recognition, the camera focusing in on a bloody corsage littering the side of the highway.

I drove a car no faster than I pushed the lawn mower, and the instructor soon lost patience.

"That license is going to be your death warrant," my father said on the day I received my learner's permit. "You're going to get out there and kill someone, and the guilt is going to tear your heart out."

The thought of killing myself had slowed me down to five miles per hour. The thought of killing someone else stopped me completely.

My mother had picked me up from a play rehearsal one rainy night, when cresting a hill, the car ran over something it shouldn't have. This was not a brick or a misplaced boot but some living creature that cried out when caught beneath the tire. "Shit," my mother whispered, tapping her forehead against the steering wheel. "Shit, shit shit." We covered our heads against the rain and searched the darkened street until we found an orange cat coughing up blood into the gutter.

"You killed me," the cat said, pointing at my mother with its flattened paw. "Here I had so much to live for, but now it's over, my whole life wiped out just like that." The cat wheezed rhythmically before closing its eyes and dying.

"Shit," my mother repeated. We walked door to door until finding the cat's owner, a kind and understanding woman whose young daughter shared none of her qualities. "You killed my cat," she screamed, sobbing into her mother's skirt. "You're mean and you're ugly and you killed my cat."

"She's at that age," the woman said, stroking the child's hair.

My mother felt bad enough without the lecture that awaited her at home. "That could have been a child!" my father shouted. "Think about that the next time you're tearing down the street searching for kicks." He made it sound as if my mother ran down cats for sport. "You think this is funny," he said, "but we'll see who's laughing when you're behind bars awaiting trial for manslaughter." I received a variation on the same speech after sideswiping a mailbox. Despite my mother's encouragement, I surrendered my permit and never drove again. My nerves just couldn't take it. It seemed much safer to hitchhike.

My father objected when I moved to Chicago, and waged a full-fledged campaign of terror when I announced I would be moving to New York. "New York! Are you out of your mind? You might as well take a razor to your throat because, let me tell you something, those New Yorkers are going to eat you alive." He spoke of friends who had been robbed and bludgeoned by packs of roving gangs and sent me newspaper clippings detailing the tragic slayings of joggers and vacationing tourists. "This could be you!" he wrote in the margins.

I'd lived in New York for several years when, traveling upstate to attend a wedding, I stopped in my father's hometown. We hadn't visited since our grandmother moved in with us, and I felt my way around with a creepy familiarity. I found my father's old apartment, but his friend's shoe store had been converted into a pool hall. When I called to tell him about it, my father said, "What shoe store? What are you talking about?"

"The place where your friend worked," I said. "You remember, the guy whose eye you shot out."

"Frank?" he said. "I didn't shoot his eye out; the guy was born that way."

My father visits me now in New York. We'll walk through Washington Square, where he'll yell, "Get a look at the ugly mug on that one!" referring to a three-hundred-pound biker with grinning skulls tattooed like a choker around his neck. A young man in Central Park is photographing his girlfriend, and my father races to throw himself into the picture. "All right, sweetheart," he says, placing his arm around the startled victim, "it's time to get comfortable." I cower as he marches into posh grocery stores, demanding to speak to the manager. "Back home I can get this exact same cantaloupe for less than half this price," he says. The managers invariably suggest that he do just that. He screams at waiters and cuts in line at tony restaurants. "I have a friend," I tell him, "who lost his right arm snapping his fingers at a waiter."

"Oh, you kids," he says. "Not a one of you has got so much as a teaspoon of gumption. I don't know where you got it from, but in the end, it's going to kill you."

naked

52

the women's open

My sister Lisa became a woman on the fourteenth hole of the Pinehurst golf course. That's what she was told by the stranger who led her to the women's lounge. "Relax, sugar, you're a woman now."

We had gone unwittingly, shanghaied by our father, who had offered to take Lisa and me for a ride in the secondhand Porsche he'd recently bought. His sherbet-colored pants should have tipped us off, but seeing as there were no clubs in the backseat, we thought we were safe.

"Just a short little jaunt," my father said. He folded back the car's canvas roof and crouched into the driver's seat. "Hell, maybe we'll just tool up to the fairground and back, drive by the correctional center and watch the guys in the exercise yard — you both seem to enjoy that. Maybe we'll go out to the highway and get ourselves some soft ice cream, who knows! Live a little, why don't you? You're not going to experience a thing sitting in the house with your nose pressed up against the TV. It's a beautiful day, let's smell the goddamned flowers."

We shot past the prison so fast, I could barely make out the guards in their gun towers. Both the fairground and the ice cream stand faded in the distance as my father regarded his watch and nervously tapped his fingers against the leather-jacketed steering wheel. He knew exactly where we were headed and had it timed so that we'd arrive just in time for the tee off. "Well, what do you know," he said, pulling off the road and into the crowded golf-course parking lot. "I wonder if there's some kind of a tournament taking place? What do you say we take a quick peek? Gosh, this is a beautiful place. Wait'll you get a look at these fairways.

Lisa and I groaned, cursing our stupidity. Once again we'd been duped. There was nothing worse than spending an afternoon on a golf course. We knew what was in store for us and understood that the next few hours would pass like days or maybe even weeks. Our watches would yawn, the minute and hour hands joining each other in a series of periodic naps. First, our father would push us to the front of a large, gaily dressed crowd. Robbed of their choice spots, these spectators would huff and grumble, whispering insults we would pretend not to hear.

"They're kids," our father would say. "What do you want them to do, stand on my shoulders for Christ's sake? Come on, pal, have a heart.

The big boys were playing that day, men whose names we recognized from the tedious magazines my father kept stacked beside the toilet and heaped in the backseat of his Mustang. We'd seen these players on television and heard their strengths and weaknesses debated by the bronzed maniacs who frequented the pro shop of our country club. These people chipped and parred. They birdied and eagled and double-bogeyed with an urgency that failed to capture our imagination. Seeing the pros in person was no more interesting than eating an ice-cold hamburger, but it meant the world to our father, who hoped their presence might kindle a passion, inciting us to take up our clubs and strive for excellence. This was, for him, an act of love, a misguided attempt to enrich our lives and bring us closer together as a family.

"You kids are so damned lucky." He placed his hands on our shoulders, inching us closer to the front. "These are the best players in the PGA, and here you are with front-row seats."

"What seats?" Lisa asked. "Where?"

We stood on the grassy embankment, watching as the first player teed off.

"Lisa," our father whispered, "go get it. Go get Snead's tee."

When Lisa refused, it was up to me to wander onto the green, searching for the spent wooden peg that might have been whacked anywhere from six to twenty feet from its point of origin. Our father collected these tees as good-luck charms and kept them stored in a goldfish bowl that sat upon his dresser. It was forbidden to wander onto the green during a tournament, so he used us to do his legwork, hoping the officials might see us as enthusiastic upstarts who decorated their rooms with posters of the masters working their way out of sand traps or hoisting trophies over their heads following stunning victories at Pebble Beach. Nothing could have been further from the truth. No matter how hard he tried to motivate us, the members of my family refused to take even the slightest interest in what was surely the dullest game ever invented. We despised golf and everything that went with it, from the mushroom-capped tam-o'-shanters right down to the cruel spiked shoes.

"Oh, Lou," my mother would whine, dressed for a cocktail party in her muted, earth-tone caftan. "You're not going to wear *that*, are you?"

"What's wrong with this?" he'd ask. "These pants are brand-new."

"New to you," she'd say. "Pimps and circus clowns have been dressing that way for years."

We never understood how a man who took such pride in his sober tailored suits could spend his weekends in Day-Glo pants patterned with singing tree frogs or wee kilted Scotsmen. You needed sunglasses to open his closet door, what with all the candy-colored sweaters, aggressive madras sportscoats, and painfully bright polo shirts all screaming for attention. Highway workmen wore such shocking colors so that motorists could see them from a distance. It made sense for them, but what perils did these golfers face? There were no jacked-up Firebirds or eighteen-wheelers racing down the fairway threatening to flatten their comfortable little foursomes. We were taught at an early age never to yell or even speak in a normal tone of voice while on the golf course. Denied the full use of their vocal cords, these people let their outlandish clothing do the shouting for them, and the results were often deafening.

"I don't feel so well," Lisa whispered to my father as we marched from the sand trap to the putting green on the eighth hole. "I really think we need to leave."

My father ignored her. "If Trevino bogeys this hole, he's screwed. That last bunker shot pinned his ass right to the wall. Did you see his backswing?"

"I'm concerned right now about *my* back," Lisa said. "It's aching and I want to go home and lie down."

"We'll be just another minute." My father fingered the collection of tees in his pocket. "The problem with both you kids is that you're not paying enough attention to the game.

naked

First thing tomorrow morning I'm signing you up for some more lessons, and then you'll see what I'm talking about. Jesus, this game is just so exciting, you won't be able to stand it."

We had serious doubts that it was exciting, but he was right when he said we wouldn't be able to stand it. A tight man with a dollar, our father had signed us up for our first lessons when we could barely hold a rattle. No, we could not have a nude maid, but he was more than happy to give us an expensive set of child-sized clubs, which sat in the dark corners of our bedrooms, the canvas bags clawed and tattered by our cat, who was the only one who seemed to enjoy them. He bought green carpet for the living room and called us in to observe his stance as he sank balls into a coffee can. The driving range, the putt-putt courses — he just didn't get it. We didn't want advice on our swing, we wanted only to be left alone to practice witchcraft, deface fashion dolls, or sit in the privacy of our rooms fantasizing about anything other than golf. He had hoped that caddying might provide us with a better understanding of the game. My sisters and I collapsed beneath the weight of his clubs, barely conscious when he called out for a nine iron or a sand wedge. Caddying was a thankless job, especially in North Carolina, where by mid-March the humidity is fierce enough to curl paper. Ninety-eight degrees on the second hole and we'd crumple to the green, listening as children our own age shouted and splashed in the nearby pool.

The tournament dragged on, and by the time we reached the fourteenth hole, Lisa had begun to bleed, the rust-colored spot visible on her white culottes. She was close to tears, sunburned and frightened when she whispered something into my father's ear.

"We'll just get one of the gals," my father said. "They'll take care of you." He turned to a handsome white-haired

the women's open

woman wearing a lime green visor and a skirt patterned with grinning pandas. "Hey, sweetheart, I wonder if you could help me out with a personal problem." Like my father, this woman had followed these players from hole to hole, taking note of their every move. She had come out that day to bask in the glow of the masters, and now a strange man was asking her to accompany his daughter to the clubhouse and outfit her with a sanitary napkin.

She didn't seem to appreciate being called "sweetheart" and bristled when my father, his eyes never leaving the ball, suggested that if she shake a leg, she might make it back in time for the next tee off. She looked at my father as if he were something she had scraped off the bottom of her shoe. It was a withering gaze that softened once it shifted direction and settled on Lisa, who stood shamefully staring at the ground, her hands cupped to hide the stain. The woman nodded her head and, placing her hand on my sister's shoulder, reluctantly led her toward a distant cluster of buildings. I didn't understand the problem but very much wanted to join them, thinking perhaps we might talk this person into giving us a ride home, away from this grinding monotony and the cruel, remorseless sun. With Lisa gone, it would become my sole responsibility to fetch the splintered tees and pester the contestants for their autographs. "Lou," I would say, holding out my father's scorecard. "My name is Lou."

The game finally over, we returned to the parking lot to find Lisa stretched out in the backseat of the Porsche, her face and lap covered with golf towels.

"Don't say it," she threatened. "Whatever it is, I don't want to hear it."

"All I was going to do was ask you to take your lousy feet off the seat of the car," my father said.

"Yeah, well, why don't you go fuck yourself." The mo-

naked

58

ment she said it, Lisa bolted upright, as if there might still be time to catch the word between her teeth before it reached our father's ears. None of us had ever spoken to him that way, and now he would have no choice but to kill her. Some unprecedented threshold had been passed, and even the crickets stopped their racket, stunned into silence by the word that hung in the air like a cloud of spent gunpowder.

My father sighed and shook his head in disappointment. This was the same way he reacted to my mother when anger and frustration caused her to forget herself. Lisa was not a daughter now but just another female unable to control her wildly shifting emotions.

"Don't mind her," he said, wiping a thin coat of pollen off the windshield. "She's just having lady problems."

Throughout the years our father has continued his campaign to interest us in the sport of golf. When Gretchen, Amy, and Tiffany rejected his advances, he placed his hopes on our brother, Paul, who found the sprawling greens an excellent place to enjoy a hit of acid and overturn the golf carts he borrowed from their parking lot beside the pro shop.

Our father bought a wide-screen TV, an enormous model the size of an industrial-sized washing machine, and uses it only to watch and record his beloved tournaments. The top of the set is stacked high with videocassettes marked 94 PGA and 89 U.S. OPEN — UNBELIEVABLE!!!!

Before our mother died, she put together a videotape she thought Lisa might enjoy. The two of them had spent a great deal of time in the kitchen, drinking wine and watching old movies on the black-and-white portable television that sat beside the sink. These were just a few favorites my mother had recorded. "No big deal," she'd said, "just a little something to watch one day when you're bored."

A few weeks after the funeral Lisa searched my parents'

house for the tape, finding it on the downstairs bar beside my father's chair. She carried the cassette home but found she needed a bit more time before watching it. For Lisa, these movies would recall private times, just her and our mother perched on stools and reeling off the names of the actors as they appeared on the screen. These memories would be a gift that Lisa preferred to savor before opening. She waited until the initial grief had passed and then, settling onto her sofa with a tray of snacks, slipped in the tape, delighted to find it began with *Double Indemnity*. The opening credits were rolling when suddenly the video skipped and shifted to color. It was a man, squatting on his heels and peering down the shaft of his putter as though it were a rifle. Behind him stood a multitude of spectators shaded by tall pines, their faces tanned and rapt in concentration. "Greg Norman's bogeyed all three par fives," the announcer whispered. "But if he eagles here on the fifteenth, he's still got a shot at the Masters."

true detective

My mother had a thing for detectives, be they old, blind, or paralyzed from the waist down — she just couldn't get enough. My older sister shared her interest. Detective worship became something they practiced together, swapping plotlines the way other mothers and daughters exchanged recipes or grooming tips. One television program would end and then the next would begin, filling our house with the constant din of gunfire and squealing tires. Downstairs the obese detective would collect his breath on the bow of the drug lord's pleasure craft while up in the kitchen his elderly colleague hurled himself over a low brick wall in pursuit of the baby-faced serial killer.

"How's your case coming?" my mother would shout during commercial breaks.

Cupping her hands to the sides of her mouth, Lisa would yell, "Tubby's still tracking down leads, but I'm betting it's the Chinesey guy with the eye patch and the ponytail."

Theirs was a world of obvious suspects. Looking for the axe murderer? Try the emotionally disturbed lumberjack loitering near the tool shed behind the victim's house. Who kidnapped the guidance counselor? Perhaps it's the thirty-year-old tenth-grader with the gym bag full of bloody rope. It was no wonder these cases were solved so quickly. Every clue was italicized with a burst of surging trumpets, and under questioning, the suspects snapped like toothpicks, buckling in less time than it took to soft-boil an egg. "You want to know who set fire to the retirement home? All right, it was ME, you satisfied now? That's right, ME. I did it. ME."

It's easy to solve a case when none of the suspects are capable of telling a decent lie. Television took the bite out of crime, leaving the detective as nothing more than a lifestyle. It seemed that anyone could solve a murder as long as he had a telephone, a few hours of spare time, and a wet bar. My mother had all three ingredients in spades. The more suspects she identified over the course of a season, the more confident she became. Together, she and my sister would comb the local newspaper, speculating on each reported crime.

"We know that the girl was held at knifepoint on the second floor of her house," Lisa said, tapping a pencil against her forehead. "So probably the person who robbed her was . . . not in a . . . wheelchair."

"I'd say that's a pretty safe assumption," my mother answered. "While you're at it, I think we might as well eliminate anyone confined to an iron lung. Listen, Sherlock, you're going at it all wrong. The guy broke in, held her at knifepoint, and made off with three hundred dollars in cash, right?"

"And a clock radio," Lisa said. "Three hundred dollars and a clock radio."

"Forget the clock radio," my mother said. "The important thing is that he used a knife. All right now, what kind of person uses a knife?"

Lisa guessed that it might have been a chef. "Maybe she

naked

was at a restaurant and the cook noticed she had a lot of money in her pocketbook."

"Right," my mother said, "because that's what cooks *do*, isn't it. They crawl around the dining-room floor looking through purses while the food sits in the kitchen cooking itself. Come on now, *think*. Who uses a knife to commit a crime? In a world of guns, what kind of person would use a knife? Give up? It's just two little words: drug addict. It's that simple. A professional thief would use a gun, but even secondhand, a gun costs money. Drug addicts can't afford guns. They need all their money for their dope and smack — the hard stuff. These dopers have a habit to feed every minute of every day, which means they're always on the lookout for their next mark. This was a heroin addict who followed the girl home from the bank, parked his car around the corner, broke into the house, and robbed her at knifepoint."

"If he can't afford a gun, what's he doing with a car?" Lisa asked. "And what about the clock radio?"

"Screw the damned clock radio," my mother said. "And as for the car, it was stolen. He took it last Thursday from that couple on Pamlico. You saw the report in the paper. The brand-new Ford Mustang, remember? You thought it had been stolen by Gypsies, and I said we don't even *have* Gypsies in this part of the country. I said the car had been taken by a dope addict who'd use it for a couple of burglaries before selling it to a chop shop. Bingo. And there you have it." She crushed her cigarette and used the butt to trawl an X through the residue at the bottom of her blackened ashtray, her way of pronouncing that this particular case was closed. "What's next on our roster?"

Vandalism at 318 Poole Road, breaking and entering at the Five Points Pharmacy, a hit-and-run traffic accident in the parking lot of Swain's Steak House — it was always the work of a drug addict or former police officer, a "renegade," a "rogue." To hear my mother talk, you'd think the sunny, manicured streets of suburban Raleigh were crawling with heroin addicts, the needles poking through the sleeves of their tattered police uniforms. It embarrassed me to hear her use phrases like "copping a fix" and "the pusher man." "I have to go now," she'd say to the grocery clerk. "My mother-in-law is back at the house, jonesing for her lunch."

"I beg your pardon?" they'd say. "Come again?"

Only on network television did people talk this way.

"I call the TV," my mother and sister would say. It didn't matter what you were watching, when they laid claim to one of the televisions, you surrendered it the same way cars gave up the road at the sight of an advancing ambulance. I couldn't bear the detective shows but made it a point to regularly check in with *The Fugitive*. This was the story of Dr. Richard Kimble, a man on the run, falsely accused of a crime he did not commit. We are told in the opening credits that "he changed his name . . . *and* his identity. The notion of identity was illustrated by a can of shoe polish sitting on what appeared to be the scuffed surface of a motel dresser. This had me stumped for months. "What," I asked, "would nobody recognize him with freshly shined shoes? Did he use it to blacken his face? I don't get it."

"His hair, stupid," Lisa said. "He used it to dye his hair." Lisa liked *The Fugitive* because, she said, "He's easy on the eyes."

The way she saw it, Dr. Kimble needed only two things: a one-armed suspect and the love of a good woman. She failed to understand that despite his brooding good looks, a man of his nature could never be happy. Unlike her nightly lineup of swaggering gumshoes, the Fugitive had both a soul and a memory and would remain a haunted man long after his wife's true killer had been brought to justice. Most programs

naked

64

discouraged you from concentrating on the hero's dark inner workings. If the girlfriend was gunned down at her makeup table, you knew there'd be another one to replace her, no questions asked. The Fugitive had no fancy convertible or stylish wet bar. He was cut from a different cloth, *my* kind of cloth, the itchy kind. Lisa wouldn't know a sensitive loner if he crawled into her lap with a fistful of daisies, and it annoyed me when she labeled *The Fugitive* as "my kind of show."

It was one thing to sit in front of the television second-guessing a third-rate detective program, but quite another to solve a real case. We were well into the summer reruns when our household was shaken by a series of very real crimes no TV detective could ever hope to crack. Someone in our family had taken to wiping his or her ass on the bath towels. What made this exceptionally disturbing was that all our towels were fudge-colored. You'd be drying your hair when, too late, you noticed an unmistakable odor on your hands, head, and face. If nothing else, life in the suburbs promised that you might go from day to day *without* finding shit in your hair. This sudden turn of events tested our resolve to the core, leaving us to wonder who we were and where we, as a people, had gone wrong. Soul-searching aside, it also called for plenty of hot water, gallons of shampoo, steel wool, industrial scrub brushes, and blocks of harsh deodorizing soap. The criminal hit all three bathrooms, pausing just long enough to convince the rest of us that it was finally safe to let down our guard. I might spend twenty minutes carefully sniffing the towel only to discover that this time the asshole had used the washcloth.

"Well," my mother said, thumbing through the newspaper one Sunday morning, "the person doing this is one sick individual, that much we know for certain."

"And they eat corn," Lisa added, patting her head with a

T-shirt. The most recent victim, she had washed her hair so many times it now resembled the wiry, synthetic mane of a troll doll.

Everybody had their theories but nobody had any hard evidence. Discounting my parents, that still left six children and my grandmother, all possible suspects. I eliminated myself, and because the towels were carefully folded, I excused my brother, who to this day cannot manage such a complex activity. It must smart to use a towel for such a delicate purpose. I watched as my family took their seats at the table, waiting for someone to cry out or flinch, but nothing came of it.

My mother and sister had always thought themselves so wily and smart, but when pressed for a suspect, they said only that this case was beneath them. If someone were to be murdered or kidnapped, they'd rise to the occasion and finger the guilty party within an hour. This particular case fell under the category of "aggravated mischief" and was therefore unworthy of their professional attention. Whoever it was would listen to their conscience and confess sooner or later. In the meantime, my mother would stock the linen closet with white towels. Case closed.

Later that month someone went through my father's top drawer, stealing a kneesock packed with one hundred and twelve Liberty silver dollars. I knew my father's drawers as well as I knew my own; everyone did. That was how you occupied your time when you had the house to yourself — you riffled through my father's drawers before moving on to his second hiding place in the shed. I had seen and counted these coins many times. We all had, but who would go so far as to steal them?

My father gathered us all in the dining room and listened as we each took turns denying any involvement. "Dollars come in silver? I never knew that. Does the government issue them in a kneesock or was that your idea?"

"Okay," my father said. "All right, I understand now. *Nobody* took my coins. I guess they just got tired of living cooped up in that dresser and decided to roll out the door and spend themselves on candy and magazines. That's what happened, isn't it! Oh, they're probably out there as we speak, having themselves a grand old time, aren't they?" His voice visited its highest register, and he rubbed his hands together as if he were considering a tray of rich desserts.

"Free at last with their whole lives ahead of them. Can't you just *feel* the excitement? Doesn't it make you want to throw up your hands and scream?"

He lowered his voice and delivered a series of ultimatums I didn't quite catch. My mind was snagged on the thought of those jubilant silver dollars, raucous and dizzy with their first feelings of independence. I pictured their splitting into groups and traveling by night to avoid any excess attention. It might prove difficult to roll over grass and leaves, so I imagined them huddled in the carport, deciding it best to stick to the roads and sidewalks. The thought of it made me laugh and when I did, my father said, "You think this is funny? You getting a chuckle out of this, are you? I'm glad you find it so amusing. Let's see how funny it is when I search your room, funny guy."

On television a search warrant guaranteed that your home would be trashed, and this was no different. Mine was the only clean room in the entire house. This was my shrine, my temple, and I watched in horror as my drawers were emptied and my closets brutally divorced of order. While searching my desk, my father came across a gold plated mechanical pencil he recognized as his own. It had once occupied the same drawer as his coins, and I admitted that, yes, I had "taken" the pencil but I hadn't really "stolen" it. There was a big difference between the two. You *steal* the things that you covet while you *take* the things the original owner is incapable of appreciating. The pencil had spoken to me of its neglect, and I had offered to put it to good use. Taking is just borrowing without the formality. I'd planned on returning it once it ran out of lead — what was the big deal? This wasn't the sort of case-busting clue he was making it out to be. There were no blaring trumpets or high-speed chases, just a lousy pencil I'd used only to make me feel important. The moment my father and his pencil were reunited, I became the prime suspect, tried and convicted on circumstantial evidence. There was nothing I could say to change his mind.

"Did you spend the money already or have you got it buried out in the yard?" my sister Lisa asked. Buried? Now I was a thief *and* a pirate.

Falsely convicted of a crime I didn't commit, there was only one thing I could do. The shoe polish was kept in the linen closet. I chose black, massaging it into my scalp in an attempt to change my identity.

The Fugitive's hair always looked perfectly natural. It blew in the breeze created by oncoming trucks as he stood beside the lonesome road, bidding farewell to a town unable to appreciate his unique gifts. My natural hair looked pretty much the same way, but once the polish dried, my hair hardened into a stiff, unified mass that covered my head like a helmet. I went to bed and awoke to find my sheets and pillows smudged and ruined. My face and arms were bruised-looking, and everything stank with the rigid, military odor of a buffing rag. It was no wonder the Fugitive was a loner. I liked the sheen and color of my hair but found I needed to slick it back to maintain a clean forehead. This hair of mine was bulletproof. You could have pounded my head with a golf club and I wouldn't have felt a thing. I carried my soiled sheets into the woods, knowing that from here on out, things were going to be different. I had crossed over the edge, and there was no turning back.

After I changed my identity, my next step was to find the real thief and clear my name. My mother and sister were fond of saying, "The criminal always returns to the scene of the crime." This was a bit of dime-store wisdom picked up from one of their television programs, but I thought it might be worth a try. It was certainly true of whoever was wiping their ass on the towels, but then again, they had no choice. The bathroom was where we kept our toilet and even if the criminal had changed their ways, they'd still need to use the john. Aside from the silver dollars, my father's drawers were home to several pocket watches, a pair of cuff links shaped like dice, tie clips, fine cigarette lighters, and a deck of nudie playing cards missing both the king of hearts and the ace of clubs.

Figuring the thief had good reason to return for more, I undertook a stakeout. My father's closet had shuttered, louvered doors that afforded a view of the entire room. I took my place, waiting a full hour before my mother entered the room shouting, "I don't give a tinker's damn what they do on Mount Olympus, in this house you don't boil a seven-dollar steak!" My intuition told me she was talking to my grandmother. Slamming the door behind her, she took a seat on the edge of the unmade bed. She stared down at her bare feet and then, as if she expected them to apologize for some trouble they'd recently caused, said, "Well, what have we got to say for ourselves?" She picked at her toenail for a moment before crossing the room to fetch a bottle of glossy polish from the top of her dresser. This was a new shade, the color of putty. Rather than highlighting the nails, it caused them to disappear into the surrounding flesh, creating a look both freakish and popular. I'd never understood why women bothered painting their toenails, especially my mother, whose crusty, misshapen talons resembled the shattered, nugget-sized Fritos found huddled in the bottom of the bag. She stood before the mirror, shaking the bottle and fretting at the sight of her brittle, frosted hair arranged into a listless style she referred to as "the devil's stomping ground." I watched then as she rummaged through her closet, returning with a tall plastic box secured with the sort of latches you might find on a suitcase. I'd been through my father's closet thousands of times, but never my mother's. "If I had something of value, this is the last place I'd put it," she'd say. "The goddamned moths don't even want what I've got." My father's closet and dresser drawers offered clues to his inner life. I enjoyed uncovering what I thought to be his secrets but felt it best to honor my mother's privacy, not out of respect so much as out of fear. I didn't want any possible handcuffs or hooded leather mask interfering with the notion that this woman was first and foremost my mother.

She carried the box to her dresser and unfastened the latches, lifting the lid to reveal a pale Styrofoam head supporting a sandy blond wig, the hair sculpted into a series of cresting waves. This was a magnificent crown of hair, so perfect that it might have been styled by God himself on one of those off days he was feeling creative rather than vengeful. After carefully removing the pins, my mother placed the wig upon her head and studied herself in the mirror. She nodded her head this way and that, but the curls, defying all laws of physics, held their position. Fumes from the shoe polish were making me nauseous, and I had begun to perspire, the inky sweat running down my forehead and staining my shirt.

"What do you say to that, missy?" my mother asked herself. She applied a coat of lipstick and brought her face close

naked

to the mirror, cocking her head and arching her eyebrows in a series of expressions that conveyed everything from heartfelt concern to full-throttle rage. Then she stepped away from the mirror, reintroducing herself slowly, as if her reflection were a guest she was meeting for the first time. I often did the same thing myself in the privacy of the bathroom. "Who's he!" I'd ask, admiring myself with a new shirt or haircut. Most often, my private sessions would end with my pants in a tangle around my ankles. Would my mother now unbutton her blouse? Would she lift her skirt and excite herself? At what point would I call out and put an end to this? How could I live with myself, knowing what she looked like naked? *Please,* I thought, *Don't do it. Don't be like me.*

"All right then" my mother said. "What do you say we paint those toenails?" Opening the jar, she took a seat on the edge of the bed. I watched then as she parted her toes and set to work, pausing every so often to regard herself in the mirror. She finished the right foot and held it out for inspection. "A little on the nail, a little on the toe, a few drops on the carpet, and everybody's happy."

When the left foot was finished, she tossed the polish onto the dresser and fashioned a mound out of pillows, something so high that she could lie on her back without crushing her wig. It looked uncomfortable, but she seemed used to it. Spreading out her arms and legs, she closed her eyes and reclined as best she could. The room, with its unmade bed and cigarette packets littering the floor, resembled a crime scene. She might have been a nightclub hostess strangled for knowing too much or a career woman who'd choked on her popcorn while watching the late movie. How strange to put on a wig, to change into someone else, and then lie down and take a nap. Was she dreaming of all the exotic things this character might do, or was her wig nothing more than a high-maintenance sleeping cap?

true detective

Television stakeouts tend to reduce the hours of monotonous waiting into a single moment of truth. The detective arrives just in time to overhear the ransom instructions or catch the jewel thieves studying the blueprints to the museum. I stood for an hour with a head full of shoe polish, a fugitive, watching my mother asleep in disguise and waiting for something to reveal itself.

After she'd woken up my mother returned her wig to its hiding place and left the room, I waited for a few minutes and then crept downstairs, where I washed my hair three times, taking care to rinse the tub with Comet and destroy my soiled shirt. At the sound of my father's footsteps coming through the front door, I darted into my bedroom, slapping my face and examining my reflection in the darkened window. I wanted to be apple-cheeked, looking fresh and innocent when he rounded up the usual suspects, herding us into the dining room in an attempt to solve the greatest mystery of all: who had smeared his shirts and jackets with shoe polish?

When the time came, I'd take a seat beside the same crooks who had stolen the coins and wiped themselves on the towels and say, "Did you say shoe polish? On your suits? Today? No, sorry, I wouldn't know anything about that."

dix hill

Growing up in Raleigh, North Carolina, one of the worst things you could say about a person was that he or she had a family member at Dix Hill, the common name for Dorothea Dix Sanitarium, the local state mental hospital. Designed by the same people who brought you Dreary Orphanage of Forsaken Children and Gabled House Haunted by Ghost of Hatchet Murderer, Dorothea Dix was a bleak colony of Gothic buildings perched upon a hilltop near the outskirts of town. In the winter its surrounding tree limbs resembled the palsied fingers of mad scientists tapping against the windows in search of fresh brains. Come summer these same trees, green and leafy, served to hide something unspeakably sinister. Whenever we passed the place, my sisters and I would stick our heads out the car window, expecting to hear a hysterical voice cackling, "I'm mad, I tell you, MAD!" The patient would embrace his lunacy as though it were a treasure he had discovered hidden beneath the floorboards. "Mad! Do you hear me, I'm mad!"

I had just completed the seventh grade when my mother

announced that until we were old enough to find a paying job, anyone above the age of fourteen would have to devote their summers to community service. My older sister, Lisa, signed up as a candy striper at Rex Hospital and as for me, I knew exactly where I was headed.

My mother was sixteen years old when she stood on her front porch and watched as men in actual white coats carried her father kicking and screaming to their local psychiatric hospital, where he received a total of thirty-seven electric-shock treatments. He had been suffering from the D.T.'s, a painful hallucinatory state marking an advanced stage of alcoholism. My mother visited him every day, and often he had no idea who she was. Once, thinking she was a nurse, he attempted to slip his hand beneath her skirt. The experience left her with a certain haunted quality I very much admired. She'd looked into the face of something horrible, and I wanted to know what that felt like.

Driving past the iron gates and up the winding driveway on my first day of work, my mother offered me a series of last-minute alternatives. I could, say, teach underprivileged children to trace — I was good at that. Or baby-sitting. I could do it for free, and she'd pay me on the sly — no one would ever have to know about it. But my mind was made up. This was what I wanted. She didn't even walk in with me, just dropped me off and told me to call when I was ready to come home. "One hour, three, however long it takes you to change your mind," she said.

The volunteer program at Dorothea Dix was so small that the receptionist doubted its existence. "Let me get this straight," she said. "You want to work here for no money? Tell me, son, are you by any chance a current resident?" She lifted the telephone and stationed her finger on the dial. "Why don't you give me your ward number, and we'll arrange for someone

naked

to carry you back and give you your medication. Would you like that, sugar? It's good, the medicine."

It was chilling to have my sanity questioned by a professional. I had the name of the coordinator I'd telephoned a few days earlier, but it seemed to take hours for me to dig it out of my pocket. Once she was satisfied that I had spoken to an actual living person, the receptionist summoned a guard to lead me to the coordinator's office. It was a short trip requiring no less than seven keys. Everything at Dorothea Dix involved locked doors, and as a result, staff members could be heard from a distance of fifty feet, their fist-sized knots of keys swinging and jangling from their belts.

If the hospital had any kind of volunteer-training program, I never knew about it. Neither did I meet anyone else introducing themselves as volunteers. I met briefly with the coordinator, who studied a list of absent orderlies before saying, "Napier's out sick, you can fill in for him. Report to Building Seven and ask them to send you up to Banes."

I was led to an infirmary, where a nurse named Banes paired me up with Clarence Poole, a plum-colored orderly who carried a transistor radio upon his person at all times. Clarence's nose lay practically flat against his cheek, causing him to look like someone from a Picasso painting. In an effort to divert attention from his face, he spent a great deal of time maintaining his hairstyle, a luminous Afro the size of a medicine ball. It was Clarence's job to show me the ropes, and my first order of business was to accompany him to the snack machines, where he bought himself an RC Cola and a bag of salted peanuts. I watched as he then proceeded to stuff the nuts down the neck of the bottle. He did it with great concentration, as if he were force-feeding a goose. After explaining that the mixture needed a few minutes to steep, he took a seat and began fluffing out his hair with a long-handled pick. He had just raised the bottle to his lips when Nurse Banes handed us our first assignment. Tucking his radio into the back pocket of his uniform, Clarence led me across the grounds to an ivy-covered building that, except for the bars covering the windows, resembled the sort of dormitory one might find on a respectable college campus. Up close these buildings were quite nice until you went inside. This was a women's ward, and the first thing I noticed was the stench. It was an aroma I grew to associate with all locked wards: urine, sweat, cigarette smoke, dirty hair, and cheap disinfectant, all marinated in an intense, relentless heat that never varied with the seasons. The women lay on iron cots and called out to us, begging for attention and cigarettes, as Clarence opened the door. "I have information that can save lives!" someone shouted. Everyone spoke at the same time: "She made me pee myself," "Tell the nigger I control all the music on his radio," "Call the embassy and have them ship the olives by plane!"

Clarence would say only, "Later, baby," speaking as if these were young girls waiting outside the stage door for his autograph. He checked the numbers on the cots and paused before an elderly woman who shifted fitfully, her shoulder-length hair the same muted yellow as her soiled pillowcase. He prepared the gurney and unstrapped her harness. "I'll take her up top and you get the feet," he said. "Come on, granny, you're going for a ride." When the sheet was lifted, I was shocked to discover that this woman was naked. I had never before seen a naked woman and hesitated just long enough for her to lurch forward and sink her remaining three teeth into my forearm. The woman then twisted her head and growled, tugging at my flesh as if she were a bobcat or wolverine, some wild creature used to hunting down its meals. Clarence raised his radio and then, thinking of the possible damage, removed one of his shoes and rapped the

naked

woman across the head until she let loose and sank back onto her pillow. Her teeth had broken the skin, but Clarence reassured me that he had seen a lot worse. A tetanus shot, some iodine, no big deal.

Our day proceeded, everything from a mongoloid teenager with an ingrown toenail to a self-proclaimed swami who had fashioned himself a turban of urine-soaked towels. Clarence and I carted them to the infirmary and later returned them to their wards. "Shipping and delivery is all it is," he said. "That's all there is to it except when they got shit on their hands and smear up the cart." The patients moaned, whimpered, and shrieked. They cackled and hooted and drooled in a drug-induced stupor. Clarence took it all in stride, but I had never imagined such a world. A bedsore would eventually heal, but what about the patient's more substantial problems? A regular hospital, with its cheerful waiting room and baskets of flowers, offered some degree of hope. Here, there were no get-well cards or helium balloons, only a pervasive feeling of doom. Fate or accident had tripped these people up and broken them apart. It seemed to me that something like this might happen to anyone, regardless of their fine homes or decent education. Pitch one too many fits or spend too much time brushing your hair, and that might be the first sign. There could be something hidden away in any of our brains, quietly lurking there. Just waiting.

"Spare me the details, Dr. Freud," Lisa said, sitting in the front seat of the car as our mother drove us home that afternoon. She had spent her day on the maternity ward, offering patients a selection of ladies' magazines and paperback novels. "God, I hope I never get that fat. Some of them looked like they'd swallowed a portable TV." She wore a crisp red-and-white-striped uniform and studied her reflection in the rearview mirror, rehearsing her smile in hopes of meeting a cute intern. Lisa didn't understand what I was talking about,

dix hill

but my mother did. Every night, rattling the ice cubes at the bottom of her highball glass, my mother knew exactly what I was talking about. Health, be it mental or physical, had never been her family's strong suit. The Leonard family coat of arms pictured a bottle of scotch and a tumor.

After his shock treatments my grandfather returned home, where he spent the rest of his life coring apples and baking pies. His children gone and his wife hypoglycemic, there was no one around to eat the pies, but that did not deter him. He baked as if the entire U.S. Marine Corps were stationed outside his front door, drumming their forks against tin plates and shouting in unison, "Dessert! Dessert!" Four pies in the oven and he'd be rolling out flag-sized sheets of dough for the subsequent crusts. Twice a year we visited my grandparents' house, where I recall pies cooling on every available surface: the window sills, the television set, even the dining-room chairs. The man never said a word, but neither did he take another drink. He just baked, dying, finally, of a stress-related heart attack.

I worked at Dix Hill all that summer and then again the following year until, at age sixteen, I took a paying job as a dishwasher at a local cafeteria that had a practice of hiring outpatients. These were both current and former Dix Hill residents, grown men who would occasionally weep in panic at the sight of a burned casserole tray. They'd get behind and take to hiding in the stockroom or, even worse, in the walk-in freezer.

I went off to college and volunteered for class credit at a nearby state hospital. At Dix Hill I had functioned as an orderly without keys. I'd had responsibilities, whereas here I was nothing more than a human cigarette machine. Two evenings a week I would visit the fetid, stagnant ward and make small talk with women who wanted nothing to do with me. I was studying Italian at the time and would attempt to practice my verb conjugation with a paranoid Tuscan named Paola, a patient in her late forties with a perpetual black eye and a pronounced mustache. Some nights Paola could be very charming and helpful, while others she seemed truly possessed, overturning the television set, attacking her fellow patients, and tossing lit cigarettes at the nurses. I might spend a few pleasant hours with someone and return three days later to find she had no memory of it. At Dorothea Dix I went from one ward to the next, while here I spent all my time with the same group of people, week after week, and none of them seemed to be getting any better. LaDonna still sat in front of the television set, boasting of her personal relationship with Lee Majors. Charlotte continued to whisper into a plastic cup and hold it to her stomach in order to communicate with what she identified as her alien fetus; it was maddening. I wanted to slam their heads against the wall and scream, "Stop acting like an idiot and get better, goddamnit!" Then I'd notice the bruises covering their bodies and realize that someone had already tried that approach.

On my last night at the hospital, a fellow volunteer was taken hostage by a wiry, manic patient who held a knife to the woman's throat and demanded freedom. The police were summoned and gathered in the snow-covered yard to negotiate her release.

"I want a girl," the man shouted. "A prettier girl than this one. I want the prettiest girl you can find and I want her dressed in a bikini. Then I want you to put us up in a motel in Akron for . . . I'll let you know when we're ready to come out. Then I want a trailer with curtains and a water bed and a truck with four new tires. And a winter coat with a zipper instead of buttons. And I want an outdoor grill, the kind with a hood."

The police captain agreed to all the demands, signaling to the four officers who were creeping up behind the wishful patient. "And I'm going to need a fish tank. And a blow-dryer for my hair, and then I want a set of matching goblets and some nice mugs for my coffee."

The officers took him from behind, and even as they dragged him toward the waiting police car, he continued to voice more requests.

I returned to Dix Hill ten years after I'd first volunteered. A friend of mine had been dating a man who had turned spooky on her. They'd been eating in a popular Raleigh seafood restaurant when he'd taken a sudden urge to pelt the neighboring table with a side order of hush puppies. The manager was called, and a fight ensued. It turned out that this fellow had been institutionalized once before, at a state hospital outside Pittsburgh.

A guard led us through a familiar series of locked doors, and the young man emerged. His face was bloated from the drugs, and his tongue protruded from his mouth, thick and lathered as a bar of soap. My friend was hoping he might be cured with bed rest and willpower.

"The restaurant manager had it coming," she said, taking his hand. "That bastard will get his soon enough; the important thing is that you're getting better." She petted his bruised knuckles. "You're getting better now, Danny. Can you hear me? You're getting better."

i like guys

Shortly before I graduated from eighth grade, it was announced that, come fall, our county school system would adopt a policy of racial integration by way of forced busing. My Spanish teacher broke the news in a way she hoped might lead us to a greater understanding of her beauty and generosity.

"I remember the time I was at the state fair, standing in line for a Sno-Kone," she said, fingering the kiss curls that framed her squat, compact face. "And a little colored girl ran up and tugged at my skirt, asking if she could touch my hair. 'Just once,' she said. 'Just one time for good luck.'

"Now, I don't know about the rest of you, but my hair means a lot to me." The members of my class nodded to signify that their hair meant a lot to them as well. They inched forward in their seats, eager to know where this story might be going. Perhaps the little Negro girl was holding a concealed razor blade. Maybe she was one of the troublemakers out for a fresh white scalp.

I sat marveling at their naïveté. Like all her previous anec-
dotes, this woman's story was headed straight up her ass.

"I checked to make sure she didn't have any candy on her
hands, and then I bent down and let this little colored girl
touch my hair." The teacher's eyes assumed the dewy, faraway look she reserved for such Hallmark moments. "Then
this little fudge-colored girl put her hand on my cheek and
said, 'Oh,' she said, 'I wish I could be white and pretty like
you.'" She paused, positioning herself on the edge of the
desk as though she were posing for a portrait the federal government might use on a stamp commemorating gallantry.
"The thing to remember," she said, "is that more than anything in this world, those colored people wish they were
white."

I wasn't buying it. This was the same teacher who when
announcing her pregnancy said, "I just pray that my first-
born is a boy. I'll have a boy and then maybe later I'll have a
girl, because when you do it the other way round, there's a
good chance the boy will turn out to be funny."

" 'Funny,' as in having no arms and legs?" I asked.

"That," the teacher said, "is far from funny. That is tragic,
and you, sir, should have your lips sewn shut for saying such
a cruel and ugly thing. When I say 'funny,' I mean funny as
in . . ." She relaxed her wrist, allowing her hand to dangle
and flop. "I mean 'funny' as in *that* kind of funny." She
minced across the room, but it failed to illustrate her point, as
this was more or less her natural walk, a series of gamboling
little steps, her back held straight, giving the impression she
was balancing something of value atop her empty head. My
seventh-period math teacher did a much better version.
Snatching a purse off the back of a student's chair, he would
prance about the room, batting his eyes and blowing kisses at
the boys seated in the front row. "So fairy nice to meet you,"
he'd say.

naked

Fearful of drawing any attention to myself, I hooted and squawked along with the rest of the class, all the while thinking, *That's me he's talking about.* If I was going to make fun of people, I had to expect a little something in return, that seemed only fair. Still, though, it bothered me that they'd found such an easy way to get a laugh. As entertainers, these teachers were nothing, zero. They could barely impersonate themselves. "Look at you!" my second-period gym teacher would shout, his sneakers squealing against the basketball court. "You're a group of ladies, a pack of tap-dancing queers."

The other boys shrugged their shoulders or smiled down at their shoes. They reacted as if they had been called Buddhists or vampires; sure, it was an insult, but no one would ever mistake them for the real thing. Had they ever chanted in the privacy of their backyard temple or slept in a coffin, they would have felt the sting of recognition and shared my fear of discovery.

I had never done anything with another guy and literally prayed that I never would. As much as I fantasized about it, I understood that there could be nothing worse than making it official. You'd seen them on television from time to time, the homosexuals, maybe on one of the afternoon talk shows. No one ever came out and called them a queer, but you could just tell by their voices as they flattered the host and proclaimed great respect for their fellow guests. These were the celebrities never asked about their home life, the comedians running scarves beneath their toupees or framing their puffy faces with their open palms in an effort to eliminate the circles beneath their eyes. "The poor man's face lift," my mother called it. Regardless of their natty attire, these men appeared sweaty and desperate, willing to play the fool in exchange for the studio applause they seemed to mistake for love and acceptance. I saw something of myself in their

i like guys

83

mock weary delivery, in the way they crossed their legs and laughed at their own jokes. I pictured their homes: the finicky placement of their throw rugs and sectional sofas, the magazines carefully fanned just so upon the coffee tables with no wives or children to disturb their order. I imagined the pornography hidden in their closets and envisioned them powerless and sobbing as the police led them away in shackles, past the teenage boy who stood bathed in the light of the television news camera and shouted, "That's him! He's the one who touched my hair!"

It was my hope to win a contest, cash in the prizes, and use the money to visit a psychiatrist who might cure me of having homosexual thoughts. Electroshock, brain surgery, hypnotism — I was willing to try anything. Under a doctor's supervision, I would buckle down and really change, I swore I would.

My parents knew a couple whose son had killed a Presbyterian minister while driving drunk. They had friends whose eldest daughter had sprinkled a Bundt cake with Comet, and knew of a child who, high on spray paint, had set fire to the family's cocker spaniel. Yet, they spoke of no one whose son was a homosexual. The odds struck me as bizarre, but the message was the same: this was clearly the worst thing that could happen to a person. The day-to-day anxiety was bad enough without my instructors taking their feeble little potshots. If my math teacher were able to subtract the alcohol from his diet, he'd still be on the football field where he belonged; and my Spanish teacher's credentials were based on nothing more than a long weekend in Tijuana, as far as I could tell. I quit taking their tests and completing their homework assignments, accepting Fs rather than delivering the grades I thought might promote their reputations as good teachers. It was a strategy that hurt only me, but I thought it cunning. We each had our self-defeating schemes, all the boys I had come to identify as homosexuals. Except for a few transfer students, I had known most of them since the third grade. We'd spent years gathered together in cinder-block offices as one speech therapist after another tried to cure us of our lisps. Had there been a walking specialist, we probably would have met there, too. These were the same boys who carried poorly forged notes to gym class and were the first to raise their hands when the English teacher asked for a volunteer to read aloud from *The Yearling* or *Lord of the Flies*. We had long ago identified one another and understood that because of everything we had in common, we could never be friends. To socialize would have drawn too much attention to ourselves. We were members of a secret society founded on self-loathing. When a teacher or classmate made fun of a real homosexual, I made certain my laugh was louder than anyone else's. When a club member's clothing was thrown into the locker-room toilet, I was always the first to cheer. When it was my clothing, I watched as the faces of my fellows broke into recognizable expressions of relief. *Faggots*, I thought. *This should have been you.*

Several of my teachers, when discussing the upcoming school integration, would scratch at the damp stains beneath their arms, pulling back their lips to reveal every bit of tooth and gum. They made monkey noises, a manic succession of ohhs and ahhs meant to suggest that soon our school would be no different than a jungle. Had a genuine ape been seated in the room, I guessed he might have identified their calls as a cry of panic. Anything that caused them suffering brought me joy, but I doubted they would talk this way come fall. From everything I'd seen on television, the Negros would never stand for such foolishness. As a people, they seemed to stick together. They knew how to fight, and I hoped that once they arrived, the battle might come down to the gladiators, leaving the rest of us alone.

i like guys

85

At the end of the school year, my sister Lisa and I were excused from our volunteer jobs and sent to Greece to attend a
month-long summer camp advertised as "the Crown Jewel of
the Ionian Sea." The camp was reserved exclusively for Greek
Americans and featured instruction in such topics as folk
singing and something called "religious prayer and flag." I
despised the idea of summer camp but longed to boast that I
had been to Europe. "It changes people!" our neighbor had
said. Following a visit to Saint-Tropez, she had marked her
garden with a series of tissue-sized international flags. A
once discreet and modest woman, she now paraded about her
yard wearing nothing but clogs and a flame-stitched bikini.
"Europe is the best thing that can happen to a person, especially if you like wine!"

I saw Europe as an opportunity to re-invent myself. I
might still look and speak the same way, but having walked
those cobblestoned streets, I would be identified as Continen-
tal. "He has a passport," my classmates would whisper.
"Quick, let's run before he judges us!"

I told myself that I would find a girlfriend in Greece. She
would be a French tourist wandering the beach with a loaf of
bread beneath her arm. Lisette would prove that I wasn't a
homosexual, but a man with refined tastes. I saw us holding
hands against the silhouette of the Acropolis, the girl begging me to take her accordian as a memento of our love.
"Silly you," I would say, brushing the tears from her eyes,
"just give me the beret, that will be enough to hold you in
my heart until the end of time."

In case no one believed me, I would have my sister as a
witness. Lisa and I weren't getting along very well, but I
hoped that the warm Mediterranean waters might melt the
icicle she seemed to have mistaken for a rectal thermometer.
Faced with a country of strangers, she would have no choice
but to appreciate my company.

naked

86

Our father accompanied us to New York, where we met our fellow campers for the charter flight to Athens. There were hundreds of them, each one confident and celebratory. They tossed their complimentary Aegean Airlines tote bags across the room, shouting and jostling one another. This would be the way I'd act once we'd finally returned from camp, but not one moment before. Were it an all-girl's camp, I would have been able to work up some enthusiasm. Had they sent me alone to pry leeches off the backs of blood-thirsty Pygmies, I might have gone bravely — but spending a month in a dormitory full of boys, that was asking too much. I'd tried to put it out of my mind, but faced with their boisterous presence, I found myself growing progressively more hysterical. My nervous tics shifted into their highest gear, and a small crowd gathered to watch what they believed to be an exotic folk dance. If my sister was anxious about our trip, she certainly didn't show it. Prying my fingers off her wrist, she crossed the room and introduced herself to a girl who stood picking salvageable butts out of the standing ash-tray. This was a tough-looking Queens native named Stefani Heartattackus or Testicockules. I recall only that her last name had granted her a lifelong supply of resentment. Stefani wore mirrored aviator sunglasses and carried an over-sized comb in the back pocket of her hiphugger jeans. Of all the girls in the room, she seemed the least likely candidate for my sister's friendship. They sat beside each other on the plane, and by the time we disembarked in Athens, Lisa was speaking in a very bad Queens accent. During the long flight, while I sat cowering beside a boy named Seamen, my sister had undergone a complete physical and cultural transforma-tion. Her shoulder-length hair was now parted on the side, covering the left half of her face as if to conceal a nasty scar. She cursed and spat, scowling out the window of the char-tered bus as if she'd come to Greece with the sole intention

i like guys

87

of kicking its dusty ass. "What a shithole," she yelled. "Jeez, if I'd knowed it was gonna be dis hot, I woulda stayed home wit my headdin da oven, right, girls!"

It shamed me to hear my sister struggle so hard with an accent that did nothing but demean her, yet I silently congratulated her on the attempt. I approached her once we reached the camp, a cluster of whitewashed buildings hugging the desolate coast, far from any neighboring village.

"Listen, asshole," she said, "as far as this place is concerned, I don't know you and you sure as shit don't know me, you got that?" She spoke as if she were auditioning for a touring company of *West Side Story*, one hand on her hip and the other fingering her pocket comb as if it were a switchblade.

"Hey, Carolina!" one of her new friends called.

"A righta ready," she brayed. "I'm comin', I'm comin'.""

That was the last time we spoke before returning home. Lisa had adjusted with remarkable ease, but something deep in my stomach suggested I wouldn't thrive nearly as well. Camp lasted a month, during which time I never once had a bowel movement. I was used to having a semiprivate bathroom and could not bring myself to occupy one of the men's room stalls, fearful that someone might recognize my shoes or, even worse, not see my shoes at all and walk in on me. Sitting down three times a day for a heavy Greek meal became an exercise akin to packing a musket. I told myself I'd sneak off during one of our field trips, but those toilets were nothing more than a hole in the floor, a hole I could have filled with no problem whatsoever. I considered using the Ionian Sea, but for some unexplained reason, we were not allowed to swim in those waters. The camp had an Olympic-size pool that was fed from the sea and soon grew murky with stray bits of jellyfish that had been pulverized by the pump. The tiny tentacles raised welts on campers' skin, so shortly after

naked

arriving, it was announced that we could photograph both the pool *and* the ocean but could swim in neither. The Greeks had invented democracy, built the Acropolis, and then called it a day. Our swimming period was converted into "contemplation hour" for the girls and an extended soccer practice for the boys.

"I really think I'd be better off contemplating," I told the coach, massaging my distended stomach. "I've got a personal problem that's sort of weighing me down."

Because we were first and foremost Americans, the camp was basically an extension of junior high school except that here everyone had an excess of moles or a single eyebrow. The attractive sports-minded boys ran the show, currying favor from the staff and ruining our weekly outdoor movie with their inane heckling. From time to time the rented tour buses would carry us to view one of the country's many splendors, and we would raid the gift shops, stealing anything that wasn't chained to the shelf or locked in a guarded case. These were cheap, plated puzzle rings and pint-size vases, little pom-pommed shoes, and coffee mugs reading SPARTA IS FOR A LOVER. My shoplifting experience was the only thing that gave me an edge over the popular boys. "Hold it like this," I'd whisper. "Then swivel around and slip the statue of Diana down the back of your shorts, covering it with your T-shirt. Remember to back out the door while leaving and never forget to wave good-bye."

There was one boy at camp I felt I might get along with, a Detroit native named Jason who slept on the bunk beneath mine. Jason tended to look away when talking to the other boys, shifting his eyes as though he were studying the weather conditions. Like me, he used his free time to curl into a fetal position, staring at the bedside calendar upon which he'd x-ed out all the days he had endured so far. We were finishing our 7:15 to 7:45 wash-and-rinse segment one

i like guys

89

morning when our dormitory counselor arrived for inspection shouting, "What are you, a bunch of goddamned faggots who can't make your beds?"

I giggled out loud at his stupidity. If anyone knew how to make a bed, it was a faggot. It was the others he needed to worry about. I saw Jason laughing, too, and soon we took to mocking this counselor, referring to each other first as "faggots" and then as "stinking faggots." We were "lazy faggots" and "sunburned faggots" before we eventually became "faggoty faggots." We couldn't protest the word, as that would have meant acknowledging the truth of it. The most we could do was embrace it as a joke. Embodying the term in all its clichéd glory, we minced and pranced about the room for each other's entertainment when the others weren't looking. I found myself easily outperforming my teachers, who had failed to capture the proper spirit of loopy bravado inherent to the role. *Faggot*, as a word, was always delivered in a harsh, unforgiving tone befitting those weak or stupid enough to act upon their impulses. We used it as a joke, an accusation, and finally as a dare. Late at night I'd feel my bunk buck and sway, knowing that Jason was either masturbating or beating eggs for an omelette. *Is it me he's thinking about?* I'd follow his lead and wake the next morning to find our entire iron-frame unit had wandered a good eighteen inches away from the wall. Our love had the power to move bunks.

Having no willpower, we depended on circumstances to keep us apart. *This cannot happen* was accompanied by the sound of bedsprings whining, *Oh, but maybe just this once.* There came an afternoon when, running late for flag worship, we found ourselves alone in the dormitory. What started off as name-calling escalated into a series of mock angry slaps. We wrestled each other onto one of the lower bunks, both of us longing to be pinned. "You kids think you in-

naked

90

vented sex," my mother was fond of saying. But hadn't we? With no instruction manual or federally enforced training period, didn't we all come away feeling we'd discovered something unspeakably modern? What produced in others a feeling of exhilaration left Jason and me with a mortifying sense of guilt. We fled the room as if, in our fumblings, we had uncapped some virus we still might escape if we ran fast enough. Had one of the counselors not caught me scaling the fence, I felt certain I could have made it back to Raleigh by morning, skittering across the surface of the ocean like one of those lizards often featured on television wildlife programs.

When discovered making out with one of the Greek bus drivers, a sixteen-year-old camper was forced to stand beside the flagpole dressed in long pants and thick sweaters. We watched her cook in the hot sun until, fully roasted, she crumpled to the pavement and passed out.

"That," the chief counselor said, "is what happens to people who play around."

If this was the punishment for a boy and a girl, I felt certain the penalty for two boys somehow involved barbed wire, a team of donkeys, and the nearest volcano. Nothing, however, could match the cruelty and humiliation Jason and I soon practiced upon each other. He started a rumor that I had stolen an athletic supporter from another camper and secretly wore it over my mouth like a surgical mask. I retaliated, claiming he had expressed a desire to become a dancer. "That's nothing," he said to the assembled crowd, "take a look at what I found on David's bed!" He reached into the pocket of his tennis shorts and withdrew a sheet of notebook paper upon which were written the words I LIKE GUYS. Presented as an indictment, the document was both pathetic and comic. Would I supposedly have written the note to remind myself of that fact, lest I forget? Had I intended to wear it

taped to my back, advertising my preference the next time
our rented buses carried us off to yet another swinging sexual playground?

I LIKE GUYS. He held the paper above his head, turning a
slow circle so that everyone might get a chance to see. I supposed he had originally intended to plant the paper on my
bunk for one of the counselors to find. Presenting it himself
had foiled the note's intended effect. Rather than beating me
with sticks and heavy shoes, the other boys simply groaned
and looked away, wondering why he'd picked the thing up
and carried it around in his pants pocket. He might as well
have hoisted a glistening turd, shouting, "Look what he did!"
Touching such a foul document made him suspect and guilty
by association. In attempting to discredit each other, we
wound up alienating ourselves even further.

Jason — even his name seemed affected. During meals I
studied him from across the room. Here I was, sweating onto
my plate, my stomach knotted and cramped, when *he* was
the one full of shit. Clearly he had tricked me, cast a spell or
slipped something into my food. I watched as he befriended
a girl named Theodora and held her hand during a screening
of *A Lovely Way to Die,* one of the cave paintings the head
counselor offered as a weekly movie.

She wasn't a bad person, Theodora. Someday the doctors
might find a way to transplant a calf's brain into a human
skull, and then she'd be just as lively and intelligent as he
was. I tried to find a girlfriend of my own, but my one possible candidate was sent back home when she tumbled down
the steps of the Parthenon, causing serious damage to her leg
brace.

Jason looked convincing enough in the company of his
girlfriend. They scrambled about the various ruins, snapping
each other's pictures while I hung back fuming, watching

naked

92

them nuzzle and coo. My jealousy stemmed from the belief that he had been cured. One fistful of my flesh and he had lost all symptoms of the disease.

Camp ended and I flew home with my legs crossed, dropping my bag of stolen souvenirs and racing to the bathroom, where I spent the next several days sitting on the toilet and studying my face in a hand mirror. *I like guys*. The words had settled themselves into my features. I was a professional now, and it showed.

I returned to my volunteer job at the mental hospital, carrying harsh Greek cigarettes as an incentive to some of the more difficult patients.

"Faggot!" a woman shouted, stooping to protect her collection of pinecones. "Get your faggoty hands away from my radio transmitters."

"Don't mind Mary Elizabeth," the orderly said. "She's crazy."

Maybe not, I thought, holding a pinecone up against my ear. She's gotten the faggot part right, so maybe she was onto something.

The moment we boarded our return flight from Kennedy to Raleigh, Lisa re-arranged her hair, dropped her accent, and turned to me saying, "Well, I thought that was very nice, how about you?" Over the course of five minutes, she had eliminated all traces of her reckless European self. Why couldn't I do the same?

In late August my class schedule arrived along with the news that I would not be bused. There had been violence in other towns and counties, trouble as far away as Boston; but in Raleigh the transition was peaceful. Not only students but many of the teachers had been shifted from one school to another. My new science teacher was a black man very adept at swishing his way across the room, mocking everyone from

Albert Einstein to the dweebish host of a popular children's television program. Black and white, the teachers offered their ridicule as though it were an olive branch. "Here," they said, "this is something we each have in common, proof that we're all brothers under the skin."

the drama bug

The man was sent to our class to inspire us, and personally speaking, I thought he did an excellent job. After introducing himself in a relaxed and genial manner, he started toward the back of the room, only to be stopped midway by what we came to know as "the invisible wall," that transparent barrier realized only by psychotics, drug fiends, and other members of the show business community.

I sat enthralled as he righted himself and investigated the imaginary wall with his open palms, running his hands over the seemingly hard surface in hopes of finding a way out. Moments later he was tugging at an invisible rope, then struggling in the face of a violent, fantastic wind.

You know you're living in a small town when you can reach the ninth grade without ever having seen a mime. As far as I was concerned, this man was a prophet, a genius, a pioneer in the field of entertainment — and here he was in Raleigh, North Carolina! It was a riot, the way he imitated the teacher, turning down the corners of his mouth and riffling through his imaginary purse in search of gum and aspirin. Was this guy funny or what!

I went home and demonstrated the invisible wall for my two-year-old brother, who pounded on the very real wall beside his playpen, shrieking and wailing in disgust. When my mother asked what I'd done to provoke him, I threw up my hands in mock innocence before lowering them to retrieve the imaginary baby that lay fussing at my feet. I patted the back of my little ghost to induce gas and was investigating its soiled diaper when I noticed my mother's face assume an expression she reserved for unspeakable horror. I had seen this look only twice before: once when she was caught in the path of a charging, rabid pig and then again when I told her I wanted a peach-colored velveteen blazer with matching slacks.

"I don't know who put you up to this," she said, "but I'll kill you myself before I watch you grow up to be a clown. If you want to paint your face and prance around on street corners, then you'll have to find some other place to live because I sure as hell won't have it in my house." She turned to leave. *"Or in my yard,"* she added.

Fearful of her retribution, I did as I was told, ending my career in mime with a whimper rather than the silent bang I had hoped for.

The visiting actor returned to our classroom a few months later, removing his topcoat to reveal a black body stocking worn with a putty-colored neck brace, the result of a recent automobile accident. This afternoon's task was to introduce us to the works of William Shakespeare, and once again I was completely captivated by his charm and skill. When the words became confusing, you needed only pay attention to the actor's face and hands to understand that this particular character was not just angry, but vengeful. I loved the undercurrent of hostility that lay beneath the surface of this deceptively beautiful language. It seemed a shame that people no longer spoke this way, and I undertook a campaign to reintroduce Elizabethan English to the citizens of North Carolina.

"Perchance, fair lady, thou dost think me unduly vexed by the sorrowful state of thine quarters," I said to my mother as I ran the vacuum cleaner over the living-room carpet she was inherently too lazy to bother with. "These foul specks, the evidence of life itself, have sullied not only thine shag-tempered mat but also thine character. Be ye mad, woman? Were it a punishable crime to neglect thine dwellings, you, my feeble-spirited mistress, would hang from the tallest tree in penitence for your shameful ways. Be there not garments to launder and iron free of turbulence? See ye not the porcelain plates and hearty mugs waiting to be washed clean of evidence? Get thee to thine work, damnable lady, and quickly, before the products of thine very loins raise their collected fists in a spirit born both of rage and indignation, forcibly coaxing the last breath from the foul chamber of thine vain and upright throat. Go now, wastrel, and get to it!"

My mother reacted as if I had whipped her with a short length of yarn. The intent was there, but the weapon was strange and inadequate. I could tell by the state of my room that she spent the next day searching my dresser for drugs. The clothes I took pride in neatly folding were crammed tight into their drawers with no regard for color or category. I smelled the evidence of cigarettes and noticed the coffee rings on my desk. My mother had been granted forgiveness on several previous occasions, but mess with mine drawers and ye have just made thyself an enemy for life. Tying a feather to the shaft of my ballpoint pen, I quilled her a letter. "The thing that ye search for so desperately," I wrote, "resideth not in mine well-ordered chamber, but in the questionable content of thine own character." I slipped the note into her purse, folded twice and sealed with wax from the candles I now used to light my room. I took to brooding, refusing to let up until I received a copy of Shakespeare's collected plays. Once they were acquired, I discovered them dense and difficult to follow. Reading the words made me feel dull and stupid, but speaking them made me feel powerful. I found it best to simply carry the book from room to room, occasionally skimming for fun words I might toss into my ever fragrant vocabulary. The dinner hour became either unbearable or excruciating, depending on my mood.

"Methinks, kind sir, most gentle lady, fellow siblings all, that this barnyard fowl be most tasty and succulent, having simmered in its own sweet juices for such a time as it might take the sun to pass, rosy and full-fingered, across the plum-colored sky for the course of a twilight hour. 'Tis crisp yet juicy, this plump bird, satisfied in the company of such finely roasted neighbors. Hear me out, fine relations, and heed my words, for methinks it adventurous, and fanciful, too, to saddle mine fork with both fowl *and* carrot at the exact same time, the twin juices blending together in a delicate harmony which doth cajole and enliven mine tongue in a spirit of unbridled merriment! What say ye, fine father, sisters, and infant brother, too, that we raise our flagons high in celebration of this hearty feast, prepared lovingly and with utmost grace by this dutiful woman we have the good fortune to address as wife, wench, or mother!"

My enthusiasm knew no limits. Soon my mother was literally begging me to wait in the car while she stepped into the bank or grocery store.

I was at the orthodontist's office, placing a pox upon the practice of dentistry, when the visiting actor returned to our classroom.

naked

"You missed it," my friend Lois said. "The man was so indescribably powerful that I was practically crying, that's how brilliant he was." She positioned her hands as if she were supporting a tray. "I don't know what more I can say. The words, they just don't exist. I could try to explain his realness, but you'd never be able to understand it. Never," she repeated. "Never, never, never."

Lois and I had been friends for six months when our relationship suddenly assumed a competitive edge. I'd never cared who made better grades or had more spending money. We each had our strengths; the important thing was to honor each other for the thing that person did best. Lois held her Chablis better than I, and I respected her for that. Her frightening excess of self-confidence allowed her to march into school wearing a rust-colored Afro wig, and I stood behind her one hundred percent. She owned more records than I did, and because she was nine months older, also knew how to drive a car and did so as if she were rushing to put out a fire. *Fine*, I thought, *good for her.* My superior wisdom and innate generosity allowed me to be truly happy for Lois up until the day she questioned my ability to understand the visiting actor. The first few times he visited, she'd been just like the rest of them, laughing at his neck brace and rolling her eyes at the tangerine-sized lump in his tights. *I* was the one who first identified his brilliance, and now she was saying I couldn't understand him? Methinks not.

"Honestly, woman," I said to my mother on our way to the dry cleaner, "to think that this low-lying worm might speak to me of greatness as though it were a thing invisible to mine eyes is more than I can bear. Her words doth strike mine heart with the force of a punishing blow, leaving me both stunned and highly vexed, too. Hear me, though, for I shall bide my time, quietly, and with cunning, striking back at the very hour she doth least expect it. Such an affront shall not

the drama bug

go unchallenged, of that you may rest assured, gentle lady. My vengeance will hold the sweet taste of the ripest berry, and I shall savor it slowly."

"You'll get over it," my mother said. "Give it a week or two and I'm sure everything will be back to normal. I'm going in now to get your father's shirts and I want you to wait here, *in the car.* Trust me, this whole thing will be forgotten about in no time."

This had become her answer to everything. She'd done some asking around and concluded I'd been bitten by what her sister referred to as "the drama bug." My mother was convinced that this was a phase, just like all the others. A few weeks of fanfare and I'd drop show business, just like I had the guitar and my private detective agency. I hated having my life's ambition reduced to the level of a common cold. This wasn't a bug, but a full-fledged virus. It might lay low for a year or two, but this little germ would never go away. It had nothing to do with talent or initiative. Rejection couldn't weaken it, and no amount of success would ever satisfy it. Once diagnosed, the prognosis was terminal.

The drama bug seemed to strike hardest with Jews, homosexuals, and portly girls, whose faces were caked with acne medication. These were individuals who, for one reason or another, desperately craved attention. I would later discover it was a bad idea to gather more than two of these people in an enclosed area for any length of time. The stage was not only a physical place but also a state of mind, and the word *audience* was defined as anyone forced to suffer your company. We young actors were a string of lightbulbs left burning twenty-four hours a day, exhausting ourselves and others with our self-proclaimed brilliance.

I had the drama bug and Lois had a car. Weighing the depth of her momentary transgression against the rich rewards of her private chariot, I found it within my bosom to

naked

forgive my wayward friend. I called her the moment I learned the visiting actor had scheduled a production of *Hamlet* set to take place in the amphitheater of the Raleigh Rose Garden. He himself would direct and play the title role, but the other parts were up for grabs. We auditioned, and because we were the youngest and least experienced, Lois and I were assigned the roles of the traveling players Hamlet uses to bait his uncle Claudius. It wasn't the part I was hoping for, but I accepted my role with quiet dignity. I had a few decent speeches and planned to work them to the best of my ability.

Our fellow cast members were in their twenties and thirties and had wet their feet in such long-running outdoor dramas as *The Lost Colony* and *Tender Is the Lamb*. These were professionals, and I hoped to benefit from their experience, sitting literally at their feet as the director paced the lip of the stage addressing his clenched fist as "poor Yorick."

I worshiped these people. Lois slept with them. By the second week of rehearsal, she had abandoned Fortinbras in favor of Laertes, who, she claimed, had a "real way with the sword." Unlike me, she was embraced by the older crowd, attending late-night keg parties with Polonius and Ophelia and driving to the lake with the director while Gertrude and Rosencrantz made out in the backseat. The killer was that Lois was nowhere near as committed as I was. Her drama bug was the equivalent of a twenty-four-hour flu, yet there she was, playing bumper pool with Hamlet himself while I practiced lines alone in my room, dreaming up little ways to steal the show.

It was decided that as traveling players, Lois and I would make our entrance tumbling onto the outdoor stage. When she complained that the grass was irritating her skin, the director examined the wee pimples on her back and decided that, from this point on, the players would enter skipping. I had rehearsed my tumble until my brain lost its mooring and

the drama bug

could be heard rattling inside my skull, and now, on the basis of one complaint, we were skipping? He'd already cut all my speeches, leaving me with the one line "Aye, my lord." That was it, three lousy syllables. A person could wrench more emotion out of a sneeze than all my dialogue put together. While the other actors strolled the Rose Garden memorizing their vengeful soliloquies, I skipped back and forth across the parking lot repeating, "Aye, my lord," in a voice that increasingly sounded like that of a trained parrot. Lois felt silly skipping and spoke to the director, who praised her instincts and announced that, henceforth, the players would enter walking.

The less I had to do, the more my fellow actors used me as a personal slave. I would have been happy to help them run lines, but instead, they wanted me to polish their crowns or trot over to a car, seaching the backseat for a misplaced dagger.

"Looking for something to do? You can help Doogan glow-tape the props," the director said. "You can chase the spiders out of the dressing room, or better yet, why don't you run down to the store and get us some drinks."

For the most part, Lois sat in the shade doing nothing. Not only did she refuse to help out, but she was always the first one to hand me a large bill when placing an order for a thirty-cent diet soda. She'd search through her purse, bypassing the singles in favor of a ten or a twenty. "I need to break this anyway," she'd say. "If they charge you extra for a cup of ice, tell them to fuck themselves." During the rehearsal breaks she huddled in the stands, gossiping with the other actors while I was off anchoring ladders for the technicians.

When it came time for our big scene, Lois recited her lines as if she were reading the words from the surface of some distant billboard. She squinted and paused between syllables,

naked

punctuating each word with a question mark. "Who this? Has seen with tongue? In venom steeped?"

If the director had a problem with her performance, he kept it to himself. I, on the other hand, was instructed to remove the sweater from around my neck, walk slower, and drop the accent. It might have been easier to accept the criticism had he spread it around a little, but that seemed unlikely. She could enter the scene wearing sunglasses and eating pizza and that was "fine, Lois. Great work, babe."

By this time I was finding my own way home from rehearsal. Lois couldn't give me a ride, as she was always running off to some party or restaurant with what she referred to as "the gang from Elsinore."

"I can't go," I'd say, pretending I had been invited. "I really need to get home and concentrate on my line. You go ahead, though. I'll just call my mother. She'll pick me up."

"Are we vexed?" my mother would ask, pulling her station wagon into the parking lot.

"We are indeed," I answered. "And highly so."

"Let it go," she said. "Ten years from now I guarantee you won't remember any of these people. Time passes, you'll see." She frowned, studying her face in the rearview mirror. "Enough liquor, and people can forget anything. Don't let it get to you. If nothing else, this has taught you to skim money while buying their drinks."

I didn't appreciate her flippant attitude, but the business with the change was insightful.

"Round everything off to the nearest dollar," she said. "Hand them their change along with their drinks so they'll be less likely to count it — and never fold the bills, keep the money in a wad."

My mother had the vengeful part down. It was the craft of acting I thought she knew nothing about.

the drama bug

103

We were in dress rehearsal when the director approached Lois regarding a new production he hoped to stage that coming fall. It was to be a musical based on the lives of roving Gypsies. "And you," he said, "shall be my lusty bandit queen."

Lois couldn't sing; everyone knew that. Neither could she act or play the tambourine. "Yours is the heart of a Gypsy," he said, kneeling in the grass. "The vibrant soul of a nomad."

When I expressed an interest, he suggested I might enjoy working behind the scenes. He meant for me to hang lights or lug scenery, to become one of those guys with the low-riding pants, their tool belts burdened with heavy wrenches and thick rolls of gaffer tape. Anyone thinking I might be trusted with electrical wiring had to be a complete idiot, and that's what this man was. I looked at him clearly then, noticing the way his tights made a mockery of his slack calves and dumpy little basket. Vibrant soul of a nomad, indeed. If he were such a big stinking deal, what was he doing in Raleigh? His blow-dried hair, the cheap Cuban-heeled shoes, and rainbow-striped suspenders — it was all a sham. Why wear tights with suspenders when their only redeeming feature was that they stayed up on their own — that's how they got their name, tights. And acting? The man performed as if the audience were deaf. He shouted his lines, grinning like a jack-o'-lantern and flailing his arms as if his sleeves were on fire. His was a form of acting that never fails to embarrass me. Watching him was like opening the door to a singing telegram: you know it's supposed to be entertaining, but you can't get beyond the sad fact that this person actually thinks he's bringing some joy into your life. Somewhere he had a mother who sifted through a shoe box of mimeographed playbills, pouring herself another drink and wondering

naked

when her son would come to his senses and swallow some drain cleaner.

I finally saw Hamlet for who he really was and recognized myself as the witless Yorick who had blindly followed along behind him.

My mother attended the opening-night performance. Following my leaden "Aye, my lord," I lay upon the grassy stage as Lois poured a false vial of poison into my ear. As I lay dying, I opened my eyes just a crack, catching sight of my mother stretched out on her hard, stone pew, fighting off the moths that, along with a few dozen seniors, had been attracted by the light.

There was a cast party afterward, but I didn't go. I changed my clothes in the dressing room, where the actors stood congratulating one another, repeating the words "brilliant" and "intense" as if they were describing the footlights. Horatio asked me to run to the store for cigarettes, and I pocketed his money, promising to return "with lightning speed, my lord."

"You were the best in the whole show," my mother said, stopping for frozen pizza on our way home. "I mean it, you walked onto that stage and all eyes went right to you."

It occurred to me then that my mother was a better actor than I could ever hope to be. Acting is different than posing or pretending. When done with precision, it bears a striking resemblance to lying. Stripped of the costumes and grand gestures, it presents itself as an unquestionable truth. I didn't envy my mother's skill, neither did I contradict her. That's how convincing she was. It seemed best, sitting beside her with a frozen pizza thawing on my lap, to simply sit back and learn.

dinah, the christmas whore

It was my father's belief that nothing built character better than an after-school job. He himself had peddled newspapers and delivered groceries by bobsled, and look at him! My older sister, Lisa, and I decided that if hard work had forged *his* character, we wanted nothing to do with it. "Thanks but no thanks," we said.

As an added incentive, he cut off our allowance, and within a few weeks Lisa and I were both working in cafeterias. I washed dishes at the Piccadilly while Lisa manned the steam tables at K & W. Situated in Raleigh's first indoor shopping center, her cafeteria was a clubhouse for the local senior citizens who might spend an entire afternoon huddled over a single serving of rice pudding. The K & W was past its prime, whereas my cafeteria was located in the sparkling new Crabtree Valley, a former swamp that made her mall look like a dusty tribal marketplace. The Piccadilly had red velvet walls and a dining room lit by artificial torches. A suit of armor marked the entrance to this culinary castle where, we were told, the customer was always king.

As a dishwasher, I spent my shifts yanking trays off a conveyor belt and feeding their contents into an enormous, foulmouthed machine that roared and spat until its charges, free of congealed fat and gravy, came steaming out the other end, fogging my glasses and filling the air with the harsh smell of chlorine.

I didn't care for the heat or the noise, but other than that, I enjoyed my job. The work kept my hands busy but left my mind free to concentrate on more important matters. Sometimes I would study from the list of irregular Spanish verbs I kept posted over the sink, but most often I found myself fantasizing about a career in television. It was my dream to create and star in a program called *Socrates and Company*, in which I would travel from place to place accompanied by a brilliant and loyal proboscis monkey. Socrates and I wouldn't go looking for trouble, but week after week it would manage to find us. "The eyes, Socrates, go for the eyes," I'd yell during one of our many fight scenes.

Maybe in Santa Fe I'd be hit over the head by a heavy jug and lose my memory. Somewhere in Utah Socrates might discover a satchel of valuable coins or befriend someone wearing a turban, but at the end of every show we would realize that true happiness often lies where you very least expect it. It might arrive in the form of a gentle breeze or a handful of peanuts, but when it came, we would seize it with our own brand of folksy wisdom. I'd planned it so that the final moments of each episode would find Socrates and me standing before a brilliant sunset as I reminded both my friend and the viewing audience of the lesson I had learned. "It suddenly occurred to me that there are things far more valuable than gold," I might say, watching a hawk glide high above a violet butte. Plotting the episodes was no more difficult than sorting the silverware; the hard part was thinking up the all-important revelation. "It suddenly occurred to me

dinah, the christmas whore

that . . ." That what? Things hardly ever occurred to me. It might occasionally strike me that I'd broken a glass or filled the machine with too much detergent, but the larger issues tended to elude me.

Like several of the other local cafeterias, the Piccadilly often hired former convicts whose jobs were arranged through parole officers and work-release programs. During my downtime I often hung around their area of the kitchen, hoping that in listening to these felons, something profound might reveal itself. "It suddenly occurred to me that we are all held captive in that prison known as the human mind," I would muse, or "It suddenly occurred to me that freedom was perhaps the greatest gift of all." I'd hoped to crack these people like nuts, sifting through their brains and coming away with the lessons garnered by a lifetime of regret. Unfortunately, having spent the better part of their lives behind bars, the men and women I worked with seemed to have learned nothing except how to get out of doing their jobs.

Kettles boiled over and steaks were routinely left to blacken on the grill as my coworkers crept off to the stockroom to smoke and play cards or sometimes have sex. "It suddenly occurred to me that people are lazy," my reflective TV voice would say. This was hardly a major news flash, and as a closing statement, it would undoubtedly fail to warm the hearts of my television audience — who, by their very definition, were probably not too active themselves. No, my message needed to be upbeat and spiritually rewarding. *Joy*, I'd think, whacking the dirty plates against the edge of the slop can. *What brings people joy?*

As Christmas approached, I found my valuable fantasy time cut in half. The mall was crazy now with hungry shoppers, and every three minutes I had the assistant manager on my back hollering for more coffee cups and vegetable bowls.

The holiday customers formed a loud and steady line that reached past the coat of arms all the way to the suit of armor at the front door. They wore cheerful Santas pinned to their baubled shirts and carried oversized bags laden with power tools and assorted cheeses bought as gifts for friends and relatives. It made me sad and desperate to see so many people, strangers whose sheer numbers eroded the sense of importance I was working so hard to invent. Where did they come from, and why couldn't they just go home? I might swipe their trays off the belt without once wondering who these people were and why they hadn't bothered to finish their breaded cutlets. They meant nothing to me, and watching them move down the line toward the cashier, it became apparent that the feeling was mutual. They wouldn't even remember the meal, much less the person who had provided them with their piping hot tray. How was it that I was important and they were not? There had to be something that separated us.

I had always looked forward to Christmas, but now my enthusiasm struck me as cheap and common. Leaving the cafeteria after work, I would see even more people, swarming out of the shops and restaurants like bees from a burning hive. Here were the young couples in their stocking caps and the families clustered beside the fountain, each with its lists and marked envelopes of money. It was no wonder the Chinese people couldn't tell them apart. They were sheep, stupid animals programmed by nature to mate and graze and bleat out their wishes to the obese, retired school principal who sat on his ass in the mall's sorry-looking North Pole.

My animosity was getting the best of me until I saw in their behavior a solution to my troubling identity crisis. Let them have their rolls of gift wrap and gaudy, personalized stockings: if it meant something to them, I wanted nothing to do with it. This year I would be the one *without* the shopping bags, the one wearing black in protest of their thoughtless commercialism. My very avoidance would set me apart and cause these people to question themselves in ways that would surely pain them. "Who *are* we?" they'd ask, plucking the ornaments off their trees. "What have we become and why can't we be more like that somber fellow who washes dishes down at the Piccadilly cafeteria?"

My boycott had a practical edge, as this year I wasn't expected to receive much of anything. In an effort to save money, my family had decided to try something new and draw names. This cruel lottery left my fate in the hands of Lisa, whose idea of a decent gift was a six-pack of flashlight batteries or a scented candle in the shape of a toadstool. Patently, joyfully normal, Lisa was the embodiment of everything I found depressing. Nothing set her apart from the thousands of other girls I saw each day, but this fact did not disturb her in the least. In her desire to be typical, my sister had succeeded with flying, muted colors. Unlike me, she would never entertain deep thoughts or travel to distant lands in the company of a long-nosed proboscis monkey. None of them would. Along with everyone else, she had traded her soul in exchange for a stocking stuffer and now would have to suffer the consequences.

As the holiday season advanced, so did my impatience. Four days before Christmas we were seated in the dining room, celebrating Lisa's eighteenth birthday, when she received a phone call from what sounded like a full-grown woman with a mouth full of gravel. When I asked who was calling, the woman hesitated before identifying herself as "a friend. I'm a goddamned friend, all right?" This caught my attention because, to my knowledge, my sister had no adult friends, goddamned or otherwise. I handed her the phone

naked

110

and watched as she carried it out into the carport, stretching the cord to its limit. It was a forbidden act, and because I felt like causing some trouble, I told on her. "Dad, Lisa carried the receiver outside and now it looks like the phone is going to spring off the wall."

He started out of his chair before my mother said, "Leave her alone, for God's sake, it's her birthday. If the phone breaks, I'll buy you another one for Christmas." She gave me a look usually reserved for eight-legged creatures found living beneath the kitchen sink. "You always have to stir the turd, don't you?"

"But she's talking to a *woman!*" I said.

My mother crushed her cigarette into her plate. "Big deal, so are you."

Lisa returned to the table in a hurried, agitated state, asking my parents if she might use the station wagon. "David and I should be back in an hour or so," she said, grabbing our coats from the front-hall closet.

"David who?" I asked. "This David's not going anywhere." I'd hoped to spend the evening in my bedroom, working on the pastel portrait of Socrates I planned to quietly give myself as an anti-Christmas present. We stood negotiating in the dark driveway until I agreed to join her, no questions asked, in exchange for three dollars and unlimited use of her new hair-dryer. Having settled that, we got into the car and drove past the brightly decorated homes of north Raleigh. Normally, Lisa demanded strict control of the radio. At the sight of my fingers approaching the dial, she would smack my hand and threaten to toss me out of the car, but tonight she gave me no grief, failing to complain even when I settled on a local talk show devoted to the theme of high-school basketball. I couldn't stand basketball and only tuned in to get a rise out of her. "How about those Spartans," I said,

dinah, the christmas whore

nudging her in the shoulder. "You think they've got what it takes to defeat the Imps and move on to the city championship?"

"Whatever. I don't know. Maybe."

Something had clearly placed her beyond my reach, and it drove me wild with something that felt very much like jealousy. "What? Are we going to meet up with the mother of your boyfriend? How much do you have to pay her to allow him to go out with you? You have a boyfriend, is that it?"

She ignored my questions, quietly muttering to herself as she drove us past the capitol building and into a defeated neighborhood where the porches sagged and a majority of the windows sported sheets and towels rather than curtains. People got knifed in places like this, I heard about it all the time on my radio call-in shows. Had my father been driving, we would have locked all the doors and ignored the stop signs, speeding through the area as quickly as possible because that's what smart people did.

"All right, then." Lisa pulled over and parked behind a van whose owner stood examining his flattened tire with a flashlight. "Things might get a little rough up there, so just do what I tell you and hopefully no one will get hurt." She flipped her hair over her shoulder and stepped out of the car, kicking aside the cans and bottles that lined the curb. My sister meant business, whatever it was, and in that instant she appeared beautiful and exotic and dangerously stupid. LOCAL TEENS SLAIN FOR SPORT the headlines would read. HOLIDAY HIJINKS END IN HOMICIDE.

"Maybe someone should wait with the car," I whispered, but she was beyond reason, charging up the street in her sensible shoes with a rugged, determined gait. There was no fumbling for a street address or doorbell; Lisa seemed to know exactly where she was going. I followed her into a dark

naked

vestibule and up a flight of stairs, where without even bothering to knock, she threw open an unlocked door and stormed into a filthy, overheated room that smelled of stale smoke, sour milk, and seriously dirty laundry — three odors that, once combined, can peel the paint off walls.

This was a place where bad things happened to people who clearly deserved nothing but the worst. The stained carpet was littered with cigarette butts and clotted, dust-covered flypaper hung from the ceiling like beaded curtains. In the far corner of the room, a man stood beside an overturned coffee table, illuminated by a shadeless lamp that broadcast his shadow, huge and menacing, against the grimy wall. He was dressed casually in briefs and a soiled T-shirt and had thin, hairless legs the color and pebbled texture of a store-bought chicken.

We had obviously interrupted some rite of unhappiness, something that involved shouting obscenities while pounding upon a locked door with a white-tasseled loafer. The activity consumed him so completely that it took the man a few moments to register our presence. Squinting in our direction, he dropped the shoe and steadied himself against the mantel.

"Why if it isn't Lisa Fucking Sedaris. I should have known that bitch would call a fucking bitch like you."

I would have been less shocked had a seal called my sister by name. How was it that she knew this man? Staggeringly drunk, the wasted, boozy Popeye charged in our direction, and Lisa rushed to meet him. I watched then, cringing, as she caught him by the neck, throwing him down against the coffee table before gathering her fists and dancing in a tight circle, thoroughly prepared to take on any hidden comers. It was as if she had spent a lifetime dressed in a black *gi*, breaking two-by-fours with her bare hands in preparation for this moment. She never faltered or cried out for help, just gave him a few swift kicks in the ribs and proceeded to carry out her mission.

"I ain't done nothing," the man moaned, turning to me with his bloodshot eyes. "You there, tell that bitch I hadn't done nothing."

"I beg your pardon?" I inched toward the door. "Oh, golly, I don't know what to tell you. I'm just, you know, I just came along for the ride."

"Guard him!" Lisa yelled.

Guard him how? Who did she think I was? "Don't leave me," I cried, but she had already gone, and suddenly I was alone with this shattered man, who massaged his chest and begged me to fetch his cigarettes off the sofa.

"Go on, boy, get 'em. Fucking bitches. Lord Jesus, I'm in pain."

I heard my sister's voice and looked up to see her fleeing the back room, dragging behind her a clownish, tear-stained woman of an indeterminate age. Her face was lined and puffy. The thick, fat, mottled body had a lot of mileage on it, but her clothing was unseasonable and absurdly youthful. While my mother's crowd favored holiday maxiskirts and turquoise squash-blossom necklaces, this woman had attempted to offset the ravages of time with denim hot pants and a matching vest that, fastened together by a cross-hatching system of rawhide laces, afforded a view of her sagging, ponderous breasts.

"Out!" Lisa shouted. "Hurry, now, step on it!"

I was way ahead of her.

"My shoes and, oh, I better take a jacket," the woman said. "And while I'm at it . . ." Her voice faded as I raced down the stairs, past the other equally dark and volatile doorways where people fought over the noise of their screeching televisions. I was out on the street, panting for breath and wondering how many times my sister would be stabbed or

naked

bludgeoned when I heard the screen door slam and saw Lisa appear on the front porch. She paused on the stoop, waiting as the woman put on a jacket and stuffed her feet into a pair of shoes that, in their bulk and color, resembled a matching set of paint cans. Instructed once again to run, her friend proceeded to totter down the street on what amounted to a pair of stilts. It was an awkward, useless style of walking, and with each step she ran her fingers through the air as if she were playing a piano.

Two young men passed down the sidewalk carrying a mattress, and one of them turned to yell, "Get that ho off the street!"

Had we been in a richer or poorer neighborhood, I might have searched the ground for a gardening tool, fearful that once again I might step on the thing and split my lip with the handle. *Ho.* I'd heard that word bandied about by the cooks at work, who leered and snickered much like the young men with their mattress. It took me a second to realize that they were referring either to Lisa or to her friend, who was squatting to examine a hole in her fishnet stockings. A whore. Of the two possible nominees, the friend seemed the more likely candidate. At the mention of the word, she had lifted her head and given a little wave. This woman was the real thing, and I studied her, my breath shallow and visible in the cold, dark air. Like a heroin addict or a mass murderer, a prostitute was, to me, more exotic than any celebrity could ever hope to be. You'd see them downtown after dark, sticking their hatchety faces into the windows of idling cars. "Hey there, Flossie, what do you charge for a lube job," my father would shout. I always wanted him to pull over so we could get a better look, but having made his little comment, he'd roll up the window and speed off, chuckling.

"Dinah, this is David. David, Dinah." Lisa made the introductions after we'd settled ourselves into the car. Apparently, the two of them worked together at the K & W and had come to know each other quite well.

"Oh, that Gene is a real hothead," Dinah said. "He's possessive, like I told you, but, Lord, that man just can't help himself from loving me. Maybe we'll just drive around the block a few times and give him a chance to cool off." She lit a cigarette and dropped it, lowering her high, teased head of hair before sighing, "Oh, well, it won't be the first car I've set fire to."

"Found it!" Lisa held the cigarette to her lips and inhaled deeply, releasing the smoke through her nostrils. A beginner would have gagged, but she puffed away like a withered old pro. What other tricks had she learned recently? Was there a packet of heroin tucked inside her pocket? Had she taken to throwing knives or shooting pool while the rest of us were asleep in our beds? She stared thoughtfully at the street before asking, "Dinah, are you drunk?"

"Yes, ma'am, I am," the woman answered. "I surely am."

"And Gene was drunk, too, am I wrong?"

"A little bit drunk," Dinah said. "But that's his way. We like to get drunk in the winter when there's nothing else to do."

"And is that good for your work-release program? Is getting drunk and having fistfights something that's going to keep you out of trouble?"

"It wasn't nothing but horseplay. It got out of hand is all."

Lisa didn't seem to mind making the woman uncomfortable. "You told me yesterday at the steam table that you were ready to break it off with that sorry little bastard and work your way up to carving. A person's got to have steady hands if she wants to carve meat all day, don't you know that?"

Dinah snapped. "I can't remember everything I said at the

goddamned steam table. Hell's bells, girl, I never would have called if I'd known you was going to hassle me half to death. Turn around, now, I want to go home."

"Oh, I'm taking you home all right," Lisa said.

The sorry neighborhood receded into the distance, and Dinah turned in her seat, squinting until her eyes were completely shut and she fell asleep.

"Mom, this is Dinah. Dinah, this is my mother."

"Oh, thank goodness," my mother said, helping our guest out of her shoddy rabbit jacket. "For a moment there, I was afraid you were one of those damned carolers. I wasn't expecting company, so you'll have to excuse the way I look."

The way *she* looked? Dinah's mascara had smeared, causing her to resemble a ridiculously costumed panda, and here my mother was apologizing for the way *she* looked? I took her aside for a moment.

"Whore," I whispered. "That lady is a whore." I'm not certain what reaction I was after, but shock would have done quite nicely. Instead, my mother said, "Well, then, we should probably offer her a drink." She left me standing in the dining room listening as she presented the woman with a long list of options delivered in alphabetical order. "We've got beer, bourbon, gin, ouzo, rum, scotch, vodka, whiskey, wine, and some thick yellow something or other in an unmarked bottle."

When Dinah spilled her cocktail onto the clean holiday tablecloth, my mother apologized as though it had been her fault for filling the glass too high. "I tend to do that sometimes. Here, let me get you another."

Hearing a fresh, slurred voice in the house, my brother and sisters rushed from their rooms and gathered to examine Lisa's friend, who clearly cherished the attention. "Angels," Dinah said. "You're a pack of goddamned angels." She was

dinah, the christmas whore

surrounded by admirers, and her eyes brightened with each question or comment.

"Which do you like better," my sister Amy asked, "spending the night with strange guys or working in a cafeteria? What were the prison guards *really* like? Do you ever carry a weapon? How much do you charge if somebody just wants a spanking?"

"One at a time, one at a time," my mother said. "Give her a second to answer."

Tiffany tried on Dinah's shoes while Gretchen modeled her jacket. Birthday cake was offered and candles were lit. My six-year-old brother emptied ashtrays, blushing with pride when Dinah complimented him on his efficiency. "This one here ought to be working down at the cafeteria," she said. "He's got the the arms of a busboy and eyes like an assistant manager. Nothing slips by you, does it, sweetheart? Let's see if he can freshen up an old lady's drink."

Woken by the noise, my father wandered up from the basement, where he'd been sitting in his underwear, drowsing in front of the television. His approach generally marked the end of the party. "What the hell are you doing in here at two o'clock in the morning?" he'd shout. It was his habit to add anywhere from three to four hours to the actual time in order to strengthen the charge of disorderly conduct. The sun could still be shining, and he'd claim it was midnight. Point to the clock and he'd only throw up his hands to say, "Bullshit! Go to bed."

This evening he was in a particularly foul mood and announced his arrival well before entering the room. "What are you, tap-dancing up there? You want to put on a show, do you? Well, the theater's closed for the night. Take your act on the road; it's four o'clock in the morning, goddamnit."

We turned instinctively to our mother. "Don't come into

the kitchen," she called. "We don't want you to see your . . . Christmas present."

"My present? Really?" His voice softened to a mew. "Carry on, then."

We listened to his footsteps as he padded down the hallway to his room and then we covered our mouths, laughing until our sight was watery. Swallows of cake revisited our throats, and our faces, reflected in the dark windows, were flushed and vibrant.

Every gathering has its moment. As an adult, I distract myself by trying to identify it, dreading the inevitable downswing that is sure to follow. The guests will repeat themselves one too many times, or you'll run out of dope or liquor and realize that it was all you ever had in common. At the time, though, I still believed that such a warm and heady feeling might last forever and that in embracing it fully, I might approximate the same wistful feeling adults found in their second round of drinks. I had hated Lisa, felt jealous of her secret life, and now, over my clotted mug of hot chocolate, I felt for her a great pride. Up and down our street the houses were decorated with plywood angels and mangers framed in colored bulbs. Over on Coronado someone had lashed speakers to his trees, broadcasting carols over the candy-cane forest he'd planted beside his driveway. Our neighbors would rise early and visit the malls, snatching up gift-wrapped Dustbusters and the pom-pommed socks used to protect the heads of golf clubs. Christmas would arrive and we, the people of this country, would gather around identical trees, voicing our pleasure with worn clichés. Turkeys would roast to a hard, shellacked finish. Hams would be crosshatched with x's and glazed with fruit — and it was fine by me. Were I to receive a riding vacuum cleaner or even a wizened proboscis monkey, it wouldn't please me half as much as knowing we were the only family in the neighborhood with a prostitute in our kitchen. From this moment on, the phrase "ho, ho, ho" would take on a whole different meaning; and I, along with the rest of my family, could appreciate it in our own clannish way. It suddenly occurred to me. Just like that.

naked

planet of the apes

It started following an all-day *Planet of the Apes* marathon held at a budget theater a mile or so from my parents' house. I had seen the original movie nine times, waiting always for Zira to ask, "What do you think he'll find in the Forbidden Zone, Dr. Zaius?" The area in question was a vast wasteland, off-limits to the intelligent chimps and warmongering gorillas who inhabited this world turned upside down. As Bright Eyes, the defiant astronaut stranded on this planet, Charlton Heston escapes his captors and rides into the Forbidden Zone accompanied by the mute human supervixen he has chosen as his mate. Their horse trots over barren deserts and sandy beaches until they come upon the half-buried remains of the Statue of Liberty. Suddenly realizing that he has been on his home planet throughout the course of the entire two-hour movie, Charlton Heston dismounts his horse and kneels in the sand. "Damn you!" he cries, shaking his fist at the blistering sun. "Damn you all to hell!"

I had entered the theater on a bright, humid morning but when I left, dazed and candy-bloated, it was dark and raining. I thought of calling my mother for a ride, but she was off wrapping potatoes in tinfoil for my sister Amy's Girl Scout troop. That left only my father.

"I'll be there in five minutes," he said. In the background I heard mention of the term "three-eighths." Not three-eighths of an inch, but three-eighths of a point, which meant he was watching the financial report and had already taken off his pants for the evening.

I called back an hour later and he answered saying, "I'm on my way out the door right this minute." A studio audience laughed and hooted from my father's end of the phone. The situation comedies had started. This meant he'd been asleep in his chair. He would sit there snoring until someone tried to change the channel. "What are you doing?" he'd yell. "I was watching that!"

It was even worse on weekend afternoons, when you'd call for a ride and hear nothing in the background. This meant he was watching golf, hours of silence interrupted every so often by the commentator whispering, "It's been bogey, bogey, double bogey for Hogan, who's nine over par coming into the fourth hole here at Oakland Hills."

You could outgrow your clothing waiting for my father to pick you up. I called a third time and he answered groggy and confused. "David who?" he asked. "What movie, where?"

I left the shopping center, walked across the road, and held out my thumb. It was just that easy. My father was always stopping to pick up hitchhikers. We'd be packed into the station wagon, on our way to the pool or the grocery store, and he would pull over, instructing us to make room for company. It was always exciting to have a stranger in the car, young men we could torment with questions. Our father, his cocktail tinkling between his legs, was outwardly gracious but

naked

also suspicious. He toyed with our guests, acting as though their stories were just that, stories, something they made up as they went along.

"All right, 'Rudy,' I'll be happy to take you to your 'grandmother's' house so you can pick up your 'laundry.'" He would shake his head and chuckle. "Always happy to help out a fine young man such as yourself."

"No, really," our passenger would say. "She is my grandmother, I swear."

"I know you swear," my father would say. "Twenty bucks says you've got a mouth like an open sewer."

As long as they were young, he was more than happy to pick them up; but the old ones — forget it. We would spot some stooped and weathered granddad standing beside a beat-up suitcase and call out, "There's one! Dad, stop." Ignoring our request, our father would drive past these men as if they were painted cutouts advertising a restaurant called Tramps or Hobos.

I held out my thumb, certain someone like my father would pick me up but instead, it was an elderly woman, her helmet of hair protected by a plastic bonnet. She rolled down her window and shouted as if the two of us had some long-standing beef. "Goddamn you, get your sorrowful butt into this car."

She wore a pale blue uniform, the outfit issued to the cashiers of a local supermarket chain. "What are you, fourteen, fifteen years old? I've got a grandson about your age, and if I ever caught him hitching a ride, I'd stick my foot so far up his ass I'd lose my shoe. What the hell do you think you're doing, taking rides from strangers? What if I was to have a pistol or a switchblade knife? You couldn't fight off a house cat, and don't bother telling me otherwise, because I know your type, Mr. Wisenheimer, I know your type only too well. What would your mother think about this foolishness? Where are your people?"

"My parents?" I hesitated a moment, realizing there was no reason I had to tell this woman the truth. Chances are, she'd never see me again; and if she did, who's to say she'd recognize me? I told her my father was attending a peace conference in Stockholm, Germany, and that my mother was a long-haul truck driver on a run to the West Coast with a loadful of . . . panty hose.

"Right," the woman said, tamping her cigarette into the smoldering ashtray, "and I breast-feed baby camels in my backyard just for the freaking fun of it. Just tell me where you live, Pinocchio, and save the baloney for lunch."

She pulled up in front of my parents' house just as my father was leaving to pick me up. "Truck driver, my pretty pink ass," she said. "Now I want you to get into that fancy house of yours and stay there before somebody carves his initials into your skull. You were lucky this time, but if I ever catch you out there again, I'll run you down just to spare you the misery."

I started hitchhiking on a regular basis. Aside from the convenience, I enjoyed spending time with people who knew nothing about me. I was free to re-invent myself, trying on whichever personality happened to suit my mood. I was a Broadway actor studying the regional accent for an upcoming show or maybe a California high-school student, here to track down the father I'd never known. "Word has it he goes by the name T-Bone, but that's all I have to go on."

Some people pulled over almost as if they'd been expecting me, while others slowed down, studying me before coming to a complete stop. They were black ministers and retired locksmiths, lifeguards, dance instructors, and floor sanders, and usually they were alone. Raleigh wasn't that big a town,

naked

and most people didn't mind going a mile or two out of their way for a stranger. "You should spend some time here, Maurice," they'd say. "It's a friendly city with plenty of opportunities for a talented concert pianist like you."

I never hitchhiked farther than the city limits until I went off to college and fell in with a girl named Veronica, whose life resembled one of the stories I'd invented. Her mother had died while confined to an iron lung parked in the family's dining room. Veronica was fourteen at the time and received the news while experiencing her first acid trip. "You want to ruin a perfectly good high, that's the way to do it," she said. Her father had remarried twice over the past four years, dragging her through two sets of stepfamilies. The experience had taught her to fend for herself. She was adventurous and independent in a way I'd never known, well instructed in the arts of camping, cigarette rolling, and sneaking out of second-story windows. Our college campus was isolated in the mountains of western North Carolina, far from the region's celebrated tourist attractions. We started off by taking day trips, first to Gatlinburg to see the fake Indians and then to Cherokee to see the real thing.

She was a take-charge kind of person, and together we crossed state lines, hitchhiking as far away as Nashville and Washington, D.C. At the end of the school year, I transferred to Kent State and Veronica packed off to San Francisco, where her brother set her up with a job in a movie theater. Her letters made my life sound hopelessly dull and predictable. "I could set you up just like that!" she'd write. "All the popcorn and hard candies you can eat, and it won't cost you a nickel. Free movies, a clean place to shit — you'll have it made!"

I lasted a year before deciding to join her, making the trip with a fellow named Randolph Feathers, a second-year college student I'd met at a party. Randolph was creating his own major in Beat literature, a subject that warranted no further attention as far as I was concerned. His collection of stained, first-edition paperbacks reflected his belief that this was to be a spiritual journey, presided over by the ghosts of his bongo-playing heroes. In order to prepare himself, he had grown a goatee and bought an Australian bush hat that he'd decorated with pins and buttons espousing the numerous political causes close to his heart. Veronica had taught me that in the hopes of squeezing out a few extra miles, it was wise never to debate or rile a driver. If they believed in, say, the enforced sterilization of redheads, it was best just to say, "Hmm, I never thought about it, but maybe you're onto something." Randolph's hat guaranteed we wouldn't be riding in any air-conditioned Cadillacs. To make matters worse, he decided to bring along a guitar. We hadn't even gotten our first ride before he pulled it out and began composing one of his mournful ballads. "Standin' on the highway, thumb up in the air/People passin' by, pretendin' not to care."

I'd sooner pick up someone waving a pistol than holding a guitar. He'd lie barefoot on the side of the road with his head propped up on his rucksack, exercising his toes and wondering why we weren't getting any rides. "It's a heartless cutthroat world, so callous and so cold/I hope to get to Frisco, before I'm bald and old."

Outside Indianapolis we were picked up by two young men in a Jeep who introduced themselves as Starsky and Hutch, names borrowed from the brazen, coltish heroes of a popular television show. They were wired and loopy, washing down their over-the-counter amphetamines with quarts of warm malt liquor. When asked where they were from, Starsky made a gagging gesture.

"That's the code for 'Delaware,'" Hutch explained.

Starsky gave the finger to the driver of an orange Gremlin.

"State bird," Hutch said. He took a swallow of his malt liquor and belched, proclaiming it the state motto.

Noticing the tank was low, they pulled into a service station where I offered them some gas money, hoping they might view my thoughtful gesture as payment enough. Starsky said he had it covered, adding that he could sure use some fudge. "Not just chocolate, but fudge. Why don't you go on into the mart there and see do they have some."

It's always best for one person to remain with the car just in case the driver gets an urge to take off with your packs, so Randolph stayed behind, squinting out at the flat, uninspired landscape and fulfilling Hutch's request for "Free Bird."

I bought a bag of potato chips and a block of something fudgelike and returned to the car just as Starsky was replacing the gas cap. "Jump in, chief." He eyed the attendant headed our way to accept payment, but just as the man reached the pump, Starsky peeled out of the station, driving over a concrete embankment and onto the interstate.

"I'm not sure how cool this is," Randolph said. "What about the police?"

"Police?" Starsky turned to look behind him. "Hey-ho, buddy, we can outrun the police, no fucking problemo." He stomped on the gas pedal and the Jeep advanced much like a plane moments before taking to the air. We passed other cars as if they were parked, Starsky hunching forward with the clenched, determined look of a bombardier preparing to destroy a village of unsuspecting peasants. He yelled out for Hutch to hold the wheel while he opened the packet of fudge, and the Jeep swerved into the other lane, barely missing a tanker filled with diesel fuel. Horns blared and brakes squealed, and for the first time in my life I thought, *This is how people die; this is exactly how it happens.* Randolph's hat flew out the window, but even if the violent wind had taken his guitar, I doubt I would have been able to appreciate it. This wasn't a situation that allowed me to laugh at someone else's misfortune. He and I were in this together. We would either die or spend the rest of our lives on the back wards of some hospital where nurses would come regularly to massage our comatose limbs and whisper words of encouragement. Beneath his goatee and tie-dyed T-shirt, we were whining, trembling brothers, frantically searching for the nonexistent seat belts and grabbing onto each other for support and comfort. Starsky and Hutch seemed to enjoy our pathetic display of fear, jiggling the steering wheel and cutting off other drivers just to watch us cower and pray. We covered an enormous amount of ground before Starsky pulled over to relieve himself behind a billboard. It struck me as odd that he could steal gasoline and threaten the lives of countless strangers, yet feel the need to hide so completely while peeing. He walked far into the tall grass, and Randolph and I took the opportunity to jump out of this death trap, our quivering hands barely able to grip our packs. "This is great," we said. "Really, this is exactly where we needed to go."

Starsky zipped up his fly and exchanged places with Hutch, who drove a few hundred feet up the road before backing up to where we stood. "And another thing," Starsky said. "Your fudge ain't worth shit." He reared back and pitched it in our direction before taking off down the interstate in a cloud of exhaust and whipped gravel. The fudge hit the billboard and bounced onto the road, where Randolph stopped to pick it up. He brushed it off and took a few bites before saying that it tasted just fine to him.

We reached Colorado, which was just as I had seen it pictured on calendars: cloudless blue skies and heroic mountains dotted with magnificent firs. Just like a calendar, with no cars, people, or houses to sully the view. Randolph used the downtime to compose a few new songs. "I'm well aware, they were from . . . Delaware."

For a brief time our brush with disaster brought us closer together. We repeated the story to drivers much like a long-married couple, one of us finishing the other's sentences. The experience seemed to fit neatly into Randolph's Beatish notions, and he spoke with growing frequency of karma and redemption. On one hot, sunny afternoon we found ourselves beside a clear, rushing river, its bed paved with smooth stones. There were no potential rides coming our way, so we took off our clothing and swam, looking down at our feet, where long, silvery fish exhausted themselves by heading in the wrong direction. The riverbank was carpeted with fragrant pine needles, and rabbits skittered through the meadow. It was, for me, one of those moments when a director might sail through the air on his cherry picker shouting, "And . . . perfect! Take five, guys, it's a wrap." While I marveled at the beauty of it all, Randolph knowingly nodded his head, referring by page and chapter to one of the books he carried in his bag. He seemed to have it all down, like a tourist holding his Michelin guide and nodding with recognition as the bus approached London Bridge. My brotherly feelings faded and were finally laid to rest a few days later when, polishing off the last of our water, he loudly belched and asked for a word that might rhyme with Utah. I didn't sleep for days.

We were stopped at the California border and asked to hand over all our fruits and vegetables, on the off chance they might introduce some new species of fly or weevil to the dry, beige fields surrounding the inspection point. I was never one of those easterners attracted by the romantic pull of California. Still, though, it felt liberating to enter a part of the country where no member of my family had ever been.

Randolph softly strummed his guitar, and I surrendered my three rotting plums as if they were my old-country surname. We crossed the border in a peach-colored Mustang belonging to a speech therapist from Barstow, and I turned briefly in my seat before vowing never to look back.

The San Francisco that awaited us bore no resemblance to the bohemian think tank described in Randolph's tattered paperbacks. The streets were crowded not with soul-searching poets but with men wearing studded vests and tight leather chaps. This was not a Beat town but rather a beat-off town. Veronica had found us rooms at a residence hotel run by a caramel-colored man whose curious Eastern religion involved bright orange robes, incessant chanting, and handcuffs. Randolph stayed for ten days, returning home by bus shortly after a neighbor cornered him in the hallway, asking if he might be so kind as to enter his penis in a blind taste test. Veronica and I left three months later, headed up to Oregon, where we hoped to make a killing picking apples and pears. *Killing* accurately described the work, and once it was over we limped up the coast to Canada, back to California, and across the country, stopping wherever we liked. It was the realization of my high-school fantasy, except that Veronica bore little resemblance to a proboscis monkey. She was, however, the perfect traveling companion, poised and even-tempered. As a couple we received rides from strangers who might not have stopped had we both been men. These were single women and truck drivers who claimed they needed company yet rarely spoke a word. Sometimes people would invite us into their homes to spend the night on their sofas. "The bathroom's down the hall, and I've laid out some fresh towels. I'm trusting you not to steal the TV or hi-fi, but help yourself to anything else, it's all garbage anyway." Other nights we slept in abandoned houses and open fields, under bridges and lean-tos, and on one occasion, in the parking lot

naked

of a Las Vegas casino. We headed down to Texas with the sole purpose of seeing an armadillo, then swept north, arriving in western North Carolina in mid-November. The next stop would be Raleigh, and wanting to postpone the inevitable, I thought I might visit some college friends in Ohio. It was the longest trip I'd ever taken alone, but having logged so many miles, I felt I was up to the challenge. Time had wisened me, I thought. Without modeling myself on someone else, I had managed to transform myself into a reckless, heroic figure, far more noble than the characters described in any of Randolph's trendy beatnik poems or novels. My college friends would view me as a prophet, and my presence would cause them to question the value of their tame, predictable lives. "Tell us again about your three days on the Mojave," they'd ask. "Weren't you frightened? Does rattlesnake really taste like chicken? What did you do with the fangs?"

I hadn't planned on lying, but it seemed a good move to embellish my stories, to pad and touch them up a bit. I stood by the side of the road, thinking that I might as well have broken wild stallions or caught trout with my bare hands — the point was that I had taken life head-on, with no regard for the consequences.

I got an interminable ride with a window salesman who spent six hours saying, "You just take and take, don't you? Out there with your thumb in the air — not a care in the world, just grabbing whatever you can get. Yes, sir, you take and take until you're ready to burst. But what about giving? Did you ever think of that? Of course not — you're too busy taking, Mr. Handout, Mr. Gimmee, Gimmee, Gimmee. Me, I'm what you call a 'taxpayer.' Tax, it's a . . . tariff that working people have to pay so that someone like yourself can enjoy a life of leisure. I give and I give until I've got nothing left! Nothing! Then I turn around and give some more. I give and I give to all of Uncle Sam's little takers, every last one of you, but what's in it for me? I've been thinking that maybe it's time I get a little something in return. Yes, indeed, maybe it's about time we try that shoe on the other foot for a change. You, my young friend, are going to wash my car, inside and out. *And* you're going to pay for it!"

He exited the interstate and headed for a car wash, the roof of which supported three artificial seals buffing a limousine with their motorized fins. The man stood beside the bumper supervising me as I shampooed and waxed his car.

"That's right, put a little muscle into it! Next I want you to empty those ashtrays and vacuum the interior, top to bottom. Come on, speedy, let's get cracking."

I had no problem with the work, but his coaching style was driving me out of my mind.

"How does it feel to be giving for a change? Not much fun, is it? Hurry up now and buff those hubcaps, I want to see them shine. Buff, boy, buff!"

I'm buffing, I'm buffing. Give it a rest already, I thought. Every headlight represented his bald, gleaming skull, and I worked the rag as if it were a sheet of sandpaper. I polished everything from the antenna to the license plate before he handed me my pack and drove away, tooting his horn as he merged into the afternoon traffic. I got a ride back to the interstate and then another that landed me twenty miles beyond Charleston, West Virginia. The sun was low and I hoped I might catch a long ride before it got dark, something that would maybe carry me through to the state of Ohio. It was cold outside and my hands were chapped from washing that lunatic's car, the skin rough but my fingernails shining with wax.

I waited twenty minutes before someone slowed and stopped twenty yards down the road. It was a pickup truck advertising an air-conditioning-and-refrigeration company. Often someone, some wise guy, would stop in the distance

naked

132

only to drive off laughing after you'd exhausted yourself running to meet him. In response, I had developed a casual trot.

The man's shirt introduced him as T. W. His fingers were soiled with grease, and the cab of the truck was littered with candy wrappers and soda cans. I asked him what T. W. stood for, and he told me it stood for T. W. His last name, he said, started with an *a*, "So when you put it all together, it has a nice ring to it." He had an open, childlike face, the features set into a continuous expression of wonder. It was as if he'd spent the last ten years in a coma and woken up to find everything new and sensational. I told him I was a medical student completing my residency, just a few more months and I'd be graduating at the top of my class.

"Really? Be a doctor and operate? On people? You must be some kind of smart to be a doctor. Operate on brains, you say?"

I'd said I'd been doing it for years and that it wasn't nearly as hard as it looked. It might seem odd for a twenty-year-old brain surgeon to be begging rides from strangers, so I told him I was hitchhiking to satisfy a bet I'd made with one of my classmates. "Fifty dollars says I can make it from Duke University to Kent State in time for tomorrow's frontal-lobe conference," I said. "It's not that I need the money or anything, this is just something we doctors do to blow off steam."

"Well, I'll see to it that you win that bet," T. W. said. He explained that he'd cut out of work early and would be more than happy to drive me to Ohio, seeing as he was a night owl and hadn't spent time with a doctor since his foot had been crushed by an air-conditioner a few years back. "Look at me," he crowed, "riding with a brain doctor!" We could get started just as soon as he dropped some documents off with a friend. He left the interstate and drove onto a series of highways and winding country roads before arriving at a tavern. It was a squat cinder-block building lit with beer advertisements and a neon sign that announced the existence of a pool table. He invited me to join him, but I was underage and had not yet developed a thirst for alcohol. "You go ahead," I said. "I'll just sit here and study for next week's lobotomy."

It killed me that T. W. actually believed I was a doctor. Once we arrived in Kent, I'd probably have him drop me off in front of the infirmary and walk the few blocks to the dorm. I hoped that between now and then we wouldn't witness any roadside accidents, but if we did, I'd just tell him I wasn't licensed to practice in this state.

It was dusk when T. W. entered the bar. I watched the sun fade behind the surrounding mountains, waiting one hour, two hours, three, until it had grown too dark for me to collect my bag and leave on my own. I had no idea where I was, and few cars passed along this road. There were no streetlights, and I could hear dogs barking off in the distance. When it started to rain I took my pack from the bed of the truck and carried it up front, rooting around for an extra sweater and a pair of socks I could wear on my hands. A car pulled into the parking lot, and I watched as the driver emptied his dashboard ashtray onto the gravel before entering the bar. It seemed a fitting gesture for this sort of place. Staring at the lights of the tavern, I wondered who might choose to live in such a dinky, do-nothing town. From what I'd seen, it was nothing more than a collection of tract houses built around a convenience store. The landscape was pretty enough; you might pass through and admire the mountains, but wouldn't person then move on to someplace more important? Travel was supposed to broaden your mind, but without Veronica's company, it had a way of depressing me. The more places I went, the more I realized I didn't matter to anyone except the family I'd left behind — and who knew them besides

naked

their friends and neighbors in a town just as pointless as this one? Raleigh would be granted a larger dot on the map, but when seen as a whole, the multitude of strange towns and cities conspired to nullify my shaky myth of self-importance. It brought me down to think about it, so I turned on the transistor radio and listened to a call-in show, the evening's topics ranging from an upcoming tractor pull to the hidden dangers of untended space heaters. Heat. It was like reading a restaurant menu to a fasting prisoner. I listened to the callers and imagined their snug, cozy homes, watching as icy clouds huffed forth from my mouth, dissipating in the frigid air.

T. W. staggered out of the bar about ten o'clock, nearly six hours after he'd entered. He had his arms around a jubilant, long-faced man and an obese woman who held her pocketbook over her head as protection against the rain.

She said something, and the men doubled over laughing, practically vomiting with merriment. I was in a foul mood but knew that I would have to swallow it, the way I always did when I was relying on someone else to do me a favor. Whatever its merits, hitchhiking robbed you of your God-given right to complain. I would have to pretend I hadn't noticed the time or temperature. "That was fast," I'd say. "No, I'm perfectly comfortable, just rubbing my hands together because I'm excited. What's up?" One look at him and anyone could tell that T. W. was drunk. He waved good-bye to his companions and proceeded to activate the truck's engine, jabbing the key here and there as though the ignition might have moved during his long absence and now might be anywhere.

"Those people are my friends," he said. "I've been knowing them all my life and they're good, *fun* people, you got that?" His face had lost all traces of innocence and had become hard and dogmatic. "Friends. Personal, *private, goddamn friends*. They're my friends, my *own* fucking friends."

He repeated the word several more times, pounding his chest for emphasis. "Friends. They *like* me. I like them. We go back."

Something told me we wouldn't be driving to Ohio anytime soon. We reached the interstate, brightly lit and teeming with traffic. I offered to get out, but T. W. wouldn't hear of it. "Oh no," he said. "You're coming home with me. Home to *my* house with *me*. I've got the place fixed up nice with rugs and TVs and all kinds of shit like that. No way are you going out alone on a night like this. Forget that crap about school and college, those people don't matter for shit."

I imagined his house with its crummy paint job and dung-colored carpets, hoping it might be located on a well-traveled road. Once there, I could probably make a run for it; in the meantime, I'd just have to humor him.

"Big brain doctor, are you? You like to stick your fat little fingers in other people's skulls and tinker around? Is that what you like to do? I'll give you something to tinker with, hot shot."

I was looking out at the road and didn't see it coming. He grabbed me by the hair and yanked my head down onto the seat, holding me there with one hand while he reached into his jacket pocket with the other. The truck swerved and skidded onto the gravel shoulder before he took the wheel and regained control. There was something cold and blunt pressed hard against my jaw, and even before I saw it clearly, I understood it was a gun. Its physical presence inspired an urgency lacking in any of the movies or television dramas in which it plays such a key role. "You like that do you?"

Only a professional maniac could ask such an inane question. I pictured his home with the same paint job and carpet, only now it was stacked with bodies, as this seemed the exact place where something like this might happen. Maybe he'd

naked

136

used his job skills and built a refrigeration chamber to prevent decay, or perhaps he'd bury me beneath some tool shed and the authorities would have to identity me through dental records. Dental records, my God. When was the last time I'd been to a dentist and why wasn't I there now, my mother smoking in the waiting room and ripping recipes from the ladies' magazines when the receptionist wasn't looking. Requested to hand over his files, my dentist would probably say that I was asking for it by taking rides from strangers. They all would. My people would hang their heads, shamed by my stupidity, while T. W.'s friends and neighbors would appear on television to say, "He was such a nice man, we had no idea."

I felt the truck slow down and take a turn. We were off the interstate now, probably on an exit ramp. He raised the gun to steady the wheel, and I scrambled across the seat, flung open the door, and jumped, thinking all the while of the many television detectives who seemed to do this on a weekly basis. My mother and older sister had sat with their faces pressed against the screen while I jeered and mocked their enthusiasm. *Jump and roll*, I thought. Wasn't that what my mother had said as her hero leaped off a train with the enemy's stolen blueprints? *Jump and roll, jump and roll.* I hit the gravel shoulder and tumbled into a muddy ditch filled with trash and brambles. My pack had landed a few yards away, so I snatched it up and ran, wondering what it carried and why. Behind me I heard the truck pull off the road, the door slam, and someone racing through the thicket. It was him, coming after me. I meant that much to him, and now I would have to work even harder to live because this man, he was determined. I thought maybe I should climb a tree, but that's what you did when pursued by bears, wasn't it? Maybe only the small bears climbed trees — the lighter ones — but still, how could I climb with socks on my hands? With the larger bears maybe you were supposed to lie down and play dead, but this was a man, so what was the point in even thinking about bears? He had a gun and now he would shoot me in the back or maybe in the head, bits of my skull scattered across the forest floor like the remnants of a melon. In the leg, maybe he'd take me there or in the shoulder, blow my arm off at the elbow and I'd consider myself lucky to massage my stump and dial the phone with the fingers of my left hand. What I needed was a weapon. Other people, hitchhikers, told me they always carried a little something, a knife or a can of Mace, and I'd laughed, thinking there was no greater weapon than the human mind. *You idiot.* A can opener. Maybe somewhere in the bottom of my pack there was a can opener I could tie to a stick. Make a spear, that's it, a spear! I'd seen them in the souvenir shops, decorated with beads and feathers. The Indians made spears, didn't they, or no, maybe I was thinking of tomahawks, they made tomahawks, but how did they do it? Didn't it take days or maybe even weeks? A broken bottle, a lance, one of those spiked cannonballs the knights used to swing around on a chain: I needed something in my hands, in my arms. I needed my mother; she'd put a stop to this. *You leave my son alone!* Where was she now and what was she doing? *I'm sorry.* I wanted her to know that and kept mouthing the word. *Sorry, so sorry.* Turning my head to look behind me, I fell into a knot of thorny bushes, thinking I should get up and run, but he was too close now. I could see him through the trees, silhouetted against the headlights. "Hey, you, Doctor Kildare or whoever you are, get back here." He looked off to my right, and I realized he couldn't see me. "I'm not going to hurt you. Come on now, get back in the truck. I was only joking. It's not even loaded, look." He pulled the trigger and the gun made a puny, clicking noise. "I was only playing with you, honest. Can't you take a joke?" He slowly returned to his truck, bending to rifle through the brush. "Hey, shithead. That's right, I'm talking to *you*. Get your ass back here. I'm through playing around." He lit a cigarette and tapped on the horn, behaving as though I'd just stepped out to urinate and had lost my way back. "You want to sleep in the woods under a wet log? Is that what you want?" He rolled down the window and drove off slowly, the door ajar and the cab lights shining, whistling, as if for a lost dog.

I worried that this might be a trick. Maybe he'd parked his truck up the road, planning to take me by surprise once I made a run for it. What if he were to circle back around? On the other hand, while I was hiding, he could be loading his gun or phoning the fellow members of his cult or posse, who would search the forest with clubs and a burlap bag in which to store my body. I stood up and crouched back down. Stood and crouched, again and again until, as if I'd been priming a pump, I shot out of the woods, down the hill, and into the center of the interstate, waving my arms and begging for someone to stop. The first two cars just missed hitting me, but the third pulled over. They were three college students headed home to Akron for the weekend. I told them what had happened, my voice breathy and high-pitched. "And then I jumped out of the truck and ran into the woods and he came after me with a gun and . . ."

"I don't mean to pry," the driver said, "but are you by any chance a faggot?"

His buddies covered their mouths and laughed into their cupped hands. This was not the sympathetic reaction I'd been hoping for. They'd picked me up hoping I might have some dope, and they were right. We smoked a few joints, and the driver popped in an eight-track of the Ozark Mountain

Daredevils. That was my punishment. My reward was that they never spoke another word until dropping me off on the road to Kent.

I continued to hitchhike for the next few years, but after the incident with T. W., something seemed to have changed. It felt as though I'd been marked somehow. I had always counted upon people to trust me, but now I no longer trusted them. A driver would introduce himself as Tony, and I'd wonder why he'd chosen that name. They were liars, every last one of them. My suspicion was a beacon, attracting the very people I'd hoped to avoid. Drivers began picking me up with the idea I had more to offer than my gratitude. Drugs were the easy part; I carried them as a courtesy and offered them whenever asked. What threw me were the sexual advances. How much did they expect to accomplish at fifty miles per hour, and why choose me, a perfect stranger? When I thought of sex, I pictured someone standing before me crying, "I love you so much that . . . I don't even know who I am anymore." My imaginary boyfriend was of no particular age or race, all that mattered was that he was crazy about me. Our first encounter would take place under bizarre circumstances: at the christening of a warship, or maybe a hurricane might bring us together in a crowded storm shelter. I thought about our courtship and the subsequent anniversaries, when our adopted children would gather at our feet saying, "Tell us again about your first date." I suppose we could have met in a car or van but not while I was hitchhiking; it would have to be more complicated than that. Maybe the driver of my vehicle would suffer a heart attack, and he would be one of the medics. The important thing was that I wouldn't be looking for it; that's what would make it so romantic.

"You fool around much when you hitchhike?" The most

naked

overt were the men with the wedding rings and the child safety seats, whose secret double lives demanded quick, anonymous partnerships. I had an unpleasant experience with a married couple outside Atlanta. Two o'clock in the morning and they were driving their Cadillac nude from the waist down. They invited me to spend the night in their home, the husband casually masturbating as his wife styled her hair. "We'll fix you something to eat," she offered. "I'm a damned good cook, you can ask anyone."

A few days later in Fayetteville I was driven down a dark dirt road by a man who offered to crush my skull like a peanut. Cowering in the bushes had become something of a hobby, and I knew it was time to ask myself some serious questions. I walked the eight miles back to town, boarded a bus, and never hitchhiked again.

I still haven't learned to drive a car. Once I was vacationing with a boyfriend who pulled into the deserted parking lot of a hamburger restaurant and demanded that I at least give it a try. After he pointed out the subtle difference between the gas and brake, we swapped seats, him howling in protest as I swerved out onto the two-lane road. It was a Sunday and there wasn't any traffic to speak of. I passed a boy on a bicycle and an elderly woman pushing a wheelbarrow. Their close proximity made me nervous, so I moved toward the center of the road, where it felt safer. I sped up, pretending that I was rushing a pregnant woman to the hospital and then I slowed down and wandered onto the gravel shoulder, making believe I'd fallen asleep at the wheel. We came upon a ranch house painted the color of a pencil eraser. A man stood in the front yard. He wore an apron and attended a smoking grill. I tapped the horn and waved, expecting him to drop his tongs and run for cover, reacting as though he had seen a chimp behind the wheel. Rather than diving into the shrubbery, the man raised his mitted hand in salute before returning to his business. It was thrilling that someone might mistake me for a driver, that I might for one brief moment appear responsible and self-reliant. I enjoyed my outing but knew I'd never make a habit of it. Driving is too dangerous, and besides that, I'm just not the type to fill out insurance forms. I moved to cities with decent public transportation systems, Chicago and then onto New York, which is even better because there are more taxis. You hold out your hand for a ride but retire your thumb, folding it against your palm. The drivers don't speak much English, but that's partly what you're paying for: the quiet.

Every now and then I'll find myself in a car driven by some friend and we'll pass someone standing by the side of the road. His hair is rowdy from the rush of passing traffic, and his lips move in what is either a curse or a prayer. I want to tell the driver to pull over and stop, but instead, pretending a sudden problem with the radio reception, I lower my head until the ghost has receded from the rearview mirror.

the incomplete quad

I spent my high-school years staring at the pine trees outside my classroom window and picturing myself on the campus of an Ivy League university, where my wealthy roommate Colgate would leave me notes reading "Meet me on the quad at five." I wasn't sure what a quad was, but I knew that I wanted one desperately. My college friends would own horses and monogrammed shoehorns. I'd spend weekends at my roommate's estate, where his mother would say things like "I've instructed Helvetica to prepare those little pancakes you're so fond of, but she's had a devil of a time locating fresh cape gooseberries." This woman would have really big teeth that she'd reveal every time she threw back her head to laugh at one of my many witticisms. "You're an absolute caution," she'd bray. "Tell me you'll at least *consider* joining us this Christmas at Bridle Haven; it just wouldn't be the same without you."

I fantasized with the nagging suspicion there was something missing, something I was forgetting. This something turned out to be grades. It was with profound disappointment I discovered it took more than a C average to attend Harvard. *Average,* that was the word that got to me. C and average, the two went hand in hand.

I was sent instead to a state college in western North Carolina where the low brick buildings were marked with plaques reading ERECTED 1974, and my roommate left notes accusing me of stealing his puka shell necklace or remedial English book. I expect someday to open the newspaper and discover the government had used that campus as part of a perverse experiment to study the effects of continuous, high-decibel Pink Floyd albums on the minds of students who could manufacture a bong out of any given object but could not comprehend that it is simply not possible to drive a van to Europe.

I spent my year buckling down and improving my grades in the hope that I might transfer somewhere, anywhere, else. I eventually chose Kent State because people had been killed there. At least they hadn't died of boredom, that was saying something. "Kent State!" everyone said. "Do you think you'll be safe up there?"

I arrived the following September and was assigned to a dormitory largely reserved for handicapped students. It had always been my habit to look away from someone in a wheel-chair, but here I had no choice, as they were everywhere. These were people my own age who had jumped into a de-ceptively shallow pool or underestimated the linebackers of the opposing team. They had driven drunk on prom night or slipped off their parents' roof while cleaning the gutters; one little mistake, and they could never take it back. The para-plegics gathered in the lobby, perfecting their wheelies and discussing their customized cars while the quads purred by in their electric chariots, squinting against the lit cigarettes propped artfully between their lips.

The first quarter I roomed with a fellow named Todd, an

naked

144

amiable Dayton native whose only handicap was having red hair. The quadriplegics had the best drug connections, so we often found ourselves hanging out in their rooms. "The hookah's over on the shelf," they'd say. "Right next to the rectal suppositories." Over time I grew accustomed to the sight of a friend's colostomy bag and came to think of Kent State as something of an I.V. League university. The state would pay your board if you roomed with a handicapped student, so second quarter I moved in with Dale, a seventy-five-pound sophomore with muscular dystrophy. I learned to bathe Dale and set him on the toilet. I turned the pages of his books, dialed the telephone, and held the receiver against his mouth as he spoke. I dressed him and combed his hair, fed him and clipped his toenails, but I can't say that we were ever close.

Midway through the term Dale was sent back home to live with his parents, and I moved in with Peg, a fun girl with a degenerative nerve disease. Peg was labeled an "incomplete quad" and liked to joke that she couldn't finish anything. Already we had something in common. She had come to school to escape her parents, who refused her any beverage after 6 P.M. They complained that at the end of a long day, they were simply too worn out to set her on the toilet. God had chosen her to suffer this disease, and if she had any complaints, she should take it up with Him. This was a nasty illness that left its host progressively incapacitated. Peg's limbs were twisted and unreliable and had a mind of their own. A cup of scalding coffee, a lit cigarette, forks and steak knives — objects sprung from her hands with no prior notice. She wore thick glasses strapped to her head and soiled sheepskin booties on her useless, curled feet. Peg's voice was slurred to the point that information operators and pizza-delivery services, thinking she was drunk, would hang up on her. Unnerved by the sight of her, Peg's professors automatically agreed with everything she had to say. "Good question!" they'd shout.

"That's very perceptive of you. Does anyone else have any thoughts on what she just said?" She might ask to use the bathroom, but because no one could understand her, it was always same answer. "Good point, isn't it class!"

In the cafeteria she was met with frantic congeniality. Rather than embarrass themselves trying to figure out her choice of an entrée, they just went ahead and piled everything on her plate.

A person in a wheelchair often feels invisible. Push a wheelchair and you're invisible as well. Outside of the dorm, the only people to address us would speak as if we were deaf, kneeling beside the chair to shout, "FATHER TONY IS HAVING A GUITAR MASS THIS SUNDAY. WOULD YOU LIKE TO JOIN US?"

Peg would beckon the speaker close and whisper, "I collect the teeth from live kittens and use them to make necklaces for Satan."

"WELL SURE YOU DO," they'd say. "THAT'S WHAT OUR FELLOWSHIP IS ALL ABOUT."

For Peg, being invisible was an old and tiresome story. To me, it definitely had some hidden potential. So began our life of crime.

We started off in grocery stores. Peg had a sack on the back of her wheelchair, which I would fill with thick steaks and frozen lobster tails. There was no need to slink behind pyramids of canned goods, hiding from the manager; we did our stealing right out in the open. Peg carried a canvas bag on her lap and stuffed it with everything she could get her hands on. Canned olives, teriyaki sauce, plastic tubs of pudding — our need had nothing to do with it. The point was to take from an unfair world. We quit going to the cafeteria, preferring to cook our meals in the dormitory kitchen, the butter dripping off our chins. We moved on to bookstores and record shops, guaranteed that no one would say, "I think I see that crippled girl stealing the new Joni Mitchell album." Circumstances prevented us from stealing anything larger than our heads, but anything else was ours for the taking.

For spring break we decided to visit my family in Raleigh. Being invisible has its merits when you're shoplifting but tends to hold a person back while hitchhiking. We parked ourselves beside the interstate, Peg's thumb twitching at odd intervals. The five-hundred-mile trip took us close to three days. It was our story that we were a young married couple heading south to start a new life for ourselves. Churchy couples would pull over, apologizing that their car was too small to accommodate a wheelchair. They couldn't give us a ride, but would we accept twenty dollars and a bucket of fried chicken?

You bet we would. "There's a hospital in Durham we're hoping might do some good," I'd say, patting Peg on the shoulder. "Here we are, a couple of newlyweds, and then *this* had to happen."

CB radios were activated and station wagons appeared. Waitresses in roadside restaurants would approach our table whispering, "YOUR BILL HAS BEEN TAKEN CARE OF," and pointing to some teary-eyed couple standing beside the cash register. We found it amusing and pictured these Samaritans notifying their pastor to boast, "We saw this crippled girl and her husband and, well, we didn't have much but we did what we could."

Someone would check us into a motel and give us cash for bus fare, making us promise to never hitchhike again. I'd take Peg out of her chair, lay her on the bed, and sprinkle the money down upon her. It was a pale imitation of a movie scene in which crafty con artists shower themselves with hundred-dollar bills. Our version involved smaller denominations and handfuls of change, but still, it made us feel alive.

We were in West Virginia when one of the wheels fell off Peg's chair. It was dusk on a rural state highway without a building in sight when an elderly man in a pickup truck swooped in and carried us all the way to my parents' front door, a trip that was surely out of his way. "Five-four-oh-six North Hills Drive? I'm headed right that way, no trouble at all. Which state did you say that was in?"

We arrived unannounced, surprising the startled members of my family. I'd hoped my parents might feel relaxed in Peg's company, but when they reacted with nervous discomfort, I realized that this was even better. I wanted them to see that I had changed. Far from average, I had become responsible in ways they could never dream of. Peg was *my* charge, *my* toy, and I was the only one who knew how to turn her off and on. "Well," I said, wiping her mouth with a dinner napkin, "I think it's time for *somebody's* bath."

My brother and sisters reacted as though I had brought home a sea lion. They invited their friends to stare from the deck as I laid Peg on a picnic blanket in the backyard. My father repaired the wheelchair, and when Peg thanked him, he left the dinner table and returned handing her a second fork.

"She didn't ask for a fork," I said. "She asked for your watch."

"My watch?" he said. "The one I'm wearing?" He tapped his fingers against the face for a moment or two. "Well, golly, I guess if it means that much to her, sure, she can have my watch." He handed it over. "And your belt," I said. "She'll need that, too. Hurry up, man, the girl is crippled."

My mother visited her hiding place and returned with a wad of cash for our bus fare back to Ohio. She called me into the kitchen and shoved the money into my hand, whispering,

naked

"I don't know what kind of a game you're playing, mister, but you ought to be ashamed of yourself." It was an actual whisper, designed to be heard only by me.

The bus ride back to Ohio was long and cheerless. The second time Peg asked to use the bathroom, I snapped. "You just went three hours ago." I shouted. "Jesus, what's your problem, do I have to take care of everything?" It got on my nerves, the way she depended on me. We'd gone on this trip, she'd had a good time, what *more* did she want? How was it that by the time we left my parents' house, *I* was considered the cripple, not her but *me*, me who had to do everything while she just sat there spilling ashes down the front of her shirt.

My mood deteriorated. We returned to school, where Peg related our adventures to a crowd of friends. I listened in, silently substituting every *we* for an *I*. "We" didn't talk a truck driver out of thirty dollars and a brand-new curling wand, *I* did that, *ME*, how dare she take half the credit. "She is some kind of brave," our classmates would say. "I wouldn't have the courage to do *half* the things that she does — and I can walk!"

The spring quarter began but by the second week, I'd stopped attending class, deciding instead to bone up on my drugs and become my own private adventurer. I signed up for sky-diving lessons at the local airfield. The training sessions were deceptively simple, but when the time came for the actual jump, they had to pry my white knuckles off the wing of the plane. I begged and pleaded and all the way down I pictured myself in a wheelchair, hoping that the person assigned to care for me would have none of my qualities. The earth was a grid, a quilt of tidy patches maintained by sensible, hardworking people who played by the rules and treated every stranger as though he were Christ in disguise. My parachute opened and I promised God that once I landed

the incomplete quad

safely, I would turn my life around. I'd spin the globe and wherever my finger landed, I would go there. Even if it was one of those countries where people squatted in the soil, eating porridge from their shit-smeared palms, I would go. I'd swat the flies from their dung-colored faces and carry them piggyback across crocodile-infested waters if that's what it took to clear my name. The harness between my legs was causing unbearable pain, and I accepted it as my first test of strength and tolerance. The Lord could have my testicles. I'd grant him a finger or two and even throw in a couple of teeth if I had to, just so long as He left me my spinal column. I hit the ground running and didn't stop until I was a half mile from my landing site. When the instructor came to gather my parachute, I stubbed out my joint, saying, "I don't see what all the fuss was about. That was nothing."

At the end of the school year I hitchhiked to San Francisco, enchanted with the idea of leading an adult life surrounded by people who could wash their own hair. My friend Veronica got me a room at a residence hotel, and I found work as a bicycle messenger. The streets of my neighborhood were fragrant with eucalyptus trees, and every passing stranger offered the hope that tomorrow just might be the day I was offered a comfortable job or a twelve-room apartment. I was far from my family and often pictured them suffering their vacations without me. They had treated me poorly, but I had come out on top because that was the kind of person I was, headstrong and independent. Me, the winner.

I was cooking spaghetti and ketchup in my electric skillet one night when I heard the pay phone ring outside my room. It was Peg, calling to say she had rolled away from home.

"Good for you," I said. "This is going to be the best thing you've ever done." When I learned she was calling from the San Francisco airport, I modified my statement, saying, "I don't know about this, Peg. Won't your parents be worried about you? What about your education?"

What followed was a lesson that college bears no resemblance to civilian life. Leaving the building involved carrying Peg up and down five flights of stairs before returning for her wheelchair. The landlord charged me a double rate for having a guest in my room, and I lost my job when Peg fell against the bathtub, taking five stitches in her head. This was a big city where people held onto their fried chicken. Nobody cared that we were a young married couple searching for a better life and not even the buses would stop to pick us up. Fed up, Veronica and I decided to head north to pick apples. I told Peg, hoping she might accept the news and return home, but she held fast. Armed with a telephone directory, she placed collect calls to government agencies whose workers held the line when she dropped the phone or took twenty minutes to locate a pen. Volunteers wheeled her to meetings in cluttered ground-floor offices where paraplegics raised their fists in salute to her determination and tenacity. She wound up living alone in a brick apartment building somewhere in Berkeley. An attendant visited every twelve hours to prepare her meals and help her onto the toilet. If a spasm sent her onto the floor, she lay there patiently until help arrived to dress her wounds. When her parents called, she either hung up or cursed them, depending upon her mood. Peg's greatest dream was to live far from her parents and enjoy a satisfying sexual encounter. She sent a postcard detailing the event. There had been three wheelchairs parked around her waterbed, the third belonging to a bisexual paraplegic whose job it was to shift the lovers into position. Within a year her health deteriorated to the point where she could no longer be left alone for twelve-hour stretches. We both wound up crawling back to our parents

the incomplete quad

151

but continued to keep in touch, her letters progressively harder to read. The last I heard from her was in 1979, shortly before she died. Peg had undergone a religious transformation and was in the process of writing her memoirs, hoping to have them published by the same Christian press that had scored a recent hit with *Joni!*, a book detailing the life of a young quadriplegic who painted woodland creatures by holding the brush between her teeth. She sent me a three-page chapter regarding our hitchhiking trip to North Carolina. "God bless all those wonderful people who helped us along the way!" she wrote. "Each and every day I thank the Lord for their love and kindness."

I wrote back saying that if she remembered correctly, we'd made fun of those people. "We lied to them and mocked them behind their backs, and now you want them blessed? What's happened to you?"

Looking back, I think I can guess what might have happened to her. Following a brief period of hard-won independence she came to appreciate the fact that people aren't foolish as much as they are kind. Peg understood that at a relatively early age. Me, it took years.

c.o.g.

The bus from North Carolina to Oregon takes four days, which breaks down to roughly seventy-five thousand hours if one is traveling without the aid of a strong animal tranquilizer. It was my fate that any AWOL marines, tear-stained runaways, or drunken parolees, would sit so close that on the off chance they might pass out, I was guaranteed to collect their bubbling saliva on the collar of my shirt. Books and magazines offered no relief. Failing to act even as a shield, their presence attracted everything from mild curiosity to open hostility.

"You think you're going to learn something from a book?" the man said, punching my headrest with his tattooed knuckles. "Let me tell you a little something, bookworm, if you really want to learn the truth, there's only one place to do it: Chatham Correctional Institute. That's the best fucking school in this whole stinking country. It taught me everything I know and then some. Hell, you'll learn more on this goddamned bus than you would in a whole . . ." He paused, attempting to recall the name given to such a place. "You'll learn more here than in a whole pyramid full of books. You could fill a racetrack with every piece of shit ever written, but you'll learn more right here."

Having never seen a racetrack full of books, I thought it premature to contradict him. "You could be right," I said, regarding the scars that ornamented his battered, sunburned face. "Pretty close to your stop, are we? If not, I can move across the aisle and give you some room to stretch out."

"I told him yes," the girl said, taking the seat beside me. "I said, 'You're goddamned right I'm having this fucking baby.' I said I'd have this stinking piece of shit whether he wanted to be the fucking daddy or not." She paused to wipe her snubbed nose with a kneesock she carried exclusively for this purpose.

"I said, 'I already took four years of this shit from Big T, and if you think I'm going to stand here and take any more, you can bend down on your knobby knees and lick the hairs on my shit-scabbed asshole, motherfucker.' I told him, 'I'm through fucking around with a white-faced nigger too busy chasing bush pussy to get up off his fat fucking asshole and find his self a motherfucking job.' I let him have it, I really did.

I said, 'motherfucker, you haven't got the fucking balls God gave a goddamned church mouse. You crawled out of your mama's tattered old pussy, grabbed hold of her milk-stained titties, and you ain't never looked back, mother-fucker.' I said, 'If you don't want this baby, then I'll find some son of a bitch who does, someone who don't look at the world through the slit of his shit-blistered, faggoty-assed, worm-sized dick.' I said, 'This baby might be a bastard, but I can guaran-fucking-tee you it won't be half the bastard its daddy is, you motherfucking bastard, you! You can suck the cream out of my granddaddy's withered old cum-stained cock before I'll ever, and I mean *ever*, let you look into this motherfucking baby's wrinkly-assed face, you stupid fucking shit-head.' That's exactly what I told him because I don't give a shit anymore, I really don't."

Having shared this information with a complete stranger, the young woman proceeded to rummage through the pocketbook that rested upon her swollen belly. She pulled out a brush and scowled, gathering the captive hairs between her fingers and pitching them down onto the floor of the bus. "I said to him, I said, 'And another thing, dick stain, after this baby is born, I'm gonna take one look at its shit-covered face and if it looks anything like you, I'll have the doctor saw its fucking head off and use it for bait. I swear to God I will, and there's not a goddamned thing in the world you can do about it.' After all the stinking shit that bastard put me through, he had the nerve to ask what I was planning on naming the baby. Can you believe that shit? I can't. I said, 'I can't believe this shit, shithead.' I said, 'Motherfucker, I'll name it what-ever the fuck I fucking want to name it.' I said, 'I got a good mind to call him Cecil Fucking Fuckwad, after his daddy, you ugly fucking fuckwad.' I said, 'How do you like them apples, you jism-stained, cocksucking sack of stinking, steaming, blood-speckled shit."

She wiped a trace of spittle off her lips and settled back in her seat. The child kicked and shifted in the womb, and she responded, calling out in pain before batting her stomach with the flat end of the brush. "Motherfucker," she said, "you try that again and I'll come in there with a fucking coat hanger and fucking give you something to fucking kick about."

This was an America conceived by Soviet propaganda chiefs, a brutal landscape inhabited by hopeless, motor-mouthed simpletons, drifting from a bad place to somewhere even worse. If you're lucky, people on the bus will wake you in order to borrow a cigarette. The man occupying the win-

c.o.g.

dow seat is likely to introduce himself with the line "What the hell are *you* staring at?" Due to the volatile nature of their passengers, the bus drivers are trained in the art of conflict management and frequently pull over to mediate a disagreement.

"He keeps taking my candy!"

"Sir, I'm very sorry, but you'll have to return this gentleman's nougats."

The bus crawled, stopping in towns I felt certain we'd passed not more than fifteen minutes earlier. *Let's get on with it,* I thought. *These people are more trouble than they're worth. Let them walk the twenty-five miles home to Wrinkled Bluffs or Cobbler's Knob or whatever godforsaken stand of cacti they call home.* Unlike the rest of them, I had places to go, real places. People were waiting for me to enrich their lives. Couldn't anyone see that?

"This bus will be running express from here to Odell, Oregon," I imagined the driver announcing into his microphone. "Anyone *not* going to Odell must disembark immediately and form a line on the edge of this forbidding desert."

My fellow passengers would moan and grumble, reaching into the seat pockets to collect their lint-specked dentures and half-empty pints of Old Spaniel. I would watch them step down onto the dusty highway, shoddy suitcases in hand, and shake their fists at the unforgiving sun. When the last of them had been evacuated, the driver would close the doors and turn in his seat, touching his fingers to the bill of his cap to say, "We'll have you in Odell in no time, sir. In the meantime, I want you just to sit back and make yourself comfortable."

Having spent close to twelve hours explaining the inconvenience of his work-release program, the man seated beside me finally reached his destination. The seat was taken by a morose, chinless smokestack of a woman wearing an ash-colored sleeveless turtleneck sweater. She never engaged in formal conversation, rather she jabbed me periodically, pointing with her cigarette at whatever she imagined I might find meaningful. "Refrigerated truck," she would whisper. "Filling station all boarded up." She never visited the toilet or shifted her position, not even during one of her many naps. Sleep seemed to overcome her without warning. "South Dakota plates on that Duster," and I'd turn to find her gently snoring, the cigarette still smoldering between her fingers.

It was almost midnight somewhere in Utah when a young woman boarded the oversold bus carrying a plastic laundry basket stuffed with shoes and clothing. Having wandered the aisle, searching in vain for a seat, she planted herself beside me, shifting her weight from foot to foot and clearing her throat with painful regularity. She acted as though I were hogging a pay phone, rambling on about nothing at all while she waited to report a round of gunfire coming from the local preschool. This made me feel uncomfortable.

"Here," I said, "why don't you take my seat for a while."

She accepted without comment. A *while*, to me, meant anywhere from fifteen to twenty minutes. If we hadn't reached her destination by then, perhaps someone else might offer her *a* seat. We could all pitch in, forging that unique bond wrought only by common sacrifice. Two minutes into my seat, the young woman was fast asleep, her slack jaw tightening every now and then to mutter what sounded to me like the word "sucker."

I moved to the front of the bus and took a seat on the stairs until the driver shooed me away, citing regulations. These were his only hours of privacy, and the man was determined to enjoy them. Come dawn, he would have his hands full with the old cranks who tended to commandeer the front seats, ignoring his DO NOT DISTURB sign to pepper him with questions like "Have you ever found a black snake curled up inside your dryer?"

I returned to stand beside my seat, hoping that someone might be leaving sometime soon, but there was nothing to stop for. The passing landscape offered no signs of life, just a fathomless, cold-hearted world of stones. I crouched for a while until, overtaken with leg cramps, I lowered myself to the floor and crawled beneath my former seat. Old Smoky sat with her legs outstretched before her while my greatest living enemy tended to thrash and fidget, literally busting my balls every chance she got. The couple seated behind me took up the rear, alternately kicking my head and spinal column with the pointed toes of what I identified as steel-tipped cowboy boots. I told myself that I'd seen worse, but try as I might, nothing came to mind. The bus's colossal engine lay just beneath my head, providing warmth for the countless bits of misplaced candy that melted to form a fragrant bed of molten taffy. Somewhere along the line something had gone terribly, terribly wrong. Why was I, the most important person on this bus, forced to spend the night curled, not on but *beneath* his rightful seat? This sort of thing would never have happened on an airplane.

"Oh," I'd said to several of my former seatmates, "you should try it sometime. It's nice, flying. They serve dinner and drinks, and you can leave your bag on the seat when you go to the bathroom."

"Really?" they'd said, "and don't nobody fuck with it?"

The look of wonder upon their faces was the reason I'd taken this bus in the first place. Having spent the last nine months washing the dishes of well-to-do college students, I thought I might get a real kick out of the Greyhound crowd, but I hadn't meant it literally. There had to be an important lesson involved in this, and one day, with any luck, these shiftless idiots would figure it out.

I lay there until sunrise, when the bus took an incline and a bottle of chocolate soda rolled across the floor, smacking me in the forehead. Crawling back toward the aisle, I stepped into the bathroom to battle the many wads of chewing gum fused to my scalp. The passengers awoke, one by one, all except for the young woman occupying my seat. A good, sound sleeper, she rose at ten, asking me to save her spot while she went to brush her teeth.

I was out in no time, waking minutes later to find her rapping on my skull with a tube of toothpaste. "Hey, wake up."

I pretended to sleep through it, figuring she'd give up sometime soon.

"Hey, this son of a bitch took my seat," she shouted. "I went to the ladies' to freshen up and now I don't got no goddamned place to sit."

"You can sit on me," I heard someone shout from the back of the bus. "I'll give you the ride of your life!"

"All right now, you've had your fun." This was a man's voice but it couldn't be the driver, as we were still moving. "Come on now, half pint, give the lady back her seat."

A hand grabbed me by the collar and lifted me effortlessly to my feet. This hand was blistered and meaty, matching both the face and personality of its owner. The man asked no questions and delivered no threats. He didn't need to. Once the seat was empty he wiped it free of crumbs and gestured for the young woman to make herself comfortable. I thought briefly of taking my case to the people, but this was clearly not my crowd. They leaned forward, craning their necks to whisper and laugh while I stood in the aisle pretending to be a foreigner, unfamiliar with the customs of this magnificent

c.o.g.

159

country. I might have accidentally taken someone's seat, but, oh, look at the way I seemed to appreciate the rugged landscape the rest of them took for granted. I bent at the waist, lowering my head to peer out the window and raising my eyebrows in delight at every passing boulder. *Look*! I seemed to say. *That one resembles a cardinal nesting on the rim of an enormous pancake! And here we have what appears to be an overturned clog, lying beneath what closely resembles the pocked, flat-featured head of the ignorant hillbilly occupying my rightful seat!*

Someone disembarked about noon, and I settled into his seat exhausted but unable to sleep, distracted by the courtship taking place across the aisle. After turning ten thousand times to thank him for his valor, seats were swapped so that Lord Beefy and Lady Laundrybasket might sit side by side and get to know each other better. Within minutes, they had their heads beneath a sweatshirt, where they were either practicing squirrel calls or sucking the acne medication off each other's faces. The sound of heavy-metal music on the radio, the piercing squall of a restless infant, the endless chatter of the nattering fogeys seated up front: I could endure anything but the noise of this couple nipping and kissing and crying out in pleasure.

She wept when he reached his stop. The sound of her muffled sobs was an absolute tonic, sending me into a deep, impenetrable sleep that lasted all the way to Reno.

This would be my second visit to the Hood River valley. The first had been an accident. My friend Veronica and I had been living in San Francisco when she laid down her copy of *The Grapes of Wrath* and announced that we'd had enough of city living. It was her habit to speak for the both of us, and I rarely minded as it kept me from having to make any decisions of my own. "We want to head up north and join our brothers and sisters in the orchards," she said, adjusting the scarf she'd taken to wearing on her head. "Migrant labor, that's the life for us." The good people of this country needed us, and we pictured ourselves reclining in sun-dappled haystacks, eating hearty lunches prepared by the farmer's gingham-clad wife.

"It's hardworking people like you that make the world go round," she would say. "Here, have another piece of my prize-winning chicken; you folks need to keep your strength up." After lunch the gentle farmer would take up his fiddle and kick up the dust with a rousing rendition of "Turkey in the Straw" or "Polly Wolly Doodle." Late afternoons would find us back at work, picking apples off the ground and lobbing them into adorable crates labeled "Li'l Redskin" or "Teacher's Pet." Our lives would be simple but unspeakably heroic. How she'd gotten this impression from a Steinbeck novel is anyone's guess, but I went along because, if nothing else, it was guaranteed to drive my father out of his mind.

We hitchhiked up into Oregon, leaping out of the car after spotting snowcapped Mount Hood, a perfect symbol for the majesty that was to become our lives. The first farmer refused to hire us because we had no experience. The second and third turned us down for the same reason. We lied to the fourth, a small elderly man named Hobbs, whose crew of Mexicans had recently been carted away by the INS.

"At this point, I'd take anyone who could pick their goddamned nose." He stared at the trees, their branches bent with fruit. "I thought for a while that maybe my wife could help me out, but she's up at the big house dying of cancer. What do you say to that, Ringo?"

If Hobbs's wife was dying, his ancient beagle couldn't be very far behind. The animal wheezed and groaned, worrying the bald patches that festered at the base of his arthritic tail.

"Goddamnit, Ringo," Hobbs would say, tossing his glowing cigarette butt onto the wet grass, "I sure am glad you're out here."

There would be no picnics taken in haystacks. No gingham, or fiddle playing. Hidden behind a thick layer of permanent storm clouds, the sun dappled nothing. Contrary to what we'd assumed, apples were not picked off the ground but from the limbs of hard-to-reach trees protected by a punishing bark that tended to retain a great deal of water following a good twelve-hour rain. This was a seven-day workweek, sunup to sundown, gentle rain or driving rain. If people like us made the world go round, it was a highly guarded secret. As pickers, we were provided with one of the half dozen cabins that formed a row alongside the gravel driveway. There was no electricity, and outside of the shower located in the barn, our only source of water was one frigid, rust-caked tap. The cooking was done on a wood stove, and we slept on mattresses stuffed with what I could only begin to identify as high-heeled shoes. These hardships were played to our favor. We took to wearing overalls, admiring our somber reflections in the candlelit windows as we huddled over steaming bowls of porridge. This would do. We were pioneers. People like us had no need for pillows or towel racks. We wore our bruises like a badge, and every chest cold was a testament to our fortitude. I was on the verge of buying myself a coonskin cap when the season ended and we traveled back home to North Carolina, where I quickly re-adjusted to a life of hot water and electricity. We'd made plans to pick again the following year, but when the time came, Veronica was forced to back out of her commitment. It seemed she had found herself a boyfriend. *Boyfriend.* The word stuck in my throat like a wad of steel wool. "It won't last," I said. "You'll see." What did she need with a boyfriend? I pictured the two of them rolling around the

naked

floor of her apartment, specks of dirt being driven into their bare backs and pale, quivering buttocks. *Boyfriend.* She'd never find anyone as good as I was, I told her that. When she agreed, I got even angrier, storming off her front porch with a ridiculous, "Yeah, well, we'll just see about that."

I told myself that it was my destiny to walk alone, but the cliché provided no comfort. Given the choice, I would much rather walk alone with someone who can cook, and I worried about spending so much time by myself. The remainder of my bus ride put the latter fear to rest. I reached Odell convinced that if I never spoke to another human being for the rest of my life, it would be too soon.

The road to Hobbs's orchard wound past a dairy farm where several dozen speckled cows passed the time grinding wet grass with their blunt teeth. I'd tried making friends with them a year earlier, standing by the fence and waving sandwiches until their owner informed me that they didn't eat chicken or pork, not even as a snack. They were dumb, these cows. Picking season began in mid-September and lasted through the end of October. Within the course of a few weeks, frost would appear and we'd awake to see our breath shooting forth in dingy clouds. I'd always thought that cows spent their winters in some sort of heated barracks; instead, it was their fate to remain outdoors, no matter how cold it got. Did these animals have any idea their summer was coming to an end? Could they remember their lives as young, carefree veal? Did they ever look forward to anything or entertain regrets? I dropped my duffel bag and approached the barbed-wire fence, hoping they might rush forward, wagging their ropy, shit-smeared tails in recognition, but they just stood there, methodically working their jaws.

Hobbs reacted in the exact same manner. "Well, look who's here, Ringo. If it isn't . . . Dennis, right?" He tossed a lit cigarette onto the grass and stepped out onto his porch, saying, "I'd invite you in, but the wife's still dying of cancer. Clifford's got it, too. You remember him, don't you? Big fat guy, used to be my foreman. He's over in Portland now, tumors up his ass the size of young Bartlett pears."

Seeing as Clifford wasn't expected back anytime soon, Hobbs offered to put me up in the foreman's trailer, which sat between the barn and the long row of cabins.

"Funny thing, cancer." He lit a cigarette, and considered the spent match. A crop duster flew overhead, and he waved his arms in greeting. "Yes, sir, it's a real mystery."

He led me to the barn, where a Mexican man stood waiting for his turn at the shower. "Whole-aah, Toe-moss," he shouted.

The man tugged at the towel he wore like a skirt around his waist and nodded his head in greeting, "Hola, Señor Hobbs."

"You speak some Mexican, don't you, Daniel?" Hobbs asked. "Well, by God, I'm learning a few words of my own. A person *has to* in order to get along in the modern world! You get me going, and I'll speak like a regular Topo Gigio, right, Ringo?"

The dog knelt at the base of a tree, doubling over to lick its blistered anus.

"These are different times we're living in, a whole new set of rules. The kids around here, they think they're too good to work. Only choice left is either trash or Mexicans, and I'll take the stupid Mexicans any day." He prodded me in the ribs, "Watch this. 'Bueños Dios, Miguel.'"

A small, dark-eyed man looked up from his wood splitting, alarmed.

"They spook easy," Hobbs said.

Yes, well, people tend to do that when you come up behind them shouting, "Good God." It's just a habit, I guess.

naked

164

Hobbs unlocked the door of the trailer, a bulbous, aqua tankard set upon cinder blocks. It worried me that the moment I crossed the threshold I might become the sort of person who lived in a trailer. A trailer, the very word set off alarms in the base of my skull. People who lived in trailers called the police to break up violent family fights. They peed in the sink and used metal buckets to barbeque tough purple steaks marked "reduced for final sale." Who did this man think I was? Did he know I'd been raised in a house with a dishwasher and central air-conditioning? It was one thing to play pioneer in a rustic cabin. This place, on the other hand, had all the charm of an oversized gas can. I hung back, watching Miguel fill his arms with firewood. He piled on the last log and then screamed, dropping his entire load to swat at his chest, calling out the words "big spider, big spider." A lot came back at that moment. I considered the row of shoddy cabins before peeking inside the trailer, where I noticed a gas stove nestled between the sink and a humming refrigerator. Miguel stood beside the barn, kicking each piece of firewood before picking it out of the mud, and I climbed the stairs to my trailer.

Apple picking is mindless work. When I'd done it with Veronica, we had worked together on the same trees, running down the names in our mental address books and discussing our friends in alphabetical order. Pickers are paid by the bin, a large wooden crate that, when full, holds roughly fifteen hundred pounds of fruit. You climb the ladder wearing a canvas sack and when it is full, you empty your load carefully into the bin. Then you climb your ladder and do it again and again and again. With two people, the time manages to pass quickly. Veronica and I might start our day recalling the false pregnancy of Beverly April and by the time we got to Lucinda Farrel's obsession with turquoise jewelry, we were ready for lunch. I tried doing it myself, speaking out loud in two distinct voices but stopped after Hobbs caught me defending Gregory Allison's use of LSD as an appetite suppressant.

Without Veronica's company, it just wasn't working. Left to my own devices, I proceeded slowly and methodically to drive myself crazy.

Once a bin was full, Hobbs would arrive on his tractor and randomly pull out three apples. If none were bruised, I would receive nine dollars. If one was bruised, I would receive eight, then seven. On a good day in young trees, it was possible to fill up to eight bins. The next day, who knew? You could spend ten hours yanking the stunted fruit off one stingy tree. Even sleep offered no relief. Night after night I dreamed of picking apples and awoke exhausted, my shoulders bruised from the heavy canvas sack. A Friday was no different than a Monday or Wednesday; with no day off, there was nothing to look forward to. During the first few weeks, Hobbs would turn off his tractor and we'd talk for a while before he carried off the bin. Once he realized just how much I had to talk about, he took to leaving the motor running. "Gotta go check on the wife," he'd shout. "You keep up the good work." The Mexicans were now jogging past my trailer on their way to the shower. A cat showed up at my doorstep, an orange tom with a neck as thick as his waist. I'd never cared for redheaded cats, always associating them with Brian O'Shea, my overbearing seventh-grade lockermate. Neither did I have a particular soft spot for male cats, who tended to spray and show up in the middle of the night, tattered and bleeding. Still, though, I was in no position to judge. The cat offered companionship, and I took him in, figuring that if he was going to have his ears chewed off, I might as well be the one to do it. I fed him sardines and stroked him until he set off sparks. He ran away.

With no one to talk to, I began putting my various

naked

thoughts and opinions into letters that were weighty in the literal rather than figurative sense of the word. I wrote my friend Evelyn a seventeen-page letter describing how I'd felt after the cat ran off. Two weeks later, having received no response, I crossed her name out of my address book. One by one, I eliminated them all. Eight pages to Ted Woestendiek on what it's like to wash your hair with laundry detergent. No answer. Twelve and a half pages to Lisa, forgiving her for being born. Nothing.

"Dear Miss Chestnut, You're probably wondering what I've been up to since the third grade . . ."

I might spend an entire evening on a single letter, but with the exception of Veronica — "No, my boyfriend has *not* left me yet, but thanks for asking" — nobody responded to any of them. This understandably put me in a foul mood. I'd thought I would return to North Carolina after the season ended, but once we moved into the Golden Delicious, I started having second thoughts. What was there to return to? How had I ever considered those people to be my friends when they were too lazy to pick up a pencil and write a letter? Surely, they missed me. Perhaps the best strategy was to see that they missed me even more. I'd live under a bridge before I'd ever go back there. Oh, they'd talk about me, wondering where I was and what I was up to. Someone would hear a rumor that I was skating my way across Europe or sharing a penthouse apartment with Michael Landon, but they'd never know anything for certain, I'd make sure of that. They'd had their chance to share in the fascinating details of my life and had blown it, every last one of them except for Veronica, who I planned to forgive as soon as she broke it off with that troglodyte.

When the last bin had been carted away, Hobbs asked if I might be interested in a job at the local packing plant. They were looking for people, and he could put in a word with the manager and let me stay on in the trailer just so long as I paid for my own electricity and promised not to knock on his door.

"It's nothing you'd want to make a career out of," he said. "The job is good for a few months, but after that I'll guarantee you'll never want to see a goddamned apple for the rest of your natural life." He studied the tip of his cigarette for a moment before lighting it. "A peach maybe, but, no sir, not an apple. Nope, no way."

The plant was located midway between town and the farm. A corrugated, ramshackle, eyesore of a building, it housed an archaic network of shuddering conveyor belts that moved as if they were powered by a team of squirrels running a treadmill somewhere in the basement. Nothing about the place was inviting, but I suspected that might change the moment they handed me my union card. I would soon be a Teamster, a title guaranteed to cost my father a good three nights' sleep and to drive my former friends wild with envy. In time, everyone would be affected. Looking out upon the busy plant floor, I imagined all these people seated in folding chairs as I addressed them from the stage of the meeting hall. "Brothers and sisters," I would yell, clutching a bullhorn in one calloused hand and a stack of documents in the other, "the time to act is *now!* They call this a contract? Well, I call it a *contrast*, the difference between the way things *are* and the way things *ought to be!*" I would need to pause here, as the applause would be deafening. "It's *us*, the working people of this country who make the world go round, and until management opens their eyes to that fact, until the fat daddies upstairs are ready to park their Cadillacs and negotiate a decent wage, *this* is what I have to say to their contract." My fellow Teamsters would stand on their seats and cheer as I ripped the contract into pieces and tossed it over my shoulder.

I had never organized so much as a dinner party, but surely

that would change as soon as my fellow workers recognized my way with words and the natural leadership qualities I had suppressed in the name of humility. I'd always had a way with the little people, making it a point to humor them without looking down my nose at their wasted, empty lives. If these people wanted to make me their leader, I had no choice but to accept with my own brand of quiet dignity. "Dav-id, Dav-id, Dav-id." The convention floor would quake with their chant.

If on the off chance these things *didn't* happen, at least I'd be working alongside other people. They might not be as perceptive as I was, but still I welcomed the opportunity to speak to something born without a stem or a tail. Somewhere in this room, a friend was waiting. "I knew it the first time I saw you," this person would say over dinner some night. "I took one look and said to myself, 'Damn, that guy is someone I'd like to know.'"

I was hired for the second shift, which began at 3 and ended at 11 P.M. My job was to stand in place and pull the leaves off the apples as they passed before me on the conveyor belt. There was a woman standing no more than four feet away from me, but the constant rattling din made it impossible to carry on a discussion. Forklifts droned in the background while men sawed and pounded wooden pallets. Sprayers, belts, and generators; the noise was oppressive and relentless. The doors to the loading dock were left open, ensuring that we'd never find ourselves complaining about the heat. I picked the leaves off the passing fruit and tossed them into a cold, wet pile that quickly grew to cover my numb feet. During my first hour I made the mistake of biting into one of the apples. Fresh from its chemical bath, it burned my lips and the flesh at the corners of my mouth, leaving a harsh aftertaste that lingered long after I'd run to the bathroom and washed my mouth out with soap.

c.o.g.

Hobbs had been right about never wanting to see another apple, but his timing was off. I was ready to banish them from my sight after my first forty-five minutes. They were merciless, pouring down the belt without interruption twenty-four hours a day, turning the concept of world hunger into either a myth or a very cruel joke. During a single half hour I had surely handled enough apples for every man, woman, and child with the teeth to bite them or the will to mash them into sauce.

It occurred to me that everything we buy has been poked or packaged by some unfortunate nitwit with a hairnet and a wad of cotton stuffed into his ears. Every ear of corn, every chocolate-coated raisin or shoelace. Every barbeque tong, paper hat, and store-bought mitten arrives with a history of abject misery. Vegetarians look at a pork roast thinking about the animal. I'd now look at them wondering whose job it was to package the shallow Styrofoam trays. *That*'s where the real tragedy lies. Cigarettes, crackers, gum: everything I saw would now be tainted by the reminder of my job. "Brothers and sisters, RUN! RUN FOR YOUR LIVES!"

The time crawled by. I'd lift my rubber glove and scrape the frost off my watch, discovering that the last hour amounted to nothing more than seven minutes. We were given a half-hour dinner break and three ten-minute rest periods, which seemed to pass before my hands regained enough feeling to hold a cigarette. Dinner was taken from coin-operated machines in a lounge overlooking the plant floor, so you could chew your sandwich without forgetting where you'd be when the time came to digest it. Except for me, all the belt workers were middle-aged women who endured the packing season and then stayed on for the canning. Their ringleader was a stocky, no-nonsense woman named Dorothy, who wore her son's football jacket beneath a soiled apron reading SHUT UP AND EAT!

naked

"Alls I can tell you about the union is they better lay off monkeying with my benefits or they'll find themselves picking their teeth from out between my bleeding knuckles," she said. "And I'll see to that personally!"

She led me to a bulletin board posted with the minutes of the last meeting. Every sentence included a long list of initials, and after a while I stopped asking what they stood for. Compared to a roll-call vote on severance payments, anything, even my job, seemed exciting. By the time I qualified for dental insurance, I'd be so old we'd be talking dentures, not fillings. "You'd be surprised," Dorothy said. "The years have a way of adding up."

I was sure they did, but couldn't they add up to something more than this?

We were taking our break one evening when I asked if anyone happened to speak Italian. "I studied it for a year back in college," I said. "And now I've completely forgotten the word for 'tragedy.' Oh, I know Spanish, too, and a wee bit of Greek, but Italian is just so, well, *bellissimo*, isn't it?"

My attempts to impress them failed miserably. The women took to calling me Einstein. "I could tell you were a smart one the first time I saw you bite into one of those apples," Trish brayed. "I said to myself, now *there's* someone with a good head on his shoulders."

The break room filled with laughter. "Hey, Einstein, what's the Latin word for 'blowhard'?"

"Tell me, Einstein," Dorothy asked, "for five bonus points, which local high-school football team is headed for the state finals?"

"Aw, leave the kid alone." This was a man's voice coming from somewhere behind me. "The guy's got better things to think about than your fat-assed son running interference for those sorry Polecats."

"My boy's a quarterback," Dorothy shouted. "And for your

c.o.g.

171

information those are the Catamounts, and they're regional champs! So put *that* in your pipe and smoke it."

The man thumbed his nose and gestured for me to join him at his table. "Goddamned flock of silly hens is what they are, but don't you worry, they'll get what's coming to them. Once they get too old to lay eggs, we take them out back and wring their necks."

"Watch it, buster," Dorothy said, tugging at the strings of her apron.

The man introduced himself as Timothy, adding that all his real friends refer to him as Curly, a curious nickname given that his thin, wheat-colored hair fell straight down from his balding scalp. "It must be hard, a person such as yourself stuck in a place like this. These morons resent anyone with brains and a decent education; it makes them feel trapped and threatened and, oh boy, we can't have that, can we! Heavens no, they can't staaannndddd that." He shuddered and hugged himself, pretending to be frightened.

"I know just what you're going through because you and me are a lot alike," he said. "I'm probably a good fifteen years older and nowhere near as smart as yourself, but come January I'm enrolling in a management class over at the community college. It's time I put on the old thinking cap and hitch this nose to the grindstone. I've wasted enough time as it is."

Curly was sort of hokey, but I was in no position to refuse anyone's friendship. I grew to appreciate his company, sometimes almost wishing we could talk about something besides me. "Say, Dave, tell me once more about that dream you had last night, the one with the shrunken heads lined up inside the egg carton. There's some powerful symbolism there, let's see if we can't figure it out." He wasn't the brightest person in the world, but his heart was in the right place.

Curly worked the first shift as a forklift operator, often

naked

staying late to collect overtime. Other nights he sometimes drove back to the plant just to join me for dinner. He spoke to the foreman and had me promoted to the position of sorter. The leafless, glistening apples passed along the belt, and my job was to separate the fancy from the extra fancy. At no point did anyone point out the distinction between these two categories. I tried asking Gail and Dorothy, but angry that I had been promoted without seniority, they ignored me. I observed and did what they did: working a stick of chewing gum, I crossed my arms and sat on a stool until a manager came into view, at which point I would rapidly and randomly discriminate, placing this apple on the fancy belt and its neighbor on extra fancy. Rotten fruit was thrown down a chute, where it would be mashed into baby food. The raise was twenty-five cents an hour. This was drier than my earlier job but no more exciting.

"Someone sure slept his way to the middle," I heard Connie whisper to Trish over the coffee machine. "Next thing you know, he'll be wearing fur-lined gloves with a cushion propped under his little fanny."

I assumed they were talking about me, as I was the only person at Duckwall-Pooley in possession of what might be described as a little fanny. Curly had been right about these women; they were just as petty and small-minded as they could be. "Slept his way to the middle." If I were asleep on the job, did they honestly think someone would have me promoted?

"It's a regular Cutthroat Island around here, and don't let anyone tell you any different," Curly would say. "You're lucky you've got someone to watch your back, my friend. They're nothing but a flock of stupid sheep, and one of these days they're going to get sheared."

I'd been at the plant for three weeks when Curly invited me to his trailer for a drink. He lived just outside Hood River in a double-wide he shared with his mother, a woman he often spoke about. "I told Mother what you said about Dorothy's mouth looking like a gunshot wound and, Lord, she just about bust a gut, she was laughing so hard. She is one funny lady, my mother. Nothing tickles her funny bone better than a knock-knock joke. You know any good sidesplitters?"

Desperate as I was for company, I understood that I was clearly dealing with a loser. Management seemed the perfect career for a person like Curly. I could easily picture him in a short-sleeved shirt, the pocket lined with pens. Someone would ask him to check the time cards and he'd probably say something goofy like "Okey-dokey, artichokey." I'd tried to straighten him out, but there's only so much you can do for a person who thinks Auschwitz is a brand of beer.

He pulled the pickup into the driveway of his trailer, which sat parked beneath a stand of fir trees. It was a cold night, and clear enough to see the steaming breath of the advancing German shepherd.

"Where's the King?" Curly asked, kneeling down to have his face licked. "Here he is! You're the King, aren't you? The King man, the King of beers. Who's the King of beers? Who is he? Where did he go?" He affectionately batted the dog's head with his cuffed fists before saying, "All right now, enough play. Go on, King. Scoot."

As he was fitting the key into the door, the dog returned to worry its head against the jamb, eager to get inside. "Motherfucker, I said NO." Curly kicked the dog with his sharp-toed boots, and the animal retreated into the yard. "Didn't I tell you no? Didn't I say we'd had enough play?" He knelt then, and his voice became soft and sweet. "King man. Where's my King of beers, King of the road, King man? Where did he run off to? The King ran off and left his crown laying in the dust. Who wants his crown back? Where did my King go? Who is the rightful owner of this crown?"

naked

The dog advanced, kneeling before Curly, who grabbed him by the collar and kicked him several times in the rear before releasing him. "It's just a game we play," he said, wiping his hands on his trousers. "He likes it rough."

It was the extreme heat combined with a low, foul odor that suggested Curly's was not a happy home. The smell was of every filthy thing you could think of and dozens more that a decent person could never imagine. The door opened onto a living room, the walls paneled in imitation walnut and hung with framed prints dedicated to the theme of simpler times, when barefoot boys snitched apples off the vendor's cart. Sofas and chairs were upholstered in red velveteen and protected by plastic jackets tailored for a snug fit. The gold-flecked coffee table supported an ornate cigarette lighter and several copies of *Oregonian* magazine arranged into the shape of a fan. Plump cherubs gamboled at the base of every lamp, and the royal blue carpet was crossed with a network of runners. It wasn't dirty or even messy, just incredibly stinky, as if the trailer itself had once been a living, breathing thing but had died about six months before, left to decompose without a proper burial.

"Mother? Are you decent? The number-one son is home." He opened a door at the end of the hallway, and I saw a thin, shriveled stalk of a woman lift herself from the toilet. I turned my head then, pretending to examine a picture of a spry granddad, spreading his arms wide to indicate the length of the one that got away.

"I thought you were one of those Taylor boys," the woman said. "I thought you were coming for that big crate of franks. Their father dropped them off, a whole big crate of them. I called and said, 'I don't know what a person would do with so many franks. Send your boy out after them.'"

Curly lowered his voice. I could not catch the words, but the tone was one of impatience.

c.o.g.

"No, sir, I do not want you to get the stick," I heard the woman say. "I want those wienies out of my closet is what I want. Call that Taylor boy on the phone and see if he can't come get them."

I heard her protest as she was lifted, heard the toilet flush and the sound of water running in the sink. "I don't have the buns for franks like that. Call them up and see won't they come."

Curly opened the door and emerged with his mother in tow, leading her past the kitchen and into a room I knew I did not want to enter. This was one of those times I literally kicked myself for never having learned to drive. What with the money I'd made picking apples, I had enough cash beneath my mattress for a secondhand model. With my own car, I could have made up some excuse and cleared out with no problem. I could have taken *his* car if only I knew how to turn it on and drive it. While I might *stay* in a trailer, it was clear that Curly actually *lived* in one; and it horrified me that he might have mistaken me for one of his own. Was it my clothing? The pallor of my skin? My tendency to let my mouth hang open while bored? People in trailers were canned and labeled much like the apple juice down at the plant, stamped with ingredients for all the world to see: chicken-fried steak, overcooked vegetables, no working knowledge of any major Italian movie directors — the list went on and on.

"Boy, is she tired or what?" Curly said, shaking his head in disbelief as he left the bedroom. "Sometimes she's just like a clock, if you know what I mean. Cuckoo. Cuckoo." He rotated his index finger against the side of his head. "You know how it is with mothers. Can't live with them, can't fit them into a burlap bag. Hey, did I say that?" He pressed a finger to the tip of his nose as if it were a button labeled REWIND. "Did we come here to relax or what?" He stepped into the kitchen and

naked

returned with a six-pack of beer, explaining that we should probably retire to his bedroom, as his mother was a light sleeper. "She can be, oh boy, a regular three-headed monster when she doesn't get her shut-eye," he said. "You're not like that, are you? Are you a cranky old werewolf when you wake up in the morning? I sure hope not, because I'm askaird of monsters." He chewed his nails and buckled his trembling knees. "I'm askaird. I'm afwaid."

Whatever Curly's theatrical fear, it could not begin to match my genuine horror as he opened the door to his bedroom, which served as a showplace for his vast collection of artificial penises. They hung from the walls, jutted from plaques, and stood upright, neatly spaced upon shelves and tabletops. Duplicated in wood, plastic, or fleshy rubber, what they had in common was their substantial size. Some were detailed to include veins and curly-haired testicles, while others existed as a minimal idea. Black or white, buffed aluminum or flesh-tone, electric or manual, the message was the same.

"So what do you think?" Curly said, lowering himself onto the waterbed.

"That's really some . . . bedspread you've got there," I said, hoping to focus the attention toward the color scheme. "It's a real . . . *orange* orange, isn't it?"

"I guess you could say that," he said, reaching over to stroke something that closely resembled a thermos. "What do you think of my toy collection? I figured you'd appreciate it more than anyone else I know. First time I saw you, I said to myself, 'There's a boy who needs a playmate.' So what do you say, Charlie Brown, you ready to play?"

"Oh, gosh," I said. "That's really nice of you to ask . . . Curly. It's just that, well, seeing that we work together . . ."

"That's all the more reason to play together," he said. "Come on now, Einstein, don't pull that shit on me. Here, you've got me worked up like a freight train." He ran the zipper of his jeans up and down the track of his fly. "You've been coming on too strong to back off now. Don't play that game with me."

"Oh, I'm not," I said. "It's just that I've got . . . these . . . damned crabs." I itched myself fiercely, silently congratulating myself on my cunning. "They're a real devil to shake, and I wouldn't want you to catch them."

"Won't be the first time," he said. "Come on now, get your ass in this bed. Curly will find those mean old crabs and spank the shit out of them."

"That sounds . . . really . . . fun," I said. "Not for the crabs though, I mean . . . it'll be bad news for *them*, won't it." I excused myself to visit the toilet. Curly had taken my coat earlier, and I groped around the dark closet looking for it. When I heard him call my name, I grabbed the down jacket and fled out the front door, running down the driveway and onto the dark road.

It wasn't until I reached a streetlight that I realized I was wearing a ladies' jacket. It was down, like my own, but this one was pink and the pockets were stuffed with wadded Kleenex. A car pulled around the corner and came speeding toward me. Just before passing, the driver veered off the road and onto the shoulder, and I fell back into a ditch. A beer can landed near my head and I heard the sound of laughter and loud music fade into the distance.

In terms of a warm, safe place, the ditch wasn't so bad. Huddled there among the decaying leaves and stray scraps of paper, I asked myself how I could have been so wrong about Curly. I'd always figured he was single because he couldn't find a woman desperate enough to put up with his juvenile personality. Would things have been any different if I'd found him attractive? If he looked like, say, William Holden in the movie *Picnic,* would I have put up with his overheated

naked

trailer and hokey stories? I recalled his collection of artificial penises and understood that the answer was definitely no. After taking on one of those monsters, the next step would involve sitting upon a greased fire hydrant. Before I knew it, I'd turn into one of those middle-aged men who wore diapers and walked with a limp. I knew that I'd worked my final shift at the packing plant. It wasn't really Curly's fault, but it's always nice having someone to blame. If anything, I should be thanking him for giving me a good excuse to quit. It suddenly seemed like a good idea to pack it in and leave town. First, though, I'd just lie in this ditch for a while, wrapped tight in a ladies' jacket and wondering where I'd gone wrong.

With the Mexicans gone, Hobbs's orchard had become a desolate place. I limped back to my trailer just after sunrise and stared out the window at the barren trees. The problem with leaving one town was that sooner or later you'd have to arrive in another. I told myself I'd head to someplace exotic, Portland maybe, or Tacoma, Washington, but deep down I knew that once my bags were packed, I'd return to North Carolina. If I could just stay here a little longer, perhaps I could form the emotional calluses people needed to leave their pasts behind them and begin new lives for themselves. It was like waiting for a fever to break, a few more weeks and I might have come out of it. Nothing, it seemed, could break one's resolve quite like spending the night in a ditch.

I hitchhiked into Hood River to turn in my library books, stopping off at the plant to explain I wouldn't be needing my job anymore.

"Yale," I shouted to the foreman over the noise of the generator. "I have to head back East because they want me to teach at Yale."

c.o.g.

179

"You what?" he shouted. "Who's going to jail?"

"No, YALE."

"All right then, just make sure you don't bend over to pick any soap off the shower floor. We'll see you when you get out."

"It looks like I'll be heading back home," I whispered to the librarian, handing in my battered, overdue copies of *Valley of the Dolls* and *Rosemary's Baby*. "They want me to teach a couple of classes at Yale, and seeing as picking season is over, I thought, why not?"

"I guess it's that or starve," the woman sighed.

I don't know why I felt the need to present any excuse at all. Except for the original owner of my pink jacket, my leaving affected no one. I'd spent several months there and they had added up to nothing. Seeing as I was not the type of person to *make* things happen, my only option was to *let* things happen. I expected opportunity to present itself to me and it had, in the way of a union card and three dozen artificial penises. Things wouldn't be any different in North Carolina than they'd been in Oregon. I thought of those people on the bus, going from one shitty place to the next, expecting nothing to change but the landscape. Soon I'd be sitting beside them, sharing my potato chips and thinking of them as my kind of crowd.

I was heading back to Odell when I got a ride in a station wagon driven by a man who introduced himself as Jonathan Combs, C.O.G.

I asked what the letters stood for, and he asked me to guess. He appeared to be in his midfifties, a doughy, square-faced man with heavy black-framed glasses and a silver crew cut.

"Go on, guess," he said.

naked

180

Cousin of Godzilla? I thought. *Chunky old geezer? Capable of genocide?*

"I can't begin to imagine," I said.

"Child of God," he said. "You're one, too! Here you had this glorious title, and you didn't even know it! I even had it put on my checks. Now if the man upstairs would only start cashing them, I'd be in business. HA!" He addressed the roof of his car. "Just teasing, Lord."

Jon said he could take me into Odell, but first he needed to drop by the studio. I asked what he did there, and he said "I'm an artist, *that*'s what I do there. Ever met an artist before? We might sometimes act a little strange, but don't worry, kid, I've had my shots and I've never been known to bite."

He pulled onto a residential street and parked before a house decorated with the remnants of Halloween. Soggy ghosts hung from the trees, bloated from the morning rain, and the jack-o'-lantern had withered, its once merry face now resembling that of a toothless, sunburned mummy. "These kind people are members of my church," he explained. "I told them I was looking for a studio, and they handed me the keys to their basement. Just like that." He smiled, shaking his head at the thought of his good fortune. "You'll meet the greatest people in the world living right here in this very town," he said. "Well, I guess I don't need to remind *you* of that. You've already met one of them."

"Who?"

"Me, ya idiot!" He reached for the two aluminum canes lying beside him and used them to support his weight as he stepped out of the car. I followed along, pretending to ignore the unmistakable sounds emanating from his trousers. Either he was suffering a terrible case of gas or he had a pint-size child practicing the trumpet in his back pocket. "You ready to see something amazing?" he asked. "You'd better hold

c.o.g.

181

onto your socks because I'm just about to knock them off."
He opened the door to a basement equipped with a washer
and dryer. In the far corner of the room sat several large,
dingy machines of an inderminate nature. He turned on the
overhead lights and made his way toward a boulder that sat
in a tray of rust-colored water. "Taa-daa! How are those
socks treating you?" he asked.

I got the distinct feeling I was missing something intended to be obvious.

"It's jade!" The man's eyes sparkled. "And I've got plenty
more where this came from. It may not be the highest quality, but still, it's enough to make me a rich man ten times
over if I don't mess up and start drinking again, knock on
wood." He sat down and rapped his knuckles against his
knees, producing a hollow sound.

I was dumbstruck.

"You want to knock wood? Go ahead, take your pick. One
leg's just as good as the other. He hitched up his trousers,
revealing sleek, putty-colored calves. "They're not real wood,
I was just pulling your leg. Ha! How do you like that one!
No, they're plastic and they're all mine and you can't have
'em." He grabbed his knees in a mock gesture of defensive-
ness.

The man was clearly some sort of a lunatic, not unlike
many of the other people who had picked me up hitchhiking, but I knew for a fact that if it came down to it, I'd be able
to outrun him. Perhaps that's why I stayed and listened as he
spoke about the many years he'd spent in Alaska. It was one
of those places I wouldn't dream of going. My childhood
fantasies of polar bears and smiling Eskimos chasing one another across the frozen tundra had been shattered by magazine articles picturing hardscrabble towns where bearded
men arm-wrestled over mail-order brides beneath the harsh

naked

midnight sun. If that was the last frontier, they were more than welcome to it.

After his first marriage broke up, Jon traveled to Fairbanks in search of fortune. "But the only gold I found was swirling around the bottom of a bottle." He lost his left leg when his car overturned, pinning him against a tree. Its partner had been amputated some months later because of gangrene. It was the pockets of air caught between the prostheses and the stumps that created the farting noises whenever he walked.

"So there I was. My legs were yesterday's news but I still had my hands, and that's all it took to reach for that bottle. Yes, indeed, the best medicine in the world is made by a fellow who goes by the name of Jim Beam. I was just a dried-up pill, nothing to do but get drunk and feel sorry for myself. And that's what I did until I met a man who told me I could walk tall even without a pair of stinking feet. A man I happened to meet by accident in the crowded hallway of a VA hospital. A man named Jesus Christ. He happened to be a close personal friend of my wife's and thought the two of us should meet. Oh, she wasn't my wife at the time, just another cute nurse with a great set of tits and an ass a man could get lost in. Jesus brought us together. Then he told us to get married and hightail it the fuck out of Alaska, and that's just what we did."

The jade was picked up later, somewhere in Washington State, where he also learned to cut and polish. "That's where the skill comes in," he said. "Take a look at this rock, it's nothing, right? Just a dusty hunk of nothing." Jon stood on his artificial feet. "Now, take a look at this!" He lifted a sheet off a nearby table, revealing a half dozen brightly polished slabs of jade fashioned into timepieces, the battery-powered minute hands jerking past blobs of gold paint used to represent numbers.

"What is it?" he asked, holding up one of the larger models. "A clock?"

"Well of course it's a clock, but what else? What's it shaped like?"

I tried to make sense of it but the best I came up with was a slice of bread, its corners chewed away by ants or mice.

"It's *Oregon*, dummy. Everyone knows the shape of Oregon. Maybe you haven't spent much time here, but that's still no excuse. The yokels in this town are going to snatch these babies up like you've never seen! I'm charging a hundred bucks a pop, which is nothing compared to what some of these jokers are getting for their wildlife paintings. What with Christmas right around the corner, I've got to get cracking and start churning these suckers out, and you know something? *You're* going to help me!"

The moment he said it, I knew he was right. Opportunity had presented itself, and I saw no reason not to run with it.

It was Jon's habit to begin each workday with a prayer. "Am I the only person in this room?" he'd ask. "My pal Jesus is looking down here saying, 'I know that's Jon, but who's that puddin'head with the stupid smirk on his face?' Hurry up now, get down on that floor and act grateful you've got the knees to bend on."

After I had assumed the position, he could commence. "Hi there, Lord. It's me again, your old buddy Jon. If it's not too much to ask, I'd like you to keep an eye on this disrespectful mutt I've got working for me. Let me be patient and try my best to teach him about you and this precious jade you've given me. And hey, thanks for the coffee, but do you have any sugar? HA!"

"You can joke with the Lord," he said one morning, removing his right leg to apply ointment to the bandaged stump. "Hey, up there. I sure hope nobody takes me to court. I wouldn't have a leg to stand on. HA!"

naked

The religious instruction was delivered with a charm that quickly faded once it was time to begin work. The jade was sliced upon a pressurized saw equipped with a hose that prevented the blade from overheating. Jon cut the rock into slices, and it was my job to sand them, using a variety of graded discs that fit upon a rapidly spinning wheel. Once they were smooth, I would polish the quarter-inch-thick slices against a rotating leather belt. The friction generated a fair amount of heat, and despite the gloves, I would occasionally let go of an advanced piece, sending it shattering onto the floor.

"You stupid, clumsy jackass," Jon would shout, pounding his canes against the table. "Do you know how much work went into that piece? You goddamned silly mutt!" Having exhausted me, he would take his case to the heavens. "Hey, Lord, why are you treating me this way? Is this some kind of a test? Did you send me this butterfingered fuckup in order to teach me a lesson? What did I do to deserve this stinking shit?"

The door leading from the basement to the first floor would open and a woman would poke her head over the banister. "Brother Jon, is there a problem?"

"Oh, I've got a problem all right. This son of a bitch just dropped four hours' worth of backbreaking work on the fucking floor. *That's* my goddamned problem."

"I'm very sorry to hear that," the woman would say, covering the ears of her five-year-old daughter.

This scenario repeated itself until the day the child addressed her mother as "shithead," and it was suggested that Jon might want to find himself a more secluded workshop.

"Get the equipment into the car," he said. "We're clearing out of this rat's nest."

He found another studio, a former beauty salon located on the outskirts of town. We moved the machinery in the morning, and by afternoon he was back to tracing the shape of Oregon onto the slabs of polished jade and cutting them on his jigsaw. Quite often during the course of our workday, we were interrupted by members of Jon's church who popped in to see how we were getting along.

"Pete, Kimberly, I'll tell you what I'm going to do. I'll let you have one of these clocks for seventy-five dollars. Don't try to talk me out of it, this is the Lord's discount, not mine. I . . . what was that?" He'd look toward the ceiling, cupping his hands to his ears as if trying to decipher information from a distant, crackling speaker. "What? OK, if you say so." Turning back to his company, he'd shrug his shoulders. "The Lord told me to throw in the batteries while I'm at it. What do you say? Seventy-five dollars."

Whether he was speaking to Phil and Dotty Frost, Walter and Linda Tuffy, Hank and June Staples, the Mangums, the Stenzels, or the Clearwaters, the response was always the same. "We appreciate the offer, Brother Jon, but I'm afraid that's a bit out of our price range."

"I'll let you have it on a payment plan, how's that?"

His fellow parishioners would chuckle, trying not to meet his eyes. "We'd love to take you up on that, we really would, but the bank's already got us on more payment plans than we can handle."

"Fucking cheapskates." Jon would stand at the window, waving as the visitors pulled out of the driveway. "Hey, Lord, why'd you send me these cheap, good-for-nothing friends?"

Until the age of seventeen I had been forced to attend the Holy Trinity Orthodox Church. The service was delivered in Greek by a robed priest and involved endless rounds of standing, sitting, and kneeling. Every few hours the altar boys would roam the aisles with smoldering tankards of incense, and one by one the congregation, woozy from fasting, would drop like flies. Because I could never understand what

naked

was being said, I formed an idea of a God who wasn't judgmental, just painfully boring. Christ was a mystery to me, and Jon and his friends were eager to fill in the blanks. There were days when I would leave work convinced that there was a five-hundred-dollar reward for the first person who could dunk my head into the nearest river or plastic baptismal pool. I was a lump of unformed clay surrounded by a guild of willing sculptors. These people were the only contact I had outside of the men and women who picked me up hitchhiking back and forth to work every day. I'd arrive at the shop, listen to Christian radio, get blessed out by Jon and blessed back in by his visiting friends and neighbors. It was like being sent to a foreign country to be immersed in a language that somehow, over time, became your own.

"Peace be with you, brethren," "You know what they say in John thirteen," "The King is coming!" I fought it like crazy, but my only alternative was talking to nobody. I'd tried that already and had wound up lecturing to cows until the farmer told me I was ruining their digestion. This God was someone I wound up turning over and over in my mind each night as I returned to my increasingly cold trailer. Was He punishing me with this meal or was He rewarding me? Did He actively watch me or take me for granted like a fish you don't notice until it's floating on the surface of the tank?

With a newfound spirit of forgiveness I wrote my friends ten- and fifteen-page letters, and again, they never responded. They couldn't manage to send a postcard while here all these people — the Halbergs, the Cobblestones, Sam and Charlotte Shelton — had mailed invitations asking me to join them for Thanksgiving dinner. When I declined, some people had taken it upon themselves to deliver a turkey to my trailer door. Unfortunately, the offering was decorated with slices of canned pineapple, but still, they'd made an effort. The gift embarrassed me, and so did the others. I found myself ducking into the bedroom several times that day. A car would pull up and I'd run into the other room, pretending I wasn't home. I was shamed by their goodwill and mortified by their cooking. There seemed to be some correlation between devotion to God and a misguided zeal for marshmallows.

"What did I tell you," Jon said. "The best people in the world, and you've got them right in your own backyard. Did your friends back home give you a basket of homemade stuffing? Did your folks bake you a marshmallow pie or a tray of crescent rolls? Of course not! They could have, but they didn't." He walked to the window and shouted up at the sky, "Hey, Lord, in case this numbskull hasn't said it, thanks for the stuffing."

From time to time during the course of the day, Jon would shut down his saw and turn to me saying, "I've got a friend who wants to have a word with you. He says he's been trying to reach you but you won't take his calls."

"Well, it's hard, seeing as I don't have a phone."

"Don't need one. This guy speaks straight to the heart. Why don't you talk to him? What have you got to lose, happiness? You're not happy now, I can tell you that much. You're searching in the weeds for something you've got right under your snotty little nose. You've got to *reach* for the joy! It's not going to drop into your lap, ya stupid nitwit, you have to *ask* for it. That's all you have to do, is ask."

My trailer had water but it wasn't hot. Since arriving, I had always boiled my bathwater, but by the last week in November it had gotten so cold that the water assumed room temperature upon impact with the tub. My heating system consisted of a space heater, the oven, and a toaster, none of which did any good unless I hovered directly over it. The warmest spot in the house seemed to be the refrigerator. I went to bed fully dressed and removed my gloves only when

naked

188

bathing and scooping the change from my pockets. Because the studio was heated, I took to spending more and more time there. Jon would leave at five, and I would remain to sweep up and work on my own projects. The clocks did nothing for me, but the jade itself could be pretty if it wasn't polished to death. Jewelry was too fussy, and bookends seemed a waste of time. The thing to make, I decided, was a stash box. Jon promoted his clocks as being both a needed object *and* a conversation piece. The problem was that you needed to be stoned in order to really talk about them. No one else was going to sit around and appreciate the fact that at three o'clock the hands fell on the cities of Eugene and Arlington. Stash boxes were the supplement that would make these clocks bearable. They needed to be simple yet charming. Not so elegant that guests would reach for them and not so luxurious that the owners would be reminded of all the other nice things they might own if only they didn't spend all their money on drugs.

There were nights when I'd work until midnight and sleep on the cot Jon kept folded in the back of the studio. Just before dawn I would wake, muddled and wondering where I was. "Go back to sleep," a voice would say. "You're in a former beauty salon surrounded by battery-operated clocks. It's nothing to worry about." Was it God talking?

I'd always thought of my life in terms of luck, but what if there was someone actually in charge of our destiny? What if all our plans amounted to nothing? Think of the guy who trains all his life for the Olympics and steps on a nail the day before the competition. What about all those perfectly nice, hardworking people who lose their homes to floods and fire? I listened to a woman on the radio. Burns covered eighty percent of her body. "The Lord doesn't send us any more than we can bear," she said. Like Jon, she didn't seem bitter about her situation, far from it. She sounded practically ecstatic, her voice so high and melodic that I thought she might burst into song. "God doesn't close one door without opening another." Was this peace, this total trust and surrender? Because I was lazy, I'd adopted the philosophy that things just happen. It was much easier to blame others than it was to take initiative. Was it accidental that Jon had picked me up hitchhiking just when I'd thought of returning home? Could I have been sent by a higher power to this small town? Had the Lord arranged for me to make stash boxes?

I was entertaining these thoughts early one morning when Jon arrived saying, "Lord, I must be doing something right today! Last night I prayed this lazy mutt would show up on time and here he is, the coffee brewed and waiting." He took no interest whatsoever in my boxes, dismissing them as a waste both of time and materials. "What are you going to put in there, three fingers? A couple dozen Q-tips? They're not even big enough to hold a deck of cards. Who needs a thing like that? A clock, on the other hand, everyone needs a clock. Someone shows up at your door asking, 'Am I early?' Where are you going to look — at a box? Of course not! A lady says 'I was supposed to boil that pudding for half an hour, maybe if I look at a box I'll know if it's done.' It's ridiculous. The point is to give people what they *need*, idiot. You want to fiddle around after work, go ahead. You have the skill and I was happy to teach you. The ability, you've got. The brains? I wouldn't hold your breath. You'll have to ask the man upstairs for help in that department." He paused to refill his mug. "Say, this coffee's good, isn't it? Let's thank our friend, Jesus, for providing the beans. Come on now, bow your empty head and then let's get to work. Time is ticking. Ha!"

Our time was ticking toward the upcoming crafts fair in Portland, where Jon planned to make a killing. He'd paid a good amount to reserve the booth but expected to make that

naked

190

money back within the first ten minutes. "These yahoos around here are all so broke, they can barely afford to pay attention. Portland, though, that's different. Portland's where the money is. If I don't clear three thousand bucks by the end of the day, you can set fire to my legs and watch me walk home on my hands. You hear that, Lord? What do you say, Big Guy, do we have a deal?"

The fair was to be held at an outdoor market on a Saturday two weeks before Christmas. We spent that Friday making price tags and loading seventy-five clocks and four stash boxes into the station wagon. Jon was in a festive mood and gave me a ride home, interrupting his lecture on salesmanship to point out a young woman standing beside the pay phone at a filling station. "Sweet merciful Christ on a cracker, look at the cacungas on that one! Oh, Jesus, I could suck on those titties till the cows come home. Lemme at 'em, lemme at 'em." I'd seen him act this way once or twice before, but this time his eyeballs were popping so far out, they were practically bumping up against the lenses of his glasses. After pulling himself back together, he dropped me off in front of my trailer and set a time when he'd pick me up the next morning.

Waiting for me on the door that evening was a plastic bag containing six letters along with a note from Hobbs apologizing for not delivering them sooner. It was his habit to drive to the mailbox each morning, and these letters, having arrived over the last few weeks, had been sitting on the dashboard of his truck. I approached my mail the way a starving person might sit down to a banquet. It seemed best to consume such bounty in small portions, but still, I couldn't help myself from devouring each letter whole, my eyes running up and down the page as if I were looking at a picture. I would swallow first and then, upon the second reading, begin to chew each word into a paste. There was a letter from my sister Lisa and another from my mother, each of them hoping I might be home for Christmas. My mother, in her familiar, slanted cursive, described an automobile accident she'd witnessed on the beltway. Lisa's letter, neatly typed, informed me that she wanted a curling iron for her birthday and a case of either shampoo or champagne for Christmas. I had apparently drawn her name in absentia and would be held solely responsible for her happiness this coming holiday season. There were two letters from Veronica, the first recounting her happy Thanksgiving and the second detailing her recent breakup with "the son of a bitch who used to be my boyfriend." There was a letter from my friend Ted and another from an old college roommate. I read each one again and again, tracing my fingers over the word *love* until I could see each of them clearly, sitting at their desks and kitchen tables. To describe the feeling as warm would be doing it an injustice. It was as though after I had mourned and planted flowers on their graves, my dead had approached me in a restaurant explaining that it had all been some terrible mistake.

I was sitting by the oven with the toaster and space heater at my feet when a harsh light shone on the wall, and Curly came to the door. "Long time, no see," he said, pushing past me and examining the contents of my refrigerator as if he had been sent for that specific reason. "I thought you'd left town until Dorothy told me she'd seen you hitchhiking on the road to Hood River. How's my mother's coat treating you, Einstein?" He had grown more forceful but no more attractive. "I could have you arrested — you know that, don't you? Stealing coats is a crime in the state of Oregon."

It didn't worry me that I might spend the night in jail for accidentally taking the jacket of a madwoman whose son considered a newel post to be an erotic object. I gave him his mother's coat and apologized for the misunderstanding, thinking that might be the end of it, but he kept coming at me, cuffing my head and inviting me to wrestle. "We can do it without the toys if that's the way you want it," he said. "I've got a bottle in my truck and we can use that. Come on now, Einstein, you owe me." Every time I brushed him off, he came back harder, driving his knuckles into my skull and working me toward the bed. "You ticklish, are you? You like being fluffed up like a pillow, is that what you like, Mr. Tickle Toes?" I'd escape his embrace for a moment or two, but the man was just too fast for me. For the first time in months, I was actually sweating. He pinned me down against the floor. "Get off of me!" I shouted. "I can't do this with you because . . . because I'm a Christian." I felt then as though both my heart and the mucus-producing glands of my nose and throat opened simultaneously. There was, upon my gloved hands, so much snot that when I united my palms in prayer, they cemented themselves together as if they'd been glued. I wept and wailed and then I sobbed. "I'm a Christian. I love Jesus, can't you see that?" The words rang true to me, and I cried even harder. "A Christian, I'm a Christian. Help me, Jesus, I'm a Christian."

"Enough already," Curly said, backing toward the door. "I didn't want your life story, just a quick fuck."

I remained on the floor long after he had gone, wondering what my life might be like now that I had finally opened my heart. Cigarettes already tasted better, but they always do after a good cry. The refrigerator, the toaster, my appliances still looked exactly the same. I thought things might appear brighter if viewed with a cheerful Christian countenance, so I walked into the bathroom as if it were a clubhouse filled with faithful friends. "Hello, soap," I said. "Hi there, toilet!"

"Lookin' good, bathmat." I moved through the kitchen and living room — "You old lampshade, you" — and wound up in the bedroom, where I leafed through my address book, forcing myself to think kind thoughts about everyone whose name I had crossed out. It was late when I finally went to bed, and I lay there, unable to sleep, wondering if God were watching. It was an uncomfortable feeling, being watched. What if I were in the bathroom, would He watch me in there, too? I guessed He had access to anywhere people are suffering, which thinking back on my Thanksgiving meal, surely included the bathroom. How then was it possible to *stop* Him from watching? I would make it a point to ask Jon the question first thing tomorrow morning. It was difficult to sleep, in part because I was so anxious to tell him my news. I was a Christian now, a Christian. Hopefully I could skip the phase of wearing large crosses and handing out pamphlets titled *The Devil in Mr. Jones* or *Satan's Slaughterhouse*. Bypassing the hopelessly corny sing-alongs and church-basement potluck suppers, I intended to move straight into a position of judgment. People would pay me to tell them what they were doing wrong, and in criticizing their every move, I would aid all mankind. With any luck I could do this without having to read the Bible or eat anything containing marshmallows. I was imagining my audience with the Pope when I finally fell asleep to the sound of awakening birds.

"Jesus, you look like shit," Jon said as I settled into his car early that morning. I thought I had my speech memorized, but I'd overslept and hadn't had time to make a pot of coffee. Groggy and thick-tongued, I started out by recounting my visit to Curly's trailer. "So, he took me into his bedroom and it turned out . . ."

"The guy was a homo, right?" Jon curled his lips in disgust. "That happened to me once back in the army. There's a

naked

194

lot of sick people in this world. The guy asked if he could hold me, that's what he said. 'Can I hold you?' I still had legs then and I used them to kick his ass. But you're that way, too, aren't you?"

I nodded my head.

"I knew it the first time I saw you operate a sander. I said, 'That guy is sick.' And you are, aren't you? You're sick."

He said it with concern, the way you might address a friend with tubes running from his nose. "You're sick." I attempted to re-create my crying jag, but it sounded false. "Boo-hoo-hoo. Aww-ha-ha-hu-hu-hu-hu." There was no mucus, and I had to provoke my eyes with my fingers to produce tears. "A-he-he-hu-hu-hu."

"Don't cry to me. Tell it to Jesus," Jon said. "Reach out to him. Tell him you're sorry. Crouch down there on the floor and pray, for God's sake."

"Oh, God, hu-hu-hu, I'm so sorry I met that guy. He was so stupid."

"And tell Him you're never going to do it again," Jon shouted.

"And I'll never do it again," I said. "No Curly, never again."

"With any man. Tell Him you're never going to lay down with any other man. Tell Him you want to get married."

"Oh, please," I said. "Please let me get married."

"To a woman," Jon said. "Married to a woman."

"Toman," I said, hoping that if the transcript were ever brought to heaven's court, I could not be accused of making promises I didn't keep. "Toman." Somewhere along the line, I had forgotten this might be part of the deal. Couldn't you be the type of Christian who judged people *and* slept with guys?

"And tell Him you're sorry for taking long lunches and being so clumsy."

"Uh-hu-hu-hu, I'm sorry for all the things I dropped. I'm really, really sorry."

"All right then," Jon said. "You can sit back in your seat. That wasn't so bad, was it? I knew you'd come along, you had the best teacher there is. I now present you with the official title, C.O.G. How does it feel? Feels pretty good, doesn't it? And who do you have to thank?"

"Curly?"

"No, me, ya idiot."

Jon mentioned a few other concessions I'd need to make and then we reached the city of Portland, where the women walked the streets in tight jeans and close-fitting jackets. "Roll down your window and ask the blonde if there's a Miss America pageant in town."

I asked and she crushed her cigarette, saying, "Beats the shit out of me."

"*Someone* needs to beat the shit out of her. Bitch. Hey, look at this one in the rabbit coat. Oh, God, sweet Jesus, look at that ass. You know there's a God when you see a keister like that. Wouldn't you just want to spend the rest of your life raising welts on that fine, fat ass? Don't you just want to bury your face all up in there until it's dark?"

I tried looking at women as a Christian, which was odd, as I thought I always had. I appreciated the fact that they were around but found it impossible to pass judgment on their breasts or bottoms, which I viewed no differently than their ears and ankles. They were just features, some smaller or larger, but none more erotically charged than the trees and mailboxes that lined the road.

"Hold on, Mamma, Daddy's coming," Jon said. "Roll down your window and ask if she applied those jeans with a brush or a roller."

He truly must believe in miracles if he thought I'd actually ask a complete stranger if she accepted deliveries in the rear.

naked

We pulled into the marketplace and I unloaded the station wagon while Jon leaned against his canes, gaping at the shapely potters and whistling at the macramé artists, their hair braided into thin, complex knots.

"The flower pots are crapola, but I sure like her jugs. HA!"

Flea market or crafts fair, the common assumption is that what interests the seller will surely captivate the public. "Are you looking at that panda? Well, it's more than a crocheted bear, it's also a blender cozy *and* a hand puppet!" I might appreciate the fact that someone has taken the time to craft wind chimes out of two dozen nickels, but no amount of talk is going to make me reach for my wallet. I'd rather be left in peace to make my own decisions.

This was not an option for the citizens of Portland. "You've got to *talk* to these people," Jon said. "Turn on the charm and make some money! Watch this: Excuse me, madam, do you happen to know what time it is?"

The woman looked at her wrist and reported that it was 9:15.

"Pardon me, sir, do you know what time it is? Well, I do, it's time for you to buy a clock. That's right, a clock! You'll know your time is precious because this is no ordinary clock, it's jade! That's right, jade! It's time for you to buy a jade clock shaped like Oregon, that's *exactly* what time it is. If you show me a picture of your wife or girlfriend, I'll give you a twenty-five percent discount. I want to see the face of the girl that's going to unwrap this clock on Christmas morning. If she's pretty, I'll knock off an extra ten dollars and let you have one of these babies for a hundred bucks. What am I, nuts? That's practically giving them away! I might be crazy, but that's what I get for being an artist. Come on now, a hundred dollars, how about it?"

I was not the only one mortified by his sales pitch. The shoppers recoiled, their faces blanched of color. Wheedled to

c.o.g.

197

within an inch of their lives, they fled toward the surrounding booths. "They'll be back," Jon said. "I planted a seed of interest, and it'll sprout any minute now. Just give it some time."

A man and woman wearing matching fringed jackets approached our table and Jon began his spiel. "I might be cuckoo, but I think it's time you two bought a clock."

The man picked up one of my boxes and turned to the woman, saying, "Nathaniel uses a pipe, doesn't he?"

Sold. Because they were already stoned, it was fairly easy to smell my customers approaching. I had priced my boxes at twenty-five dollars each, and by noon all four of them had been bought.

"Say, Goldilocks, you want a nice clock to go with that? I'm giving a thirty percent discount to anyone wearing paisley boots."

By late afternoon Jon had begun invading other people's booths in search of customers. "Stained-glass tissue dispensers? What do you want with those? Let me show you something that'll really knock your socks off."

The people of Portland winced. They shrugged and apologized, but not a single one consented to purchase a clock cut in the image of their fair state.

"Cheap sons of bitches," Jon said. "Hey, Lord, why didn't you tell me these creeps would be such tightwads?"

When the other craftspeople began packing up, Jon told me to stay put. "This way, the latecomers will have less of a selection. They stuck us all the way out in the back where nobody can find us, that's the problem. By the time the customers get here, they've already spent all their money. Now's our chance, boy. Our day is just beginning."

Vans and trucks were summoned, and I watched as our neighbors loaded up their folding tables and portable wall

naked

units, congratulating one another on their recordbreaking sales. It was after dark when Jon finally allowed me to pack up the station wagon.

We rode in silence past the city limits and onto the highway, the clocks ticking the words, "choke, choke, choke." It had been awhile since I'd spent any time in a city, and several times during the course of the day, I'd looked up thinking that this or that backpacked stranger was someone I knew. It was a heady, joyous feeling. *"Oh, look, it's Veronica; it's Gretchen."*

It was implausible, but that never stopped me from drawing a quick breath and bolting up from my folding chair. The disappointment that followed was crushing and only served to remind me just how much I missed the people I'd left behind. I watched shoppers buying Christmas gifts and pictured myself spending the holiday alone in my trailer, waiting for well-meaning Christians to deliver a ham or casserole to my doorstep. And these people *were* good. They were kind and thoughtful, but their grace was wasted on me because, regardless of my circumstances, I would never genuinely accept it. Perhaps that didn't matter to them, but it meant something to me. A chicken, a cardboard box, a jade clock: these things were much more forgiving than I could ever hope to be. I was a smart-ass, born and raised. This had been my curse and would continue to be so. Instructing me in religious faith was like trying to teach a goat to cook a fine meal — it just wasn't going to happen. I was too greedy and inattentive, and the ultimate reward meant nothing to me. I didn't want to quit my job. Quitting involved a certain degree of responsibility I didn't want to assume. Rather, I hoped that Jon might remove that burden and dismiss me as soon as possible. I had felt contempt for him, even occasional hatred, and now I was fighting the urge to feel sorry for him. He must have known it, and clearing his throat, he proceeded to cut me off at the pass.

"Let me tell you a little something," he said finally. "I don't appreciate being used. I'm not talking here about all the free coffee and rides I've given you. I mean used in here." He meant to point at his heart but, swerving to pass another car, wound up gesturing toward his lap instead. "You're a user, kid. You used my tools and my patience and now you want me to pat you on the head and tell you what a good little boy you are. But you know what? You're *not* a good boy. You're not even a good girl."

More, I thought. *More, more.*

"You swish into town, expecting everyone to bend over backward and roll out the red carpet, and, oh, some of them did it. You ate their stuffing and came back for seconds, but this is *it,* Piglet, the cupboard is bare. I taught you a skill, and now you can pay your own way for a change. That's right, let's turn the tables. Why not? It's only fair! For starters, you owe me a hundred dollars for that booth rental. Why should I pay? You're the one who reaped the benefits, not me. All I did was break my back teaching you a skill and listening to you blubber like a baby every time you skinned your delicate little knuckles. You wear me out with your sob stories and then expect me to dust you off and tell you Daddy's going to make everything all right. But you know something, kid? I'm *not* your daddy and I'm tired of being used like one."

He pulled off to the side of the highway. "I'm not your daddy *or* your chauffeur *or* your goddamned Santa Claus."

I handed him the money I'd made and stepped out of the station wagon.

"The God part I'm not charging you for," he shouted. "Him, you can have for free."

I watched him pull back onto the highway and, having selected a good-sized stone, I blessed the back of his car. It

naked

wasn't terribly far back to Odell, no more than ten miles. I walked for a ways and then held out my thumb, eager to get back to the trailer, where if I hurried, I could clean the place up and get my things together in time to catch the morning bus home.

something for everyone

The day after graduating from college, I found fifty dollars in the foyer of my Chicago apartment building. The single bill had been folded into eighths and was packed with cocaine. It occurred to me then that if I played my cards right, I might never have to find a job. People lost things all the time. They left class rings on the sinks of public bathrooms and dropped gem-studded earrings at the doors of the opera house. My job was to keep my eyes open and find these things. I didn't want to become one of those coots who combed the beaches of Lake Michigan with a metal detector, but if I paid attention and used my head, I might never have to work again.

The following afternoon, hung over from cocaine, I found twelve cents and an unopened tin of breath mints. Figuring in my previous fifty dollars, that amounted to an average of twenty-five dollars and six cents per day, which was still a decent wage.

The next morning I discovered two pennies and a comb matted with short curly hairs. The day after that I found a peanut. It was then that I started to worry.

I have known people who can quit one job and find another in less time than it takes to quarter a fryer. Regardless of their experience, these people exude charm and confidence. The charm is something they were either born with or had beaten into them at an early age, but what gives them their confidence is the knowledge that someone like me has also filed an application. Mine is a history of almosts. I can type, but only with one finger, and have never touched a computer except to clean it. I never learned to drive, which eliminates delivery work and narrows my prospects to jobs located on or near the bus line. I can sort of hammer things together but have an ingrained fear of electric saws, riding lawn mowers, and any motorized equipment louder or more violent than a vacuum cleaner. Yes, I have experience in sales, but it is limited to marijuana, a product that sells itself. I lack the size and bulk to be a guard, and the aggression necessary for store detectives, crossing guards, and elementary schoolteachers. Years ago I had waited on tables, but it was the sort of restaurant where customers considered the phrase "Have a good day" to be an acceptable tip. On more than one occasion I had found it necessary to physically scrape the cook off the floor and scramble the eggs myself, but this hardly qualified me as a chef.

It wouldn't have worked to include the job on my résumé and list it as a reference, as the manager never answered the telephone, fearful that it might be someone phoning in a take-out order. The waiters in Chicago tended to apply with a modeling portfolio in one hand and a gym bag in the other, and it seemed useless to compete. If my shirt was pressed, it was more or less guaranteed that my fly was down.

When luck was with me I tended to stumble into jobs, none of which were the type to hand out tax statements at the end of the year. People gave me money and I spent it. As a result, I seemed to have fallen through some sort of crack.

something for everyone

203

You needed certain things to secure a real job, and the longer you went without them, the harder it was to convince people of your worth. Why *can't* you work a cash register or operate a forklift? How is it you've reached the age of thirty and still have no verifiable employment record? Why are you sweating so, and what force compels you to obsessively activate your cigarette lighter throughout the course of this interview? These questions were never spoken but rather were implied every time a manager turned my application face down on his desk.

I leafed through the Art Institute's outdated employment notebook, and page by page it mocked my newly acquired diploma. Most of the listings called for someone who could paint a mural or enamel a map of Normandy onto a medallion the size of a quarter. I had no business applying for any of these jobs or even attending the Art Institute in the first place, but that's the beauty of an art school: as long as you can pay the tuition, they will never, even in the gentlest way, suggest that you have no talent. I was ready to pack it in when I came across the number of a woman who wanted her apartment painted. Bingo. I had plenty of experience there. If anything, I was considered too meticulous a painter. As long as she supplied the ladder and I could carry the paint on the bus, I figured I was set.

The woman began by telling me she had always painted the apartment herself. "But I'm old now. It hurts my hands to massage my husband's feet, let alone lift a heavy brush over my head. Yes, sir, I'm old. Withered and weak as a kitten. I'm an old, old woman." She spoke as if this were something that had come upon her with no prior notice. "All the sudden my back gives out, I'm short of breath, and some days I can't see more than two feet in front of my face."

This was sounding better all the time. I'd learned to be wary of people forced to pay others for a job they used to do themselves. As a rule they tended to be hypercritical, but with her, I didn't think there would be any problem. It sounded as if she couldn't see anything well enough to complain about it. I could probably just open the paint can, broadcast the fumes, and call it a day. We made arrangements for me to visit her home the following morning, and I hung up the phone cheering.

The apartment was located in a high-rise building on Lake Shore Drive. I knocked and the door was answered by a trim, energetic woman holding a tennis racket. Her hair was white, but except for a few spidery lines beneath her eyes, her face was smooth and unwrinkled. I asked to speak to her mother, and she chuckled, poking me in the ribs with the handle of her racket.

"Oh, I am just so happy to see a young person." She grabbed my hand. "Look what we've got here, Abe: a young fella. Why, he's practically a toddler!"

Her husband bounded into the room. Muscular and tanned, he wore a nylon fitness suit complete with a headband and sparkling sneakers. "Ahh, a youngster!"

"He's a graduate," the woman said, squatting to perform a knee bend. "A kid, thinks he's ready to paint our sarcophagus. He's looking at us thinking he's discovered a pair of fossils he can maybe sell to the museum. Oh, we're old all right. Out to pasture. Long in the tooth."

"Built the great Pyramids with my own two hands," the husband added. "Used to swap ideas with Plato and ride a chariot through the cobbled streets of Rome."

"Face it, baby," his wife said. "We're ancient. A couple of has-beens."

"Oh, no," I said. "You're not old. Why, neither one of you looks a day over fifty. Look at you, so trim and fit, you're in much better shape than I am. I'm sure you've got plenty of time left."

"Yeah, right." The woman hopped onto an exercycle. "Time to forget our own names, time to lose control of our bowels, time to stoop and blather and drool onto our bibs. We've got all the time in the world. Days were when I'd throw on a rucksack and head out for a good two-, three-week hike, but now, forget it. I'm too old."

"She's older than the hills she used to climb," her husband said.

"Oh, look who's talking, Father Time himself."

"I'm an old geezer and I'll admit it," the man said. "Still, though, I'm what you call an 'up person.'"

"That's right," she cackled. "Washed up and used up!"

I understood then that this was their act: the Squabbling Old Folks, appearing interminably.

"I guess if you're going to be painting the place, I might as well scrape these tired old bones together and give you a tour," the woman said. She guided me through their home, where every room was furnished with a piece of exercise equipment. A NordicTrack stood parked beside a rowing machine, both facing the living-room television. In the bedroom they kept a set of barbells and colorful mats upon which to practice aerobics. Swimsuits hung drip-drying in the bathroom, and athletic shoes neatly lined the floors of every closet. Except for a few smudges near the guest-room punching bag, the walls were spotless. The doors and baseboards were in fine shape, not a chip or scratch on them. They led me beneath the chin-up bar and into the study, which decorated floor to ceiling with photographs documenting their various adventures. Here they were riding a tandem bicycle through the streets of Peking or trading beads in a dusty Peruvian marketplace. The pictures spanned the course of forty years spent kneeling in kayaks and pitching tents on the peaks of snow-covered mountains, hiking muddy trails and taking the waters of frigid streams.

naked

"Look what we've got here," the woman said. "There's old Methuselah staggering up Mount Rainier. First one to make it all the way to the top with a walker."

"And here's the missus in Egypt," her husband said, pointing to a framed photograph of a mummy.

I tried to turn the subject back to painting, but they wouldn't hear of it.

"Stay for lunch, why don't you," the woman said. "I'll just hook Old Crusty up to his feeding tubes and throw us together a couple of sandwiches."

"A sandwich!" the man cried. "How are you planning to manage the bread? Those chops of yours can't take on anything harder than applesauce."

"Well, I can still chew *you* out," she said. "And they don't come any harder than that."

I drew up an estimate and phoned the next day, knowing in my heart that it was a waste of time.

"It's our young person," I heard her yell to her husband in the background. "Listen, doll, it seems we've decided not to have the place painted after all. Not much point in it, seeing as we'll probably be packed off to the nursing home before you get your ladder set up."

It was my role to contradict her. Instead, I said, "You're probably right. As feebleminded as you are, I guess it's about time to make plans for a structured environment."

"Hey now," she snapped. "No need to get ugly."

During episodes of unemployment I find it rewarding to sleep as much as possible — anywhere from twelve to fourteen hours a day is a good starting point. Sleep spares you humiliation and saves money at the same time: nothing to eat, nothing to buy, just lie back and dream your life away. I'd wake up in the afternoon, watch my stories on TV, and then head over to the sofa for a few more hours of shut-eye. It be-

something for everyone

came my habit to pick up a newspaper just after five o'clock and spend some time searching the want ads, wondering who might qualify for any of the advertised positions: vault verifier, pre-press salesman, audit technical reviewer. Show me the child who dreams of being a sausage casing inspector. What sort of person is going to raise his clenched fist in victory after reading "New Concept=Big $! High energy= Return + Comm. Fax résumé." Fax résumé for what?

I called responding to a quadriplegic looking for a part-time aide. He answered on the fifteenth ring shouting, "For the love of God, Mother, can't a man have five minutes of privacy?"

At the supermarket I dropped a five-dollar bill and turned around just in time to watch someone stuff it in his pocket. My luck was reversing itself.

"Why the hell don't you go back to school and take some *real* classes?" my father said. "Learn to program computers, that's what the Stravides boy did. He'd gone to college and studied show tunes or folklore, some damned thing — went back to school for programming, and now he's heading up the shipping department over at Flexy-Wygaart, whole damned department! Computers, that's where the action is!"

Aside from the fact I had no interest in computers, it seemed a betrayal to graduate from one school only to enter another. That would be admitting I'd borrowed ten thousand dollars and learned absolutely nothing of value, and I was not ready to face that fact.

I found the ad in a community booster paper. "Sharp, experienced go-getter wanted to strip/refinish woodwork. Enthusiasm a must." I had spent years refinishing, first in Raleigh and then again in Chicago. I always vowed I'd never do it again, but that's the problem with having a skill: once you swear off it, you know you're stuck with it forever. All work

naked

seems designed to kill you, but refinishing is tailor-made to provide a long and painful death. The chemical strippers are sold in metal cans picturing a skull and crossbones, and the list of ingredients reads like a who's who in the world of cancer-causing agents. These strippers will eat through plastic buckets, rubber gloves, and nylon brushes. One is advised to wear a respirator but I rejected it, as the cumbersome mask tended to interfere with my smoking. As a result, I found it no longer mattered what I ate. Everything tasted like benzene: scrambled eggs or barbequed pork, when I closed my eyes the only difference was the texture. After a day's work my vision was blurred and my hands were left so stained that cashiers would lay the change upon the counter rather than risk touching my nasty outstretched palm. In Raleigh my friend and I had all the work we could get since the town's foremost furniture refinisher had recently retired. Dean and I would occasionally visit him with a technical question and watch as his wife wheeled him into the parlor, fussing with the tubes that ran from his nose and swabbing the nicotine-stained hole at the base of his throat. His watery eyes would move from one of us to the other. "You boys play your cards right and you've got a fine career ahead of you," he'd wheeze.

My first couple of years in Chicago I'd worked for a man refinishing woodwork. It was much more dangerous than furniture, as it often involved brushing the chemicals onto overhead beams while at the same time attempting to follow the proceedings of *All My Children* and *One Life to Live*. No sooner would Victoria Buchanan wake from her coma than I'd discover a wad of stripper eating a quarter-sized patch of hair from the back of my head. It rained from the ceiling, destroying sofas and carpets, and we followed in its wake, pathetically attempting to restore the discolored fabric with Magic Marker. Our clients would return home to find the

something for everyone

knobs eaten off their television sets and the handle of the refrigerator looking as though someone had taken to it with a
blowtorch. We practiced our campaign of destruction until,
after accidentally setting his van on fire with a smoldering
jah stick, my boss was forced to declare bankruptcy. Once
more, I swore never to refinish again.

I responded to the ad, phoning to speak to a woman who
identified herself as Uta. "Wouldn't you know," she said. "I
just hired myself a colored guy not more than ten minutes
ago. You say you have experience? Well, that's a plus, isn't it?"

She paused, and I took the opportunity to practice the only
promotional skill at my disposal: fluttering my fingers over
the telephone's mouthpiece, I attempted to cast a spell,
silently chanting, *It's me who you want. Me, me, me.*

"Come to think of it," she said, "it *is* an awful lot of work.
Maybe I'd be better off using two people instead of one.
Would that be a problem for you? Because he seemed pretty
sharp, the colored guy did."

"Great," I said. "I love . . . sharp people."

"You a pretty sharp guy?" she asked.

"I guess so, sure." I felt the top of my head.

She asked me my last name and I told her.

"What kind of a name is that," she asked. "It's not Jewish,
is it? Greek? Well, that's fine by me. There are a lot of sharp
Greeks out there. So, listen, my Greek friend, the colored guy
can't start until Monday, so how about you come in tomorrow
morning and give Uta a chance to see how sharp you are,
sharp guy."

I took down the address and agreed to meet her on Saturday morning at 9 A.M. "Sharp."

She met me in front of the building, a three-story six-flat
not far from Wrigley Field. Uta was a stout, muscular woman
with a boxy face, heavily caked with putty-colored founda-

naked

tion that ended at the borders of her formidable jawline. Her hair was dyed a dirty blond, cut short in the back and long up front, the bangs falling to the bridge of her nose. Brushing it off her face gave her something to do with her hands since she had quit smoking several months earlier. "You like that?" she asked. "I thought it was pretty clever." When speaking, she tended to hold her arms close to the body, her fists balled and head cocked, as if she were a boxer scoping out her next punch. "You ready to roll up your shirtsleeves and show Uta what you can do, sharp guy?"

I followed her up the back porch to one of the third-floor apartments and waited as she emptied the contents of her pocketbook, sorting through a knot of keys. She and her sister had recently bought this building, the fourth in what they hoped to be their empire. The family had fled Lithuania in the midforties and settled on the South Side of Chicago, where their father had taken a job in the stockyards.

"We all worked," she said. "Worked our little fannies off. Nobody ever handed Uta anything, I'll tell you that right now. Unlike some people I could mention, I had to start at the bottom and work my way up." She stared off toward the baseball stadium and shook her head in thought, her eyes assuming that haunted, faraway quality sought after by therapists and documentary filmmakers. "It all started with an innocent, pigtailed girl standing on the bow of a ship headed for the new world. The child watched as the beautiful fields of her homeland gave way to the stinking chaos of the stockyards. And she cried, oh, how she cried. She and her family had nothing but gumption and a few loaves of hard, stale bread, but they didn't let that stop them. You see, that little pigtailed girl was me. People ask how I got to where I am today, and I tell them that it took a lot of work. Umpteen and a half years of backbreaking hard work."

It is always a bad sign when an employer offers an image

of themselves doing anything other than getting drunk and throwing money around. Uta gave me the creeps that way. It was fine for her to slave and scrimp, just so long as she didn't expect that sort of behavior from me. I preferred to put in my time, go home, and spend my money as soon as possible. My father's story involved selling newspapers on the snow-covered streets in order to create a better life for himself. It was my destiny to cast off everything he had worked so hard to achieve and mire myself in the very activities that were bringing this country to its knees.

I understood that working for Uta would be an exercise in nodding my head. "Yes, it's a shame the government insti-tuted those crippling child labor laws." "No, these chemical burns don't bother me in the least bit, why would they?" At the end of the day it wasn't my arms that were sore. It was my neck.

"Let's see what we've got here," Uta said, entering the kitchen. "What sort of mess did our little Jewess leave be-hind?"

I was thrown by her use of that expression. Like the term *Negress*, it had a musty, clinical ring to it. She spat the word out of her mouth as if it were a worm she had discovered nesting beneath her tongue. "You buy a building but until the old tenants move out, your hands are basically tied. Lucky for me our fat little Jewess was the first to go. She was a little short thing with an ass the size of a beanbag chair, and Christ Almighty, was she ever a slob. I had the place sprayed yesterday afternoon so we could get started with a clean slate." She spotted a roach shuddering in the sink and smacked it flat with her palm. "Huge ass on that girl, enor-mous. Then again, that's what happens when you sit on your duff expecting the world to do you a favor."

Jews and Jewesses were a big thorn in Uta's side. She tried explaining it to me once, but I found the story difficult to

naked

follow after hearing the date 1527. According to Uta, Adolf
Hitler was completely misunderstood, "as most great thinkers
frequently are." She spoke at length of a conspiracy between
the Jews and Stalin, who had their sights set upon her native
Lithuania for a variety of reasons. The communists wanted
the country in order to enslave the independent, hardworking population. The Jews wanted it for the many forests they
hoped to use as paper with which to wipe their fat asses. Uta
despised these Jews and blamed them for everything from
traffic snarls to the high cost of cable TV.

She walked me through the apartment, which was large
and bright, equipped with nice little touches such as built-in
cabinets and two wood-burning fireplaces. The woodwork
had been painted beyond recognition by sixty years' worth of
tenants who seemed to have sloshed their preferences
straight from the can without benefit of a brush. This spelled
more work, but unfortunately, a great deal of it would involve a heat gun, a high-powered blow-dryer that melts paint
and tends to leave a bad taste in one's mouth. It is slow and
tedious work, aiming the gun until the paint blisters and
then scraping it away with a blade. On a good day you walk
away with a pounding headache. On a bad day you set fires.

"You get this paint off and then the fun starts," Uta said.
"You, me, and the colored guy are going to work some magic,
get this place looking sharp. What do you say? Are you up for
that, you pint-sized Greek, you? Uta's up for it. The colored
guy is up for it. How about it, you ready to join the team?"

She left to run a few errands, and I started bubbling the
paint off the kitchen door. While working I listened to the
radio, a local AM station that broadcast old serials and com-
edy programs every Saturday. I enjoyed both *Suspense* and
The Shadow but when *The Life of Riley* began, I found my
mind beginning to wander. William Bendix plays the sort of
predictable, good-natured idiot guaranteed to get his finger

something for everyone

213

stuck in a bowling ball the night of the big fellowship dinner. He's a garden-variety doofus who seemed to set some sort of standard for generations of succeeding television programs featuring overstuffed closets and family dogs who snatch the holiday turkey off the table while everyone's eyes are closed in prayer. In real life you'd beat a dog senseless for pulling a stunt like that, instead, these are the sort of characters who sit down to a meal of frankfurters and stuffing, pretending they've learned the true meaning of Thanksgiving. This was a world where people were enlightened by a single word or deed. Lessons were learned and lives were changed over the course of twenty-three minutes. Even as a child I had trouble accepting the concept of such rapid spiritual growth. If it were that easy to change people, surely I would be sitting upon a padded velvet throne before a nation of willing servants. Who didn't want to change people? When Uta spoke of the Jews, I'd done nothing more than stare down at my feet. I could have named countless Jews who didn't fit her bill, but that wouldn't have changed her opinion, as her mind had been made up a long time ago. The most you could do with a woman like Uta was to change the subject to a medical mishap, hoping that a good turn to the stomach might shut her up for a while.

I once worked as a runner on a construction site and lost my job when the head carpenter, a fully grown man with a Sir Lancelot haircut, discovered I was a homosexual. We'd gotten along fine all summer, but the moment I questioned his thirst for beating up transsexual prostitutes, he came at me with a hammer. The foreman had let me go as gently as possible, explaining that if he ever hired an all-girl crew, I'd be the first person he called. For a long time afterward I thought of this head carpenter, always placing him in a position of grave, physical danger. The walls of his cell were closing in. A train was headed for his bound-and-gagged body. A

naked

214

bomb was set to go off and only one person could save him. "But first you have to take it all back," I imagined myself saying. "And this time you have to say it like you really, really mean it." I fantasized about it for a few months and then moved on to something else. My hands tend to be full enough dealing with people who hate me for *who* I am. Concentrate too hard on the millions who hate you for *what* you are and you're likely to turn into one of those unkempt, sloppy dressers who sag beneath the weight of the two hundred political buttons they wear pinned to their coats and knapsacks. I haven't got the slightest idea how to change people, but still I keep a long list of prospective candidates just in case I should ever figure it out.

Uta returned at five and enthusiastically inspected my work. The melted paint chips had hardened and littered the floor, as crisp and curled as Fritos. She scooped up a handful, running them through her fingers like a pirate discovering a chestful of golden doubloons. "Hey, Mr. Sharpie, are you sharp or what? Old Uta made a smart move signing you on, didn't she!" She stamped her feet upon the fallen chips, turning in a circle and snapping her fingers.

It occurred to me that she might be drunk, but Uta was the sort of person who didn't need alcohol in order to make a spectacle of herself. I had apparently passed her test and was invited to report back to work on Monday morning, when I could meet "what's-his-hootle, the colored guy."

What's-his-hootle was a tall, solidly built fellow in his early thirties who went by the name of Dupont Charles. In his moments of repose, his eyes were hooded and sensually sleepy, peering out from a handsome face the color of the dark walnut stain Uta planned to use on the woodwork. In the presence of authority, his expression would change completely. As if his features were activated by an invisible pulley, his

something for everyone

eyes would bulge from their sockets and his lips would stretch to comic proportions, revealing a smile of frightening intensity.

"Well, I have a feeling you're a pretty sharp guy," Uta said to Dupont as I entered the room. "And that's just what the doctor ordered. Yes, sir, I need all the sharp guys I can get. What do you say, sharp guy, are you with us?"

"Oh, Miz Uta," he said, "you know I is. I bees wit chu every stepa da way! You can't find no harder worker than Ole Dupont, less you puts ten regular mens together an' beats 'em wid a whip."

He rubbed his hands together and grinned in a way that made my jaws ache. Uta introduced us to each other and stood to watch as we got started.

"You best be careful not to be holdin' dat heat gun too close to the wood," Dupont instructed me. "Elseways all this pretty lady's dreams be goin' up in smoke and we sho' don't want dat happnin', do we?"

"No, Dupont, we certainly don't," Uta said. "You keep on top of him and show him what's what."

"I sho' will. Lord, I must be doin' somethin' right to have got me this fine job workin' fah a nice lady such as yo'self. I waked up dis moanin' jus' prayin' you be haf as nice as you already is. Now here I bees workin' longside you and this tiny little man — oh, you done made me one happy fella, Miz Uta. One happy, happy man."

Uta chuckled, brushing the hair away from her eyes. "You are an absolute treasure," she said. "Both of you are just as sharp as tacks. I guess I'm just one lucky somebody, aren't I?"

"Pretty too," Dupont added. "You bees jus' as lucky an' pretty as you can be."

"You keep that up, mister, and I'm liable to get a swelled head."

"Oh no, Miz Uta. Your head bees jus' right. T'aint too big *or*

naked

216

small. Your head bees perfect. I wished I had me a right-sized head like yours. 'Stead mine be all swolled up an' lumpy."

"Well, it's supporting a nice big brain," Uta said. "You've got a good head on your shoulders, Dupont. You both do."

Dupont beamed and I held my fingers to my throat, attempting to hold back the rising tide of vomit induced by this conversation. Either he had been preserved in a block of ice for the past sixty years or this was some sort of an act. I prayed in favor of the latter possibility, as I could not see myself having to spend eight hours locked in a kitchen with Stepin Fetchit.

When Uta finally left, Dupont stood at the window waving as her car disappeared into traffic. "Sayonara, fathead." His voice had changed both in pitch and timbre, and he no longer spoke with an accent. After turning on the radio, he took a seat on the radiator and lit a cigarette. "You ever been to Tijuana?" he asked. Most of Dupont's stories began with a question and ended with an insatiable woman, buck naked and begging for more. In Tijuana it had been the dark-eyed innkeeper's daughter who reportedly shouted out the words "bueño!" and "grande!" as he took her from behind. Afterwards he had visited a nightclub where, for no cover charge and a two-drink minimum, he had witnessed a prostitute get it on with a braying donkey. "For real. After the show the club owner offered me the girl for free, but I said no because she was all stretched out. Say, you ever put a saddle on a fat girl's back and ride her until she drops?"

Dupont lived with his girlfriend on the north side of town. He said that being white and Jewish, she was so desperate for a real man that she not only paid the rent and bills but also provided him with a clothing allowance. There were, he said, some pictures he'd show me after his brother got through with them. "Have you ever gotten two sisters pregnant in the same month?" he asked.

something for everyone

217

Uta's car pulled up later that afternoon, and Dupont scrambled to collect his cigarette butts before turning on his heat gun. "Dat's how come I bees workin' so hard," he said to me as she entered the room. "I dreams a goin' off ta college some day and maybe bein' a doctah or lawyah. Oh, hey, Miz Uta. You go get yo' hairs done? It sho' be lookin' pretty."

Uta said no, she'd just run a comb through it, nothing special. "What's this garbage on the radio?" she asked, referring to the station Dupont had settled on after she'd left.

"Is dat da radio I been hearin'? Sound ta me like two cats clawin' they way outta a bag. When jew turn on da radio, Mistah Dave? Lord, I guess I bees workin' so hard I ain't had da time ta hardly notice it."

"Well *I* do and it's giving me a big fat headache," Uta said, resetting the dial to a classical station.

"Oh, I likes dat!" Dupont sang. "Dat dere bees the exact typo music I listens to at home." He waved and glided his hands through the air as if he were conducting a symphony, his heat gun shooting helter skelter and singeing the hair on my arms.

"Oh, Dupont, you are certainly one very special person."

It was my habit to stop for a cigarette once every hour, and I saw no reason to stop just because Uta was around.

"That, mister, is one nasty habit," she said. "You ought to do like me and quit cold turkey. It was hard, sure it was, but I toughed it out and now I can finally see just how disgusting it really is."

"It smell bad, too," Dupont said, as if he could detect anything over the stench of burning paint. "It stink up da vironment and cause folks ta get cansah, too."

"That's telling him," Uta said.

"I don't wanna get me no cansah, Miz Uta. No ma'am, I don't want nothin' preventin' me from achievin' my goals. I mona go to medical school and learn how to be a doctah.

naked

218

Then I mona go to anotha school an be a lawyah, and then I ain't stoppin' till I bees the president of da YOUnited States!"

"You see there," Uta said. "Speaking on behalf of a doctor, lawyer, and the future president of the United States, there will be no more smoking in this apartment."

I carried my cigarette out onto the back porch, listening as Dupont promised Uta a position as his secretary of health. His health was something he definitely needed to worry about, as I planned to kill him as soon as possible.

"Don't think I'm not docking you for that little cigarette break, mister," Uta said when I returned. "It was Dupont's idea, and I think it's a good one. Why should he work like a dog while you sit on your duff puffing away like a chimney? Maybe a dent in the old pocketbook will be the very thing that leads you to quit. Some people just have to learn the hard way."

"Dat's right!" Dupont said.

I asked him later why he bothered going through that foolish routine. He lit a cigarette and shrugged, explaining that he needed the money. I said that I needed the money, too, but there was more than enough work to go around. Why bust my chops and act like a moron when it wasn't necessary?

"She likes it," he said. "Big deal. If you want her to like *you*, maybe you should try a little harder, sharp guy." He wiped the tips of his sneakers with a paper towel, saying "Hey, did you ever fuck a stout frecklefaced girl while her boyfriend was passed out in front of the TV?"

I enjoyed Dupont's stories in part because I never quite believed them. It wasn't, say, his seventh-grade math teacher measuring his erect penis with a slide rule that captivated me, rather it was the notion that he thought I might be impressed. He knew I had a boyfriend, yet he persisted with his

something for everyone

219

questions. "When was the last time you poured motor oil on a college girl's titties?" Like the act he presented for Uta, this seemed tailored to accommodate his notion of what he thought I expected him to be. To the landowning business-woman, he was the grinning minstrel, standing upon an overturned bucket to deliver his hopeless State of the Union Address. To what he considered a sex-crazy homosexual, he was the indefatigable stud, roaming from haystack to canopied bed to service his ever-expanding flock of enthusi-astic bitches. I suppose we all bend ourselves to what we per-ceive as other people's expectations, but to go so far as to outlaw smoking suggested a serious personality disorder. Who was he to his mother? To his girlfriend or father? In his attempt to be all things to all people, Dupont had succeeded in being one of the most mysterious people I'd ever met. Coma patients reveal more about themselves than he did.

For lunch we usually took forty-five minutes and ate cheeseburgers from a stand down the street. When Uta was around, Dupont suddenly switched to eating rice cakes and a cup of plain yogurt, her personal favorite as she was trying to work off the weight she'd gained since calling it quits with cigarettes. He'd shovel it down in five minutes, wipe his lips with the sleeve of his shirt, and return to work, regarding me as if I personified everything that was wrong with shiftless, fat-dazed America.

"I likes to eat da natural things what God set upon the plate of Adam an Eves," he'd say. "Don't take much ta make *me* happy, no ma'am; the littler I eats, the happier I bees."

"That's because you're like me," Uta would say. "You're a sharp person who eats smart."

We'd been at it for close to three weeks when finally it was time to switch off our heat guns and move on to the next phase. Uta had a system for stripping wood that involved us-ing sawdust rather than steel wool. We painted the chemicals

naked

onto a patch of woodwork, packed it with sawdust, and scrubbed the area with a brush, removing the varnish to expose the natural oak that probably hadn't seen the light of day since Uta's friend Hitler was a young boy in lederhosen. Her method was quicker than using steel wool — cheaper, too — as the sawdust was given away free by the neighborhood lumberyard. The problem was that the sawdust had a way of infiltrating any unguarded part of the body, coating our hair and settling into the ears and nostrils. It crept through the eyelets of my shoes, into my socks and pockets, and clung to the sweat of our faces so that by the end of the day we all looked frighteningly alike. With our matte, beige faces; red eyes; and plush, dusted hair, Uta, Dupont, and I could have easily passed as members of the same grotesque family.

Uta was away one morning, visiting her accountant, when Dupont asked, "Have you ever loaned pictures of your girl-friend to your brother and gotten them back all covered with stains?" The answer was clearly so obvious, he did not hesi-tate for a reply but rather handed me a stack of Polaroids wherein a washed-out, naked, and bored-looking white woman posed upon a brown corduroy sofa, clutching a vari-ety of household objects in her vagina: a flashlight, a hair-brush, a family-sized tube of toothpaste, and what looked to be a bottle of either shampoo or dish detergent. "That's my girl!" Dupont said proudly. It was his hope to get the pictures published in what he referred to as "one of the magazines." Toward the bottom of the stack were portraits of Dupont, sitting on a rattan throne and wearing nothing but pale blue socks and a pair of aviator sunglasses. His face was twisted into a sneer, and he was leaning forward, propping his chin upon the handle of a cane carved to resemble the head of an angry lion.

In situations like this I tend to comment on the details that

something for everyone

might allow me to walk away as quietly as possible. "That's some chair," I said. "Where did you get that picture you've got hanging on the wall there? It always cheers me up to see a kitten sleeping in any kind of a basket."

"You ever fuck a Jewish girl up the butt with the tip of a cane?" he asked.

We had finished stripping all the woodwork and were preparing to apply the stain when Uta announced that following this next stage of the game, she would no longer be needing us both. Her friend Briggs would drive in from Michigan to lend a hand when it came time to apply the finish. "I'm sorry, guys," she said. "You're both as sharp as you can be, but Briggs is practically family and has a lot of experience with polyurethane."

"Jus' like me!" Dupont said. "I bees experiencin' with polyuratain all my life. Mistah Dave complain that it gives him a headache, but it bees like a tonic for me." He paused to tap his brush against the rim of the can. "I's jus' hopin' that, seein' as you can't afford to keep us both on, you'll at least let me stay on and work fo free as a volunteer."

Uta said she appreciated the gesture but wouldn't think of having someone work for no pay. "Besides," she said, "what makes you think I'd be letting *you* go?"

"It jus that, well . . ." He hung his head. "You know how it bees for people like me. Bein' . . . a colored man the way I is."

"I understand it's very hard for you people," Uta said. "You get all kinds of flak from the southern rednecks and now I read in the paper where you're getting it from the Jews to boot."

"They'se the people who kilt Jesus!" Dupont said. "Hung him up on a cross and poked him wit sticks."

"Well, I wouldn't mind poking a few of *them* with a stick," Uta said.

naked

"Me neither." Dupont looked my way and smiled.

Over the next few days he shifted into high gear, pointing out my countless flaws while pretending to share an interest in Uta's many views and hobbies. Every few hours he would ask a question about crochet or ice-skating, but mainly he stuck to the Jews. "Las' night I got to thinkin' about how you said the Jews was tryin' ta take ovah the world banks, Miz Uta. An' it don't hardly seem fair to me, seein' as how them peoples already gots so much already."

"Well, Dupont, some people are just plain greedy. It's in their genes. I guess they're just born that way."

"I reckon you'se right. Some folks like Mistah Dave be born jus' to show up late, even when he *ain't* wearin' jeans. Other folks come into dis whorl jus' wantin' to have everthang they can get they hands on. Me, I jus' wish everybody be borned like you, Miz Uta, wantin' to be sweet an' pretty an' fair-minded 'stead of bein' late and tryin' ta take ovah da world banks. When I bees elected to president, I mona pack them Jews an' lazy folks off to wherever they come from and have me a country dats got somethin' for everyone!"

"Well, you've got *my* vote," Uta said.

The closer we came to the end of the week, the more ruthless Dupont became. I was returning from lunch, changing back into my work pants, when I heard him delivering what he hoped might be the final nail in my coffin.

"Miz Uta, did you know David be sick?"

"What, does he have a cold or something? I haven't noticed anything."

"Nome, I mean he be sick . . . in here."

I couldn't see anything but imagined he was pointing to the space between his ears.

"He tole me that he likes to go with mens, Miz Uta. In bed, I mean. Said he been doin' it all his life. Said now he be livin' wit another man, the two of 'em together like a regu-

something for everyone

223

lah man and wife. And it . . . it jus' ain't right. No, ma'am, it jus' is . . . wrong. T'aint natural in the eyes o' God or the eyes of me neither. Way I see it, people like that be preyin' on youngsters an' ruinin' folks' lives just like the Jews be doin', don't you think?"

"I think it's time for you to stop sticking your nose into other people's business, that's what I think," Uta said. "David can do whatever he wants to do after he leaves this apartment. We're not here to discuss anyone's private life; we're here to stain this wood, do you understand?"

"It jus' that . . . well, it make me uncomfortable, the way he bees lookin' at me sometimes, Miz Uta. Make me feel all spooky. It like . . . he can see right through my clothes or somethin'. I don't know how he do it."

"It's not all that difficult to see through you, Dupont," I heard her say. "Take my word for it, the hard part is listening to you."

Stunned, he spent the next few hours trying to regain her good graces. In his haste to please her, he overturned a can of stain. "That's coming out of *your* pocketbook, my friend," Uta said.

He ran to her with a cigarette butt he'd found in the pantry. "Miz Uta, somebody done been smokin' in the apartment again. I tole him it was dangerous on account of the fumes and all but he said . . ."

"Oh, for the love of Pete," Uta snapped. "Could you please shut your stupid mouth for just five minutes!"

Friday quietly came and went. Dupont returned on Monday morning with the pocket of his jeans slashed. "You ever been robbed, Miz Uta?" He said it happened on his way home from church. "I usually goes to church with my Moms, but she got carried away to the hospita' Saturday night wiff a turrible pain in her stomach. Doctor tole her that a tumor

naked

224

done settled in there and like to eat her whole kidney clean off unless she have herself a operation."

"Oh, Dupont, that's terrible."

"Yes'm, so I stayed up all night wiff her and then the next day I goes to church and on the way home I bees so tired I falls asleep on the train."

"I'll bet you were just exhausted," Uta said.

"Yes'm, I sho' was. I sat in that seat and felled stoned asleep while some pickpocket done slashed my pants with a razor and stole my wallet."

"You've got to be sharp when you're riding those trains, Dupont. Keep your eyes open and look out for danger."

"I wished I had ahad my eyes open, Miz Uta. They took my wallet wiff all my money and my ID card and the pay-check you gave me last Friday."

"Well, that's a shame," Uta said. "But look at it this way, at least you learned a lesson."

"I suspect I did. Yes'm, I sho' be awake now. Can't sleep a note thinkin' 'bout that paycheck I worked so hard for and now it be stole. All that money I was hopin' to save for med-ical school be stole, and my whole dream be gone."

"Don't worry," Uta said, laying her hand on his shoulder. "There'll be other dreams." She really seemed to be enjoying this.

"I reckon there will, Miz Uta, but I need this dream *now*. I's hopin' I could go to medical school . . . real soon so maybe I could . . . operate on my mother."

"That's very thoughtful of you," Uta said. "I'm sure your mother's very proud."

"What's left of her," Dupont said. "Po' thing be coughin' up specks of her throat into a napkin and can't nobody do nothin' 'bout it."

"Well, that's certainly tragic," Uta said. "It's a sad, sad

story you've got there. I only wish I could do something to help."

"Well, maybe there is *one* thing," he said, scratching his head with the point of a pencil. "Maybe if you was to maybe write me anotha check, make up fo' the one what got stole. What if you was to make me a new check and call the bank tellin' 'em to cancel out the first check 'fore anybody have a chance to cash it."

"Don't you think someone might have cashed it already?" she asked, looking down at his feet. "Hey, nice new sneakers, Dupont. Those are really sharp."

"Chances most likely that nobody *did* cash it yet," he said, changing the subject. "Seein' how the banks be closed on Sunday."

"Then they probably took it in first thing this morning," she said.

"Naw, probably most likely they ain't on account that it take a while for 'em to work up the nerve to forge my hand-writin' on the back of the check."

"You might be right about that," Uta said. "Chances are it would take a thief a good three or four days to work up that kind of confidence."

"Oh, please, Miz Uta, you know I weren't be axin' if it wadn't such a mergency. If somethin' happen and you find out dat first check done already been cashed, I swear I'll make it up to you, even though it weren't my fault to begin wiff. I'll come over to you house and chop some wood or dig you a pool, you know I will."

Uta sighed. Drying her hands, she reached for her pocket-book.

"Oh, you is one sweet white lady," Dupont said. "I don't care what nobody says, you jus' as nice an' sweet as you can be." He folded the check in half and placed it in his shirt pocket, tapping it for safekeeping.

naked

226

"You'd better get down to the bank and deposit that in your savings account right away," Uta said dryly. "Otherwise, you might lose it, then you'll never be able to attend eight years of medical school in time to cure your mother of cancer."

"Yes'm, I reckon you's right. I'll jus' run to da bank right quick and be back sooner'n you can blink yo' pretty blue eyes." He bolted out the door, managing to contain his laughter until he hit the street.

"I know what you're thinking," Uta said to me. "But you're wrong. I was born at night but it wasn't *last* night. Thinks he's so sharp, does he? Well, he doesn't know the half of it. I was going to give him that money anyway, hand it to him as a severance check as soon as I let him go. Goddamned apple polisher. Promising to dig me a pool, ha! I was paying him a lot less than what I've been giving you, but what the heck, I figure I got my money's worth out of him. Five dollars says he'll run down to the bank and keep on running. What do you say, five bucks, let's wager, sharp guy."

There was no point in throwing my money away, as I knew she was right.

Uta's friend, Polly Briggs, arrived the following morning but didn't start work until after the Cubs game. She was a back-slapper, forthright and loud with short curly hair and a spray of freckles across her nose. Briggs — "Call me Polly one more time and you'll be wiping vomit off your shoes. Can't stand the name. Never could." — spent most of the year in northern Michigan, where she taught physical education at a public high school. During her summer vacations she often came to Chicago to attend baseball games and help Uta with whatever little project she happened to be working on. They struck me as unlikely friends, different in age, temperament, and tastes. Uta did not look unhealthy, but Briggs, with her

something for everyone

227

hale complexion and robust physical stature, appeared as if she had spent the wee hours tossing bales of hay onto a horse-drawn wagon. She was casual and cloddish, while Uta tended to be much more guarded, preferring to think herself infallible, especially in the presence of her employees.

When Briggs complained that she'd gotten bad seats to that afternoon's game, Uta remarked that all the good spots had been taken by the Jews, who, according to her, also controlled the hot-dog concessions and souvenir sales. "The parking, the players' salaries, even the making of bats and mitts, it's all controlled by the Jews. They've been shooting the prices right through the roof. Here I am, two blocks from the ballfield, and they're driving my property taxes sky-high. They want to make it so . . ."

"Aw, shut up, already," Briggs said. "You've been carping about the Jews ever since you left that dump of a country. Open up a third-grade history book and maybe you'd learn something. Besides, you didn't think the Jews were so bad back when you were chasing Brandy Fleischman."

Uta brushed the bangs back from her forehead the way she had a thousand times before, but now the gesture was openly nervous. She pulled the hair back over her eyes as if to hide herself and, after a lengthy pause, muttered, "Well, Brandy was only *half* Jewish."

"Yeah? Which half, top or bottom?" Briggs turned to me and winked while Uta huffed and fidgeted, her face rising in color. Dupont and I had often speculated about her sex life. He'd insisted she wanted all the black men she could get her hands on, while I had a hard time imagining her with anyone but one of those retired Nazi generals holed up in the jungles of Argentina. We were both way off the mark.

"Say, Uta, whatever happened to that little Collins girl, the one that used to go with us down to the dunes? You know the one I'm talking about. She used to sell fire insurance or some

naked

damned thing, liked to skeet shoot." Briggs sloshed on the polyurethane with all the delicacy of a toddler, and I followed along behind her, trying to smooth out the drips before they hardened. After the first few days Uta loosened up a bit and allowed herself to enjoy her friend's company. Their gentle bickering assumed a harmless and comfortable tone, and I tuned in and out according to my interest. They were debating the merits of a high-fiber diet one afternoon when I looked out the window, certain I saw Dupont standing on the corner in front of the small neighborhood grocery. A woman came out of the store carrying two large paper sacks. Dupont said something, and she shook her head no. He moved toward her, his arms positioned to embrace the bags, and she backed away, calling through the screen door. The grocer stepped out and Dupont threw up his hands in what appeared to be either frustration or denial. After exchanging a few more words, he walked away, rounding the corner and out of sight.

We had applied the first coat of finish and were halfway through the second when Briggs accidentally dropped a full cup of Gatorade into the gallon bucket of polyurethane. "That's coming out of *your* paycheck, baby," Uta said.

They squabbled back and forth until Briggs offered to buy a whole tanker of the stuff if it would get Uta to shut her yap.

"All right, then," Uta said, "but *I'm* coming with you to make sure you don't walk out of there with a cheaper brand. And we're taking *your* car because I've wasted enough gas on you already. *And* we're going to listen to what *I* want to hear on the radio. How do you like them apples?"

They left the apartment carrying on and had been gone for no more than three minutes when Dupont entered the room.

something for everyone

"Hey," I said, "what happened? We've been wondering what you've been up to. Uta's not here right now, she . . ."

"Took off in a car talking shit to some curly-headed bitch. I saw them leave. Tell me when she's coming back."

I said fifteen, maybe twenty minutes. "Say, guess what? It turns out that Uta is a . . ."

"Give me twenty dollars," Dupont said, lighting a cigarette. "I'll pay you back next week." He stood in front of the fireplace mirror, inspecting his hair, which had been treated with oils and now hung in lank curls. For a moment I hardly recognized him. It wasn't just his hair that had changed, it was his whole manner. The question mark had been removed from both his speech and his posture. He stood straight, his shoulders squared and his head positioned as if it had been screwed to a post. "Give me twenty dollars," he repeated.

When I told him I didn't have it, he closed his eyes and let out an impatient sigh, the sort you deliver the moment you decide someone needs to learn a lesson.

I pulled out my wallet, "Look, see for yourself. I spent my last five dollars on lunch." It's always nice when, by some freak of nature, you can rely upon the truth to get you out of an uncomfortable situation. There was a checkbook in my knapsack, but in terms of cash, my wallet held nothing but an outdated school ID, my library card, and the telephone numbers of people I could no longer recall.

"Well, I need twenty dollars," he said. "That's just the way it is. I need it."

"Maybe you can wait until Uta gets back, and she'll let you work for a few hours."

He looked at me as though I'd suggested he pan for gold in the gutter.

"OK, maybe you could borrow the money from your girl-friend," I offered.

"Right," he said. "My girlfriend. You're real quick, aren't

naked

230

you. I guess I'd forgotten just how smart you really are." His voice had a hard, bitter edge to it. "You're just as sharp as a fucking ice pick, aren't you." He paced the room. "Sharp as a jackknife, aren't you, Boy Scout."

I looked in the mirror and watched as he picked Uta's purse off the window ledge. "That's Uta's," I said. "Maybe you should talk with her before opening it because, well, it's hers and you know how she is about her things."

This was about as forceful as I get. Were America's safety in my hands, we would all be wearing burlap sacks, polishing the boots of any invader capable of pronouncing the word *boo*.

Dupont found her wallet and removed three twenties, a five, and two singles. He arranged the bills into a flaccid fan and waved them before his face, as if the tiny breeze were all he had intended them for. Then he folded the money, placed it in his pocket, and walked out the door.

I left shortly afterward, mounting my bicycle and riding toward the bank for three twenties, a five, and two singles. Uta was the type of person who knew exactly how much she had riding in her wallet. She kept lists of withdrawals and carefully tabulated all her receipts. "Can you believe I spent seventeen dollars at the Osco? And for what? One tiny bag I walked out with." She would certainly notice that her money was missing. I couldn't tell her that Dupont had taken it, as she would have yelled, "You let him into this apartment? And then what, he rifles through my pocketbook and you didn't think to stop him? You just let him take my money and waltz out the door?"

I would have felt the same way had I been her. If I'd told her that Dupont had stolen the money, she probably would have called the police and I'd have had to go through the entire conversation again. "And you *let* him take the money?" the officer would ask. Had the case gone to court, *I* would have been the one to run into Dupont late some night after he'd served his thirty days or whatever the going rate is for petty larceny.

Neither could I have lied, telling Uta that I'd left for some small errand and neglected to lock the door behind me. "You did *what?* Why not just roll out a red carpet and hang up a sign inviting every crook in Chicago to come on in and rob me blind? That sixty-five dollars is coming out of *your* paycheck, mister." And again, that would have been my reaction, too, were I an aggressive or forthright person. Instead, I am not, and because of that, I felt a real hatred, not for Dupont or Uta, but for myself for being so weak and cowardly with the both of them. They had presented themselves, each in their own way, and it was always my option to draw some sort of a line, to voice my opinion or defend myself; to be brave or be frank or just *be* something. It had nothing to do with changing people — forget that, on a good day you're lucky if you can talk someone into changing his socks. Neither could I tell myself that this was strictly job-related behavior. My spine retains this buttery consistency with or without a paycheck. Unlike other people I have known, my silence will never be interpreted as wisdom. It is my chattering teeth that give me away every time.

Uta and Briggs were back at it by the time I returned. "Say, David, we've got a little wager going here. Who won the pennant back in fifty-seven?"

I told Briggs I had no earthly idea.

"I still say it was the Oreos," Uta shouted.

"The Oreos, listen to this one!" Briggs rolled her eyes and squatted to pry open the new can of polyurethane.

I waited until it was time to leave. The women were in the other room changing out of their work clothes, and I crept over to replace Uta's money, feeling more anxious than I would have if I were stealing it. Opening her pocketbook, I thought of how unfair it was that, of all the involved parties,

naked

I was the one who would have to pay. Dupont knew that I wouldn't have stopped him or told on him. Uta had a half dozen rental properties and a thick portfolio of stocks under her belt. They were having a ball, never questioning their actions or the things that they said. What made them so sure of themselves and why couldn't I feel the same way? I told myself that as opposed to them, I had a conscience, but the moment I thought it, I knew it was a lie. Had it been a sense of goodness that motivated me, I would have thought nothing of it. Instead, this was a soft and flabby cowardice that had assumed the shape of virtue.

She was in her stocking feet, and wallet open, radio blaring, I didn't hear Uta coming up behind me. "What is it you're doing in my purse?" she asked. "What, I don't pay you enough, is that it?" She cupped her hands to her mouth, "Hey, Briggs, get in here. I just caught our friend going through my wallet."

The air rushed out of the room, through the open windows and the cracks beneath the door, leaving, in its wake, a vacuum. "So tell me about it, friend. Just what exactly is it you're looking for?"

The mind plays tricks on the memory. Time is skewed to benefit convenience. Events are compressed for greater efficiency or expanded to accommodate a false sense of triumph. This being the case, it's hard to say exactly, but it seems to me that I spent close to fifteen thousand years standing stock-still in that exact same spot, searching for an answer to her question.

ashes

The moment I realized I would be a homosexual for the rest of my life, I forced my brother and sisters to sign a contract swearing they'd never get married. There was a clause allowing them to live with anyone of their choice, just so long as they never made it official.

"What about children?" my sister Gretchen asked, slipping a tab of acid under her tongue. "Can I *not* marry and still have a baby?"

I imagined the child, his fifteen hands batting at the mobile hanging over the crib. "Sure, you can still have kids. Now just pick up your eyebrow pencil and sign on the dotted line."

My fear was that, once married, my sisters would turn their backs on the family, choosing to spend their vacations and holidays with their husbands. One by one they would abandon us until it was just me and my parents, eating our turkey and stuffing off TV trays. It wasn't difficult getting the signatures. The girls in my family didn't play house, they played reformatory. They might one day have a relationship — if it happened, it happened; but they saw no reason to get bent out of shape about it. My father thought otherwise. He saw marriage as their best possible vocation, something they should train for and visualize as a goal. One of my sisters would be stooped before the open refrigerator, dressed in a bathing suit, and my father would weigh her with his eyes. "It looks like you've gained a few pounds," he'd say. "Keep that up and you'll never find a husband." *Find.* He said it as though men were exotic mushrooms growing in the forest and it took a keen eye to spot one.

"Don't listen to him," I'd say. "I think the weight looks good on you. Here, have another bowl of potato chips."

Marriage meant a great deal to our neighbors, and we saw that as another good reason to avoid it. "Well, we finally got Kim married off." This was always said with such a sense of relief, you'd think the Kim in question was not a twenty-year-old girl but the last remaining puppy of an unwanted litter. Our mother couldn't make it to the grocery store and back without having to examine wallet-size photos of someone's dribbling, popeyed grandbaby.

"Now *that's* different," she'd say. "A living baby. All my grandchildren have been ground up for fertilizer or whatever it is they do with the aborted fetuses. It puts them under my feet but keeps them out of my hair, which is just the way I like it. Here's your picture back. You tell that daughter of yours to keep up the good work."

Unlike our father, it pleased her that none of her children had reproduced. She used the fact as part of a routine she delivered on a regular basis. "Six children and none of them are married. I've taken the money we saved on the weddings and am using it to build my daughters a whorehouse."

After living with her boyfriend, Bob, for close to ten years, my sister Lisa nullified our contract when she agreed to marry him. Adding insult to injury, they decided the wedding would take place not at a drive-through chapel in Las Vegas but on a mountaintop in western North Carolina.

"That's nice," my mother said. "Now all I need is a pair of navy blue hiking boots to match my new dress and I'll be all set."

The first time I met my future brother-in-law, he was visiting my parents' home and had his head deep in the oven. I walked into the kitchen and, mistaking him for one of my sisters, grabbed his plump, denim-clad bottom and proceeded to knead it with both hands. He panicked, smacking his head against the oven's crusty ceiling. "Oh, golly," I said, "I'm sorry. I thought you were Lisa."

It was the truth, but for whatever reason, it failed to comfort him. At the time Bob was working as a gravedigger, a career choice that suggested a refreshing lack of ambition. These were not fresh graves, but old ones, slotted for relocation in order to make room for a new highway or shopping center. "How are you going to support my daughter on that?" my father asked.

"Oh, Lou," my mother said, "nobody's asking him to support anyone; they're just sleeping together. Let him be."

We liked Bob because he was both different and unapologetic. "You take a day-old pork chop, stab it with a fork, and soak it in some vinegar and you've got yourself some good eatin'," he'd say, fingering the feathery tip of his waist-length braid. Because of his upbringing and countless allergies, Bob's apartment was a testament to order and cleanliness. We figured that someone who carefully shampooed the lining of his work boots might briefly date our sister but would never go so far as to marry her. Lisa couldn't be trained to scoot the food scraps off her soiled sheets, much less shake out the blanket and actually make the bed. I underestimated both his will and his patience. They had lived together for close to three years when I dropped by unan-

naked

nounced and found my sister standing at the sink with a sponge in one hand and a plate in the other. She still hadn't realized the all-important role of detergent, but she was learning. Bob eventually cut his hair and returned to college, abandoning his shovel for a career in corporate real estate. He was a likable guy; it was the marrying part that got to me. "My sister's wedding" was right up there with "my recent colostomy" in terms of three-word phrases I hoped never to use.

Three weeks before the wedding, my mother called to say she had cancer. She'd gone to a doctor complaining about a ringing in her ear, and the resulting tests revealed a substantial tumor in her lung. "They tell me it's the size of a lemon," she said. "Not a tiny fist or an egg, but a lemon. I think they describe it in terms of fruit so as not to scare you, but come on, who wants a lemon in their lung? They're hoping to catch it before it becomes a peach or a grapefruit, but who knows? I sure as hell don't. Twenty-odd tests and they still haven't figured out what's wrong with my ear. I'm just hoping that whatever it is, it isn't much larger than a grape. This cancer, though, I realize it's my own fault. I'm just sorry your father's still around to remind me of that fact every fifteen goddamned seconds."

My sister Amy was with me when my mother called. We passed the phone back and forth across my tiny New York kitchen and then spent the rest of the evening lying in bed, trying to convince each other that our mother would get better but never quite believing it. I'd heard of people who had survived cancer, but most of them claimed to get through it with the aid of whole grains and spiritual publications that encouraged them to sit quietly in a lotus position. They envisioned their tumors and tried to reason with them. Our mother was not the type to greet the dawn or cook with oats and barley. She didn't reason, she threatened; and if that

ashes

237

didn't work, she chose to ignore the problem. We couldn't picture her joining a support group or trotting through the mall in a warm-up suit. Sixty-two years old and none of us had ever seen her in a pair of slacks. I'm not certain why, but it seemed to me that a person needed a pair of pants in order to defeat cancer. Just as important, they needed a plan. They needed to accept the idea of a new and different future, free of crowded ashtrays and five-gallon jugs of wine and scotch. They needed to believe that such a life might be worth living. I didn't know that I'd be able to embrace such an unrewarding future, but I hoped that she could. My brother, sisters and I undertook a campaign to bolster her spirits and suggest new and exciting hobbies she might explore once she was cured and back on her feet.

"It'll be great," I said. "You could, I don't know, maybe you could learn to pilot small planes or volunteer to hold crack babies. There are a lot of things an older person can do with her time rather than smoke and drink."

"Please don't call me stoned on pot and tell me there are lots of things I can do with my life," she said. "I just got off the phone with your brother, who suggested I open up a petting zoo. If that's what being high does for a person, then what I really need to do is start smoking marijuana, which would be a bit difficult for me since the last time I saw my right lung it was lying in the bottom of a pan."

In truth, her lungs were right where they'd always been. The cancer was too far advanced and she was too weak to survive an operation. The doctor decided to send her home while he devised a plan. The very word sounded hopeful to us, a plan. "The doctor has a plan!" my sisters and I crowed to one another.

"Right," my mother said. "He plans to golf on Saturday, sail on Sunday, and ask for my eyes, kidneys, and what's left of my liver on that following Monday. That's his plan."

naked

We viewed it as a bad sign when she canceled her subscription to *People* magazine and took to buying her cigarettes in packs rather than cartons. She went through her jewelry box, calling my sisters to ask if they preferred pearls or gems. "Right now, the rubies are in a brooch shaped like a candy cane, but you can probably get more money if you have them removed and just sell the stones." In her own way she had already begun to check out, giving up on the plan before it was even announced. *But what about us?* I wanted to say. *Aren't we reason enough to carry on?* I thought of the unrelenting grief we had caused her over the years and answered the question myself. It was her hope to die before one of us landed in jail.

"What's Amy planning on wearing to this little Pepsi commercial," my mother asked, referring to the mountaintop ceremony. "Tell me it's not that wedding dress, please."

Lisa had decided to be married in a simple cream-colored suit, the sort of thing one might wear to work on the day of their employee evaluation. Figuring that at least somebody ought to look the part, Amy had the idea to attend the ceremony dressed in a floor-length wedding gown, complete with veil and train. In the end, she wound up wearing something my mother hated even more, a pink cocktail dress outfitted with detachable leg-o'-mutton sleeves. It wasn't like her to care what anyone wore, but she used the topic to divert attention from what we came to refer to as her "situation." If she'd had it her way, we would never have known about the cancer. It was our father's idea to tell us, and she had fought it, agreeing only when he threatened to tell us himself. Our mother worried that once we found out, we would treat her differently, delicately. We might feel obliged to compliment her cooking and laugh at all her jokes, thinking always of the tumor she was trying so hard to forget. And that is exactly what we did. The knowledge of her illness forced everything

ashes

239

into the spotlight and demanded that it be memorable. We were no longer calling our mother. Now we were picking up the telephone to call our mother with cancer. Bad day at work? All you had to do was say, "I'm sorry I forgot to vacuum beneath the cushions of your very lovely, very expensive Empire sofa, Mrs. Walman. I know how much it means to you. I guess I should be thinking of more important things than my mother's inoperable cancer."

We weren't the ones who were sick, but still, the temptation was so great. Here we could get the sympathy without enduring any of the symptoms. And we deserved sympathy, didn't we?

Speaking to our mother, we realized that any conversation might be our last, and because of that, we wanted to say something important. What could one say that hadn't already been printed on millions of greeting cards and helium balloons?

"I love you," I said at the end of one of our late-night phone calls.

"I am going to pretend I didn't hear that," she said. I heard a match strike in the background, the tinkling of ice cubes in a raised glass. And then she hung up. I had never said such a thing to my mother, and if I had it to do over again, I would probably take it back. Nobody ever spoke that way except Lisa. It was queer to say such a thing to someone unless you were trying to talk them out of money or into bed, our mother had taught that when we were no taller than pony kegs. I had known people who said such things to their parents, "I love you," but it always translated to mean "I'd love to get off the phone with you."

We gathered together for the wedding, which took place on a clear, crisp October afternoon. The ceremony was held upon a grassy precipice that afforded magnificent views of the surrounding peaks, their trees resplendent in fiery red and orange. It was easy to imagine, looking out over the horizon, that we were it, the last remaining people on the face of the earth. The others had been wiped out by disease and famine, and we had been chosen to fashion a new and better world. It was a pleasant thought until I pictured us foraging for berries and having to bathe in ice-cold streams. Bob's family, hearty and robust, could probably pull it off, but the rest of us would wither and die shortly after we'd run out of shampoo.

My father wept openly during the ceremony. The rest of us studied his crumpled face and fought hard not to follow his example. What was this emotion? My sister was getting married to a kind and thoughtful man who had seen her through a great many hardships. Together they shared a deep commitment to Mexican food and were responsible card-carrying members of the North American Caged Bird Society. The tacos and parrots were strictly between Lisa and Bob, but the rest of her belonged to us. Standing in a semicircle on top of that mountain, it became clear that while Lisa might take on a different last name, she could never escape the pull of our family. Marriage wouldn't let her off the hook, even if she wanted it to. She could move to Antarctica, setting up house in an underground bunker, but still we would track her down. It was senseless to run. Ignore our letters and phone calls, and we would invade your dreams. I'd spent so many years thinking marriage was the enemy that when the true danger entered our lives, I was caught completely off guard. The ceremony inspired a sense of loss directed not at Lisa, but at our mother.

"No booze?" she moaned. My mother staggered toward the buffet table, its retractable legs trembling beneath the weight of sparkling waters, sausage biscuits, and decaffeinated coffee.

"No booze," Lisa had announced a week before the ceremony. "Bob and I have decided we don't want that kind of a wedding."

"Which kind?" my mother asked. "The happy kind? You and Bob might be thrilled to death, but the rest of us will need some help working up the proper spirit."

She didn't look much different than she had the last time I'd seen her. The chemotherapy had just begun, and she'd lost — at most — maybe five pounds. A casual acquaintance might not have noticed any change at all. We did only because we knew, everyone on that mountaintop knew, that she had cancer. That she was going to die. The ceremony was relatively small, attended by both families and an assortment of Lisa's friends, most of whom we had never met but could easily identify. These were the guests who never once complained about the absence of alcohol.

"I just want you to know that Colleen and I both love your sister Lisa so much," the woman said, her eyes moist with tears. "I know we've never been formally introduced, but would you mind if I gave you a big fat hug?"

With the exception of Lisa, we were not a hugging people. In terms of emotional comfort, it was our belief that no amount of physical contact could match the healing powers of a well-made cocktail.

"Hey, wait a minute. Where's *my* hug?" Colleen asked, rolling up her sleeves and moving in for the kill. I looked over my attacker's shoulder and watched as a woman in a floor-length corduroy skirt wrestled my mother into an affectionate headlock.

"I heard what you're going through and I know that you're frightened," the woman said, looking down at the

naked

242

head of thinning gray hair she held clasped between her powerful arms. "You're frightened because you think you're alone."

"I'm frightened," my mother wheezed, "because I'm *not* alone and because you're crushing what's left of my goddamned lungs."

The scariest thing about these people was that they were sober. You could excuse that kind of behavior from someone tanked up on booze, but most of them hadn't taken a drink since the Carter administration. I took my mother's arm and led her to a bench beyond the range of the other guests. The thin mountain air made it difficult for her to breathe, and she moved slowly, pausing every few moments. The families had taken a walk to a nearby glen, and we sat in the shade, eating sausage biscuits and speaking to each other like well-mannered strangers.

"The sausage is good," she said. "It's flavorful but not too greasy."

"Not greasy at all. Still, though, it isn't dry."

"Neither are the biscuits," she said. "They're light and crisp, very buttery."

"Very. These are some very buttery biscuits. They're flaky but not too flaky."

"Not too flaky at all," she said.

We watched the path, awkwardly waiting for someone to release us from the torture of our stiff and meaningless conversation. I'd always been afraid of sick people, and so had my mother. It wasn't that we feared catching their brain aneurysm or accidently ripping out their IV. I think it was their fortitude that frightened us. Sick people reminded us not of what we had, but of what we lacked. Everything we said sounded petty and insignificant; our complaints paled in the face of theirs, and without our complaints, there was nothing to say. My mother and I had been fine over the telephone, but now, face to face, the rules had changed. If she were to complain, she risked being seen as a sick complainer, the worst kind of all. If I were to do it, I might come off sounding even more selfish than I actually was. This sudden turn of events had robbed us of our common language, leaving us to exchange the same innocuous pleasantries we'd always made fun of. I wanted to stop it and so, I think, did she, but neither of us knew how.

After all the gifts had been opened, we returned to our rooms at the Econolodge, the reservations having been made by my father. We looked out the windows, past the freeway and into the distance, squinting at the charming hotel huddled at the base of other, finer mountains. This would be the last time our family was all together. It's so rare when one knowingly does something for the last time: the last time you take a bath, the last time you have sex or trim your toenails. If you know you'll never do it again, it might be nice to really make a show of it. This would be it as far as my family was concerned, and it ticked me off that our final meeting would take place in such a sorry excuse for a hotel. My father had taken the liberty of ordering nonsmoking rooms, leaving the rest of us to rifle through the Dumpster in search of cans we might use as ashtrays.

"What more do you want out of a hotel?" he shouted, stepping out onto the patio in his underpants. "It's clean, they've got a couple of snack machines in the lobby, the TVs work, and it's near the interstate. Who cares if you don't like the damned wallpaper? You know what your problem is, don't you?"

"We're spoiled," we shouted in unison.

We were not, however, cheap. We would have gladly paid for something better. No one was asking for room service or a heated swimming pool, just for something with a little more

naked

244

character: maybe a motel with an Indian theme or one of the many secluded lodges that as a courtesy posted instructions on how to behave should a bear interrupt your picnic. Traveling with our father meant always having to stay at nationally known motor lodges and take our meals only in fast-food restaurants. "What?" he'd ask. "Are you telling me you'd rather sit down at a table and order food you've never tasted before?"

Well, yes, that was exactly what we wanted. Other people did it all the time, and most of them had lived to talk about it.

"Bullshit," he'd shout. "That's not what you want." When arguing, it was always his tactic to deny the validity of our requests. If you wanted, say, a stack of pancakes, he would tell you not that you couldn't have them but that you never really wanted them in the first place. "I know what I want" was always met with "No you don't."

My mother never shared his enthusiasm for corporate culture, and as a result, they had long since decided to take separate vacations. She usually traveled with her sister, returning from Santa Fe or Martha's Vineyard with a deep tan, while my father tended to fish or golf with friends we had never met.

The night before the wedding, we had gone to a charming lodge and eaten dinner with Bob's parents. The dining room had the feel of someone's home. Upon the walls hung pictures of deceased relatives, and the mantel supported aged trophies and a procession of hand-carved decoys. The night of the wedding, Lisa and Bob having left for their honeymoon, we were left on our own. My sisters, stuffed with sausage, chose to remain in their rooms, so I went with my parents and brother to a chain restaurant located on a brightly lit strip of highway near the outskirts of town. Along the way we passed dozens of more attractive options:

steak houses boasting firelit dining rooms and clapboard cottages lit with discreet signs reading HOME COOKING and NONE BETTER!

"What about that place?" my brother said. "I've never tasted squirrel before. Hey, that sounds nice."

"Ha!" my father said. "You won't think it's so nice at three A.M. when you're hunched over the john, crapping out the lining of your stomach."

We couldn't go to any of the curious places, because they might not have a sneeze guard over the salad bar. They might not have clean restrooms or a properly anesthetized staff. A person couldn't take chances with a thing like that. My mother had always been willing to try anything. Had there been an Eskimo restaurant, she would have been happy to crawl into the igloo and eat raw seal with her bare hands, but my father was driving, which meant it was his decision. Having arrived at the restaurant of his choice, he lowered his glasses to examine the menu board. "What can you tell me about your boneless Pick O' the Chix combination platter?" he asked the counter girl, a Cherokee teenager wearing a burnt orange synthetic jumper.

"Well, sir, there isn't much *to* say except that it doesn't got any bones and comes with fries and a half-gallon 'Thirsty Man' soda."

My father shouted as if her dusky complexion had somehow affected her hearing. "But the chicken itself, how is it prepared?"

"I put it on a tray," the girl said.

"Oh, I see," my father said. "That explains it all. Golly, you're a bright one, aren't you? IQ just zooming right off the charts. You put it on a tray, do you? I guess that means the chicken is in no position to put itself on the tray, which tells me that it's probably been killed in some fashion. Am I correct? All right, now we're getting somewhere." This con-

naked

246

tinued until the girl was in tears and we returned empty-handed to the car, my father muttering, "Jesus, did you hear that? She could probably tell you everything you needed to know about trapping a possum, but when it comes to chicken, she 'puts it on a tray'."

Under normal circumstances my mother would have worked overtime to protect the waitress or counter help, but tonight she was simply too tired. She wanted to go somewhere that served drinks. "The Italian place, let's go there."

My brother and I backed her up, and a short time later we found ourselves seated in a dimly lit restaurant, my father looking up at the waitress to shout, "*Rare*, do you know what that means? It means I want my steak the color of your gums."

"Oh, Lou, give it a rest." My mother filled her wine glass and lit a cigarette.

"What are you doing?" He followed his question with an answer. "You're killing yourself is what you're doing."

My mother lifted her glass in salute. "You got that right, baby."

"I don't believe this. You might as well just put a gun to your head. No, I take that back, you can't blow your brains out because you haven't got any."

"You should have known that when I agreed to marry you," she said.

"Sharon, you haven't got a clue." He shook his head in disgust. "You open your mouth and the crap just flies."

My mother had stopped listening years ago, but it was almost a comfort that my father insisted on business as usual, despite the circumstances. In him, she had found someone whose behavior would never vary. He had made a commitment to make her life miserable, and no amount of sickness or bad fortune would sway him from that task. My last meal with my parents would be no different than the first. Had we been at home, my mother would have fed him at seven and then waited until ten or eleven, at which time she and I would broil steaks. We would have put away several drinks by then, and if by chance the steaks were overcooked, she would throw them to the dog and start all over again. Before moving to New York, I had spent two months in Raleigh, painting one of my father's rental units near the university, and during that time our schedule never varied. Sometimes we'd eat in front of the television, and other nights we would set a place for ourselves at the table. I try recalling a single one of those evenings, wanting to take comfort in the details, but they are lost to me. Even my diary tells me nothing: "Ate steaks with Mom." But which steaks, porterhouse or New York strip? What had we talked about and why hadn't I paid attention?

We returned to the motor lodge, where my parents retired to their room and the rest of us hiked to a nearby cemetery, a once ideal spot that now afforded an excellent view of the newly built Pizza Hut. Over the years our mother had repeatedly voiced her desire to be cremated. We would drive past a small forest fire or observe the pillars of smoke rising from a neighbor's chimney, and she would crush her cigarette, saying, "That's what I want, right there. Do whatever you like with the remains; sprinkle them into the ashtrays of a fine hotel, give them to smart-assed children for Christmas, hand them over to the Catholics to rub into their foreheads, just make sure I'm cremated."

"Oh, Sharon," my father would groan. "You don't know what you want." He'd say it as though he himself had been cremated several times in the past but had finally wised up and accepted burial as the only sensible option.

We laid our Econolodge bedspreads over the dewy grass of the cemetery, smoking joints and trying to imagine a life without our mother. If there was a heaven, we probably

naked

248

shouldn't expect to find her there. Neither did she deserve to roam the fiery tar pits of hell, surrounded for all eternity by the same shitheads who brought us strip malls and theme restaurants. There must exist some middle ground, a place where one was tortured on a daily basis but still allowed a few moments of pleasure, taken wherever one could find it. That place seemed to be Raleigh, North Carolina, so why the big fuss? Why couldn't she just stay where she was and not have cancer? That was always our solution, to go back in time. We discussed it the way others spoke of bone marrow transplants and radiation. We discussed it as though it were a viable option. A time machine, that would solve everything. I could almost see its panel of blinking lights, the control board marked with etched renderings of lumbering dinosaurs and ending with Lisa's wedding. We could turn it back and view our mother as a young girl, befriend her then, before her father's drinking turned her wary and suspicious. See her working in the greeting-card section of the drugstore and warn her not to drop out of school. Her lack of education would make her vulnerable, causing her to overuse the phrase "Well, what do I know" or "I'm just an idiot, but . . ." We could turn it back and see ourselves as babies, our mother stuck out in the country with no driver's license, wondering whom to call should someone swallow another quarter or safety pin. The dial was ours, and she would be at our mercy, just as she had always been, only this time we would pay attention and keep her safe. Ever since arriving at the motor lodge, we'd gone back and forth from one room to another, holding secret meetings and exchanging private bits of information. We hoped that by preparing ourselves for the worst, we might be able to endure the inevitable with some degree of courage or grace.

Anything we forecasted was puny compared to the future that awaited us. You can't brace yourself for famine if you've

ashes

never known hunger; it is foolish even to try. The most you can do is eat up while you still can, stuffing yourself, shoveling it in with both hands and licking clean the plates, recalling every course in vivid detail. Our mother was back in her room and very much alive, probably watching a detective program on television. Maybe that was her light in the window, her figure stepping out onto the patio to light a cigarette. We told ourselves she probably wanted to be left alone, that's how stoned we were. We'd think of this later, each in our own separate way. I myself tend to dwell on the stupidity of pacing a cemetery while she sat, frightened and alone, staring at the tip of her cigarette and envisioning her self, clearly now, in ashes.

naked

It is disconcerting to talk to someone on the phone and know that he is naked. Every now and then I might call a friend who says, "You caught me on my way to the shower," but that's different. The man at the nudist colony sounded as though he had been naked for years. Even his voice was tanned.

"All right, then, have you ever visited us before? No? Well, you're in for a real treat. We've got a heated pool, a sauna, Jacuzzi, and a fully stocked pond for fishing."

I tried to imagine what one's ass might look like having spent several hours pressed against an overturned log, but the mental picture was too brutal and I forced it out of my mind.

"We can give you a tour, show you around the place once you arrive, and in the meantime, I'd be happy to send you a brochure. Let me just . . . get your . . . information here . . ."

Where, I wondered, *did he keep his pen?* Unlike me, he would never instinctively reach for his breast pocket. Keys, lighters, cigarettes, change — all the things a reasonable person might carry were jumbled together somewhere else, and it took him awhile to find something to write with. He took my name and address saying, "All right then, we look forward to seeing you."

"Yeah, right. You bet." Freak. I'd just called for the brochure, wanting to give it as a joke to my brother, Paul, a floor sander who, due to a recent polyurethane spill, had been discovered naked by the startled owners of the condominium in which he'd been working. Ever since he'd told me about it, I've been calling him to suggest other nude activities he might enjoy.

"I keep telling you it was a goddamned accident." He yells so loud, I have to hold the phone away from my ear. "I had clean clothes down in the kitchen, motherfucker, I was just trying to get *to* them when . . ."

Ignoring him, I plow ahead. "Or boating, you might like doing that naked. There are plenty of things a person like you can do without having to wear clothes. There's no need to feel ashamed of your desires. 'If it feels good, do it!' Isn't that what you young people like to say?"

I keep at it until he slams down the phone, threatening to cross state lines and kick my ass. This brochure will be just the thing to send him over the edge. It occurred to me later that I should have had it mailed directly to his house in North Carolina. It would have been much more effective that way, but I don't want to call the colony again. They might think I'm a nut.

In this afternoon's mail I received my brochure which reads, "Body acceptance is the idea. Nude recreation is the way. Bring your towels and suntan lotion and relax with us. You will experience a freedom of movement that cannot be felt with clothes: the freedom to be yourself."

The brochure pictures a swimming pool, the fully stocked

naked

pond, a sundeck, and the inevitable volleyball court, which leaves me to wonder: What *is* it with these people and volleyball? The two go hand in hand. When I think nudist, I don't think penis — I think net.

Included in the envelope is a calendar of events. Late April marked the reopening of the snack bar, which goes by the name Bare Necessities. In May they held a golf-cart rally, several theme campfires, a chili cook-off, and something called "Wild West horseback riding."

Test eye shadow on all the rabbits you want. Strap electrodes to the skulls of rhesus monkeys and shock them into a stupor, but it is inhumane to place a nudist on horseback the day after a chili cook-off. ("Was he *always* an Appaloosa?") The calendar is filled with mystifying events such as nude bowling night, the Hobo Slumgullion, and Nudeoween. The restaurant opened the first week of June. A nude restaurant. They seem to have taken care of just about everything. Under the heading of "What to Bring," they list only towels, suntan lotion, and a smile.

Last night I was in a foul mood and provoked Hugh into a fight, goading him until he left the bedroom, shouting, "You're a big, fat, hairy pig!"

Big is something I can live with. *Fat* is open to interpretation, but when coupled with the word *hairy*, it begins to form a mental picture that is brought into sharp focus when united with the word *pig*. A big, fat, hairy pig. Well, I thought, pigs provide us with bacon and watchbands, and that's saying something. Were they able to press buttons and operate levers with their sharp hooves, they would have been sent into space long before monkeys. Being a pig isn't so bad. I wiped a driblet of snot from the tip of my snout and lay there feeling sorry for myself. If I were a nudist, Hugh's words wouldn't have hurt me, as I would have accepted myself for

naked

253

who I am. There were, of course, other options. I could trot down to the local gymnasium and tone myself up. It's a nice word, *gymnasium*, unfortunately it's also archaic. Gone are the jump ropes and medicine balls of my youth. Now there are only health clubs and one-syllable *gyms* where sweat-drenched he-men bulk up through the use of weight machines and StairMasters. I've seen them through the front windows of the city's many fitness centers. Dressed in costumes as tight as sausage casings, these men and women intimidate me with their youth and discipline. It's them who have removed both the *g* and the *h* from the word *light*, reducing it to its current, slender version. Everything is "lite" now, from mayonnaise to potato chips, and the word itself is always printed in bright colors so your eyes won't get fat while reading the label. Diet and exercise are out of the question as far as I'm concerned. My only problem with nudism is that I don't even walk around my house barefoot, let alone naked. It's been years since I've taken off my shirt at the beach or removed so much as my belt in the presence of strangers. While I long to *see* naked people, I'm not so sure I'm ready to be naked myself. Perhaps the anxiety will cause me to drop a few pounds and I'll come out a double winner. The less I have to accept of myself, the easier it will be. Already I can feel my appetite waning.

This afternoon, after a half dozen false starts, I phoned the nudist colony to make a reservation, speaking to the same fellow who'd mailed me the brochure. This time I could hear people in the background, splashing and yelling with glee. The sound of them made me giddy, and I unbuttoned my slacks. The brochure had mentioned rental cabins, and I was wondering what it might cost to stay for a week.

"You want a trailer for how long?" he asked.

I refastened my pants. I had imagined tree-shaded bunga-lows paneled in knotty pine. That, to me, is the essence of the word *colony*.

This place was, instead, a nudist trailer park.

"We don't use the word *colony* anymore because it's too spooky. No, what we have are trailers. The smaller units run thirty dollars a night, but if you want your own kitchen and bathroom, your only option is the double-wide, which will run you an extra seventy dollars a week."

He'd lost me way back. How was the word *colony* spooky, but not *trailer* or even *nudist* for that matter?

"I can let you have the front bedroom of the double-wide; that's not booked yet."

Front bedroom suggested the evidence of a back bedroom, which, I was told, would be rented out separately. "You could have one roommate or maybe it'll be a couple. They might stay for a night or two or maybe they'll spend the whole week. Don't worry, though, you won't get lonely."

I was still wrestling with the idea of a trailer, and when he introduced the possibility of a roommate, my vision blurred. A roommate at a nudist trailer park. The combination of those elements presented a staggering tableau, made all the more incomprehensible when I heard the man shoulder the phone and raise his voice to shout, "Mom! Hey, Mom, where's the weekly price list for the two-bedroom rental trailer?"

This person was not only standing around naked in broad daylight, he was doing it with his mother. I heard a screen door slam, followed by the wary voice of a woman shouting, "Hold your hollering, loudmouth. Looking for the weekly price sheet? You're probably sitting on it, just like the last time. See, I told you so! Phew, somebody needs a shower."

I made my reservation and planned to arrive in one week.

naked

255

I called the nudist park again today and a woman answered. When asked if they provide sheets and pillows, she said, "Yes, but no towels. You'll have to bring your own towels because we can't be doing that. Bedding yes, towels no."

I asked if the trailer's kitchen was equipped, and she replied, "Kind of."

Seeing as I would be there for a week, I was hoping she might elaborate.

"Well, it kind of has some things but not some others."

"Does it kind of have a stove and refrigerator?"

"Oh, sure," the woman said. She seemed busy with something else and spoke lazily, not wanting to talk but not wanting to get off the phone either. "There's a sink up there and probably some pans and so forth, but definitely no towels, you'll have to pack your own because we can't be running back and forth like that. We haven't got the time for that kind of thing."

I told her I understood perfectly.

"A lot of folks think we keep a nice fluffy stack of towels out by the pool for their own private use, but we don't do that. Not here we don't. Not anymore. Towels are personal things, and you'll have to bring your own."

I truly had gotten the message.

"Course sometimes a person might come in for the day and leave their towel behind by accident, but we put that into the lost-and-found box in case they come back looking for it. You can't use those towels because they're not clean and they don't belong to you. That somebody might come back one day to claim their towel, and it wouldn't do for them to walk in here and find you using it without their permission. It wouldn't be right. If it was lotion, I might say, 'Go ahead and use it; I'll do your back,' but not towels, no way. You'll have to bring your own."

I underlined the world *towels* on my list of things to pack and placed question marks beside everything else.

I arrived at the nudist park early this afternoon, the cabdriver pulling up to the clubhouse in a light rain. He'd been very nervous on the ride over. "I'm not here to judge," he'd said. "Hell, I give rides to all kinds of people, even drunks. Whatever floats your boat, partner." Something about me seemed to make him uncomfortable, and I frequently caught him studying me in the rearview mirror with a look that said, "Keep your hands where I can see them."

I collected my bags and entered a low, clapboard building where five fully dressed senior citizens sat hugging themselves against the cold and watching the local news on a color television set bolted to a high shelf. On the screen a weatherman pointed to a map studded with frowning suns, his arm positioned as though he were drawing a heavy curtain. The inhabitants of the room leaned forward in their chairs, biting the ridges of their clenched fists and groaning when confronted with the words, *cold front.* They booed the weatherman. They cursed him and then they pounded on the tabletops, much like prisoners unhappy with their food. The room was filled with the rhythmic thuds of protest when I set down my suitcase and approached the front desk.

"He did this!" An elderly man pointed his crooked finger in my direction. "Brought this nastiness with him down from the lakes!"

"You from the lakes?" the woman behind the counter asked. The corners of her mouth hung so low, they grazed the line of her jaw. She narrowed her eyes upon my suitcase as if expecting it might bluster across the floor, packed as it was with storm clouds and unseasonable winds.

"I don't know anything about any lakes." There was a rising panic in my voice. "It was hot and sunny when I left New York this morning, really, it was. It turned cold around Scranton, but I didn't even get off the bus. It's the truth, you can ask the driver." It was ridiculous to stand before a group of strangers denying my responsibility for the weather, but surrounded by their stern accusatory faces, the charges seemed frighteningly plausible.

"Well, it's supposed to clear by tomorrow afternoon, but if it doesn't, I'll know where to find you." The woman pointed out the window. "It's that trailer there with the orange trim. Front bedroom, that's what I've got you down for."

"You mean the one with the rust-colored band?"

"You call it rust, I say it's orange, but you get the idea. It's the one with the picnic table in the front yard. Can we agree that that *is*, in fact, a picnic table?"

Without meaning to, I seemed to have offended her.

"I painted that trim myself and the can distinctly identified it as 'burnt orange.' If it had said 'rust', I never would have bought it. It only *looks* rusty under those clouds you brought. Sunny day comes, you'll see that color for what it is. I'm sorry I can't rush out there and repaint it to suit your needs, but I've got other things to do, other duties."

I asked where I might find the key to my trailer and heard a round of muffled laughter coming from the far corners of the room.

"Key!" She acted as though I had requested a prayer rug or a life-sized statue of Buddha. "We don't believe in locked doors, not here we don't. Maybe where you come from, people barricade themselves behind closed doors, but here we have no reason." She placed her elbows upon the countertop and framed her face between her fists. "We don't lock our doors because, unlike certain other people, we have nothing to hide."

The clubhouse was furnished with tables and chairs. Be-

naked

258

side the front desk was a small kitchen, its serving window framed with packages of freeze-dried beef and bags of potato chips. There was a grill, a deep fryer, and a menu board offering possible choices for breakfast and lunch. This was clearly the snack bar, but where was the restaurant?

"Snack bar by day, restaurant at night." The woman said. "But only on Saturdays, when nothing else is planned."

Why hadn't they told me this earlier? I'd been led to believe the restaurant was open every night. All I'd brought with me was a salami and a box of crackers. What was I supposed to do, with no car?

"I can fry you up a hamburger if you want, but you'll have to make up your mind. Snack bar closes at one P.M. on weekdays unless it's good weather or a holiday, then we're open until three-thirty. There's a little restaurant on the road into town, but they close at three." She studied her watch for a moment. "If you start now, you can probably make it before they close, but you really should have brought a car. A person needs a car for this kind of lifestyle. You need a car and plenty of towels."

My only choice was to take a taxi into town and buy myself a week's worth of groceries. Where might I find a pay phone?

"It's out on the deck." The woman waited until I reached the screen door to add, "But it doesn't work. Storm knocked it out last Thursday and hasn't nobody come to fix it yet. We have a devil of a time getting repairmen out here. I guess our money's not good enough for them. Most things we just patch up ourselves, but not that phone. Tricky thing, a pay phone. I can let you use my phone, but you'll have to make it quick, I'm expecting a call."

The taxi driver said he could pick me up in an hour, and I wondered what he might charge to drive me all the way back home. This wasn't what I had in mind at all. No key, no

naked

259

restaurant, just a handful of cranks moaning about the weather.

I walked up the gravel lane to my trailer, which had been sprayed with so much insecticide that it curled the hair in my nose. Raisin-sized flies lay gasping on the countertops, their upturned legs signing the words, "Get out of here, quick, while you still have a chance." I set down my suitcase and fled, trotting past the clubhouse to the soggy volleyball court. The same pool I had seen in the brochure was now covered by a tarp, as was the hot tub. Even the flag was at half mast.

My trailer's main room is paneled with artificial walnut planks, and the low, fiberglass tiled ceiling is stained with water marks. A linoleum floor separates the kitchen area from the carpeted living room, which is furnished with a worn, gold velvet sofa and two matching easy chairs that face a low table bearing the scuff marks of a now absent television set. Two of the walls are lined with windows, and the other supports a large, ornamental carpet picturing a family of polar bears occupying an ice floe. My bedroom, like that of my potential roommate's, is cell-like in both its size and simplicity, furnished with only a bed and a small chest of drawers that easily accommodates the little I brought with me.

By the time I'd unpacked and put away my groceries, it was early evening and the rain had stopped. After staring at the spot where the television used to be, I took a walk past the clubhouse and up into the park's more established neighborhoods. These were mobile homes that had been soundly grounded upon carefully manicured lots, many with built-on decks made of pine and redwood. Some of the trailers had been sided to resemble log cabins, and others were fronted by shingled, A-framed entrance halls. The homeowners' names were displayed on wooden plaques along with slogans such as

"Bare with us" or Smile if you talk naked!" Flowerbeds were marked with wooden cutouts of bare-bottomed pint-size children and silhouettes of shapely, naked women were painted onto the doors of tool sheds and nailed like FOR SALE signs onto the trees. Most everyone seemed to have a golf cart parked in the driveway, and these, too, were personalized with bumper stickers and hand-painted slogans. I passed a sign reading SHEEP CROSSING 20 FEET and came across a trailer whose lawn played host to a flock of artificial sheep tended to by an oversized, bonneted doll equipped with a crooked staff. Time had not been kind to the shepherdess, nor to her charges, whose waterlogged wool was stained with the evidence of a long and unforgiving winter. Farther along the road these homes gave way to tents and campers equipped with pop-up roofs and jury-rigged awnings made of plastic and fronted by mosquito netting. The lack of space had forced both the kitchens and bathrooms outdoors, and the yards were home to outhouses and picnic tables surrounded by coolers and grills that sat positioned beneath festive paper lanterns. A trailer door opened and a young woman stepped out, leading a child who beat upon her legs with a wooden spoon. The woman was topless, and her breasts hung like two kneesocks, each stuffed with a single orange. I knew when I signed up that I would encounter exposed breasts, but this being my first pair, I reacted with alarm. She wore her hair in a neglected shag and scolded the child for a moment or two before gathering him up in her arms and burying her sharp-featured face into his stomach. Topless. She was topless, walking the streets of what amounted to her neighborhood. The boy howled with pleasure and then rapped her over the head with his spoon.

"He's at that age," the woman said, and I nodded in agreement, pretending to recall the first time I had tweaked my mother's nipple while standing in the front yard of our trailer. I looked into her face, trying my hardest not to stare at her breasts. "Well, all right," I said, "OK then."

On the way back to my trailer, I caught sight of various nudists through lit windows, washing dishes and enjoying a quiet evening at home. Curtains wide open, doors unlocked, and there they were with their legs spread apart, chuckling along with the situation comedies. A car came up the lane in my direction, driven by a shirtless man smoking a pipe. As he passed I glanced down into the front seat and saw that he was naked. He raised his pipe in salute and proceeded down the road. Where, I wondered, was he going? Was he driving in circles in order to blow off steam? Or did he plan to leave the grounds and take to the highway?

It took a few drinks before, drawing the curtains of my double-wide, I was able to remove my shirt and shoes. The table was littered with beer cans by the time I finally stepped out of my briefs and started to prepare my dinner, trying hard to convince myself that it's natural to broil pork chops in the nude. As they sizzled away, I pretended that my roommate had just arrived. "You're just in time," I said, taking two plates from the overhead cabinet. "Have a seat, dinner will be ready in a couple of minutes. Say, don't mind those beer cans, I pulled them out of the neighbor's trash thinking I'd carry them down to the recycling bin the next time I head into town. Never touch the stuff myself, but then again, that's just me, 'the health nut.' Let me give you a quick look around." I was showing my invisible guest the back bedroom when the smoke alarm went off. The searing, high-pitched squeal sent me into a panic, and before I had time to think about it, I was standing with the door open, brandishing a dishcloth in an attempt to clear the air. Naked. I was drunk

naked

262

and naked for all the world to see. It was a sobering thought that continued to haunt me as I sat down to my blackened dinner.

It's begun to thunder and rain is beating down upon the metal roof of my trailer. Ten o'clock and, from what I can see, everyone's lights are out for the evening. I've been reading over the list of rules handed me this afternoon by the matron behind the front desk.

Conduct — We are a family park and expect your conduct to reflect the moral standards of a family campground.

Towels — Carry a towel with you at all times and please SIT ON YOUR TOWEL FOR SANITARY REASONS."

Towels. It suddenly made sense. Noticing the wide range of short curly hairs beside me on the sofa, I leaped up and fetched a towel that, from this moment on, would never leave my underside.

Photography — Cameras and camcorders are permitted only by special permission of the management. ANY PHOTOGRAPHY EQUIPMENT NOT APPROVED BY THE MANAGEMENT WILL BE TAKEN FROM YOU. Prior written permission MUST BE OBTAINED from any person being photographed.

Pets — No pets are allowed in common sunning areas. They should be under your control at all times. You must clean up after your pet and dispose of all feces.

Alcohol — Alcoholic beverages may be consumed only in moderation. Intoxication will not be permitted on the grounds.

Pool Etiquette — Take a SOAP SHOWER before entering
the pool or hot tub. NON-POTTY-TRAINED CHIL-
DREN ARE NOT ALLOWED INTO EITHER THE
POOL OR THE HOT TUB.

Dress — We dress or undress for comfort. When using our
recreational facilities, YOU MUST BE NUDE. INTI-
MATE APPAREL, BATHING SUITS, AND INTIMATE
BODY JEWELRY ARE INAPPROPRIATE ON OUR
GROUNDS. YOU MUST BE NUDE IN THE POOL,
HOT TUB, AND SHOWER."

What, I wonder, is intimate apparel and body jewelry?
Doesn't the word lose meaning when everyone is nude?

I know it's probably against the rules, but I can't shake the
hint of sexual excitement I'm feeling. It's not an erection,
just a tingling sensation in the tip of my penis. Outside of the
bathtub or an occasional doctor's visit, the only time I'm
naked is when I've talked someone into having sex with me.
Sitting here with nothing on, I keep expecting some guy to
walk out of the bathroom saying, "So what are you planning
to do with the prize money?" It feels silly to wander about
my trailer this way, and I realize that it has long been my
habit to stretch my T-shirt over my knees while sitting alone
at a table. I'm also used to pulling my pants above my navel
and tightening my belt to diminish my gut. Jangling the keys
in my pocket, thoughtlessly gnawing at the collars of my
shirts: these things are lost to me now. It feels dangerous to
drink a cup of hot coffee, and twice in the last hour I've
hopped up to brush glowing cigarette ash off what I once
considered to be my private parts.

I awoke this morning to a fog so thick, I couldn't see the picnic table in my front yard. From the sky to the ground, every-

thing was the exact same shade of gray. It wasn't until early evening that the weather finally cleared. At six o'clock I looked out my window to see a naked couple strutting across the grounds with a pair of tennis rackets in their hands. The man wore his hair long in the back and carried himself as though he were dressed in a fine suit, his stride confident and purposeful, while the woman trotted along behind him wearing a sun visor, kneesocks, and sneakers. These were the first active, out-of-door nudists I had seen, and I threw on my clothes and followed them to the pavilion, where I pulled a book from my pocket and pretended to read. The man had an ample stomach and a broad, dimpled ass that jiggled and swayed as he leaped about the court, attempting to return his partner's serves. They played for no more than five minutes before he placed his hands on his knees, released a mouthful of bile onto the grass, and called it quits. They left the court and I followed them into the clubhouse, where the man stepped into the bathroom, returning ten minutes later with a bright red ring around his ass. Here, I thought, was a real nudist. There was a tuft of toilet paper, just slight, clinging to his bottom, and when the woman pointed it out to him, he ran his hand along his crack and casually shrugged, as though it were no more significant than a dab of mayonnaise on his lip.

I tried to start my day naked but made it no farther than my picnic table before returning to my trailer and throwing on a T-shirt that covered me to midthigh. Walking out past the pavilion, I came upon a group of elderly men and women gathered around a gravel court. It was midmorning, and I got the idea that something important was about to begin. A woman stooped to rake the stones. She wore a short-sleeved shirt but no skirt or pants, and her ass was a landscape of pocks and wrinkles, the blue veins crossing her thighs like a topographical map of creeks and rivers. Seated on a nearby bench were two other women, each dressed in T-shirts. One wore a visor, while the other favored the type of bonnet I associate with the milkmaids of old. This was a broad-brimmed, ruffled contraption tied in a bow beneath the lowest of her several chins. "Howdy," she said. "Hey, look, everybody, we've got ourselves some new blood!"

"Aah, a fresh face, that's just what we need to keep the game interesting." The speaker was a deeply tanned gentleman, naked except for a golf hat upon which he'd pinned the key to the equipment locker. "Have you ever played *pétanque* before?" He placed his hand on my shoulder and led me to the court. "It's the French cousin to the Italian game of bocci. Stan Friendly and his wife used to play it down in Florida, and when they brought it up north, we all said, 'What the heck kind of game is that?' We were all playing volleyball and thought these *pétanque* players were a pair of cuckoo birds, didn't we, Frank?"

"We thought they were a couple of loons." Frank said. Scratching his mosquito-bitten buttocks, he joined us on the court. "Now we say, 'To hell with volleyball,' and we're playing *pétanque* three times a day. It's a great game, you'll see. Hey!" he shouted. "Somebody give our friend here a pair of balls. We've got ourselves a new player."

It was curious to see the various states of undress and the way clothing was shed over the course of the game. Like me, Jacki and Carol had arrived wearing T-shirts, while Bill, Frank, and Celeste wore nothing but hats. Phil and Millie drove up in sweatsuits, which they immediately discarded and placed in a heap on the picnic table. A man named Carl wore a shirt and vest, which coupled with his black socks and sensible street shoes, suggested he was just passing time while his pants and underwear tumbled in the dryer.

naked

266

Bill, the man with the golf hat, had a long scar running from the center of his back to his right underarm. The wound was once level with his skin, but now the tight, slick scar tissue resembled a narrow road surrounded on either side by barren, amber hills. Frank's body, on the other hand, was a regular ATM machine, with surgeons making routine withdrawals from his back, chest, and stomach. He tossed a small wooden ball onto the court, explaining that this was to be our target, and then handed me what appeared to be a croquet ball made out of metal that looked like something a person might fire from a cannon. Taking another for himself, he mounted a flat concrete slab at the edge of the court, closing one eye and holding the thing much like Hamlet reflecting on the skull of his deceased jester. Because he was naked, his stance seemed strangely heroic, as if he were posing for a statue used to commemorate the geriatric wing of a hospital devoted to sports medicine. Then, without warning, he reared back, swung his arms a few times for practice, and released the ball, which sailed through the air, landing with a thud two inches from the target.

"Now you give it a try, Dave." My ball missed the mark by a good six feet.

"Good throw!" Frank said. "Say, Bill, did you see that? Looks like we've got a natural on our hands. Try it again, young fella."

My second ball missed the court entirely and landed in the damp grass. It was clearly bad, as was my next shot, and the one after that. Yet, each attempt garnered the same response: "Good throw!" Either their eyes were clouded with cataracts or these were indeed the best sports I had ever met.

The game went on forever, its details discussed with passion. Often there was a debate over which ball was closest to the target. "I think it's Carl's, but why don't we check. Phil's ball looks neck and neck." A tape measure was brought forth, handled gently and with great reverence, as if it might once and for all prove the existence of God. The team captains would squat down on their heels, their testicles bobbing against the gravel court. "Carl's is eight and three-quarters and Phil's is . . . what do you know, eight and nine-sixteenths! Looks like Phil's team gets the point!"

The tedium of the game allowed me to forget the fact that I was wearing nothing but a T-shirt and sneakers. At first, I'd hung around the outer edges of the court and retrieved my balls like a white-wigged countess, twisting my way toward the ground as if the queen were passing through the gardens. Now I hardly gave it a second thought. No one cared what my ass looked like. They were thinking of the game and nothing else until I lit a cigarette and my teammates asked me to put it out. You could be naked outdoors but apparently you couldn't smoke outdoors. What sense does that make?

Looking out my bedroom window, I can see the clubhouse and its parking area. This afternoon I watched as a large trailer pulled up, led by a four-door, late-model car bearing out-of-state license plates. This was someone arriving to park themselves and stay awhile. The car door opened and a man stepped out, completely naked. He'd been driving that way on the highway. I guess he just couldn't wait.

I went tonight to the clubhouse to watch TV and sat there alone for twenty minutes or so when Jacki, the bonneted woman from the *pétanque* court, traipsed naked from the bathroom, asking if I'd care to join her in the sauna. I had never before visited a sauna and wasn't quite sure what it involved. Did I need a bar of soap?

"A towel, silly. All you need is a towel. Now get those clothes off and get out there. I'll be waiting for you."

naked

268

Because it was delivered as an order, it seemed useless to argue. Sooner or later I would have to appear naked, and this seemed as good a time as any. I ran back to my trailer, grabbed a towel, and lowered my pants, thinking I might inspect my ass in the mirror but knowing that if I did, I'd never leave the house again. *Don't think about it, don't think about it, don't think about it.* I swabbed myself with a washcloth just for good measure and returned to the clubhouse, where I undressed in the bathroom, folding my clothes and piling them neatly on the countertop. *It's all right,* I thought, *this is a bathroom.* It's natural to be naked in a bathroom. It was not, however, quite so natural to *leave* the bathroom and walk past the tables and chairs of a clubhouse. Other people did it with no problem whatsoever, and look at them! Jacki had breezed through the room, and I'd looked at her as though she were a goat that had wandered into a hotel lobby. The tennis player had done it this afternoon. Thousands of people had walked naked through this room, eating lunch and playing cards. Now it was my turn! I tried looking at it as a privilege, and when that didn't work, I threw the towel over my shoulder, closed my eyes, and ran straight into the bookcase.

The sauna, a squat wooden hut, was located beside the pool. A stifling antechamber led to a sweltering hellhole heated by a smokeless cauldron filled with white-hot rocks. Jacki sat upon a wooden shelf, mopping at the sweat that ran down her breasts, over her considerable stomach, and collected in a puddle beneath her childlike, shaved vagina. She was a plump woman, tight as a tick, her head balanced on her shoulders with no discernible neck.

"Nasty bump you've got there on your forehead, Dave. You should put some ice on that before you go to bed tonight." She aimed a squeeze bottle toward the cauldron and released a stream of fragrant water upon the rocks, caus-

naked

269

ing the chamber to grow even hotter. "You like that?" she asked. "It's eucalyptus. I can't use it when Barb is here, because she's allergic, makes her facial cheeks swell up like they were stuffed with cotton. You're not allergic, are you? If so, you'd better run while you still have a chance. I threw my back out a few years ago and can't drag a cat, much less a full-grown man. The most I can do is run to the clubhouse and call out for help but even that will take me awhile. You could be dead by the time I get back — so make up your mind, are you allergic or not?"

I was not.

"Good." Once again she aimed her bottle toward the furnace. "Can you feel that? Eucalyptus is a healing ointment, very big back in ancient Greece and Egypt. It opened the sinuses of Socrates and King Ramses the Second, allowing them to concentrate on more important things like ... democracy and snakes. It frees the mind, eucalyptus. I get some wild thoughts here in the sauna, I don't mind telling you! Thoughts like, well, what if everybody in the world were allowed one wish, but in order to get it, it meant they'd have to crawl around on their hands and knees for the rest of their life? That's a real puzzler, isn't it! If you wanted to be rich, you'd have to crawl around your palace, just like a baby with your mink coat dragging the floor. World peace, a cure for cancer, an end to hunger and suffering, what'll it be? What's your wish?"

The eucalyptus had obviously not cleared my mind the way it had hers. Still, though, once the question had been introduced, I found it impossible not to think about it. If I could have the face and body of my dreams, what good would it do me if I had to walk around like an animal? Maybe if I were to wish for happiness, I wouldn't mind crawling — but what kind of a person would I be if I were naturally happy?

I've seen people like that on inspirational television shows, and they scare me. Why did I have to think about this in the first place? I looked over at Jacki's round, glistening face, her hands folded over her belly like a wizened, patient genie. "If I had one wish, I'd wish for an unlimited amount of wishes," I said.

She shook her head in a way that suggested she had heard this answer countless times before. "Don't get greedy on me, Dave, you only get one wish."

The room filled with steam, and in my woozy state, it occurred to me that this woman might actually possess some musty, supernatural power. The circumstances were so bizarre that maybe she *had* been sent to grant me my one, true desire. I thought of having my mother back, but often these are trick wishes. I might ask for my mother and receive an urnload of talking ashes that would complain bitterly at the sight of her son racing back and forth across the room like a bloodhound. Curing disease is a nice idea, but if we all got one wish, surely some enthusiastic fourteen-year-old would take care of that. "I'd wish," I said, "I'd wish I could fly."

"Fair enough." Jacki scratched a mosquito bite on her upper arm and sighed, "I have to go away this weekend and am definitely not looking forward to it at all. I'd live here year-round if I could, but my trailer's not winterized, and with this bad back, I wouldn't be able to shovel my driveway. It's gotten to the point where I hate to leave for any length of time. This coming weekend I have to go home for a church fund-raiser and then next Tuesday I leave for my granddaughter's birthday. I can tell by the look on your face that you're surprised by that one! Most everyone tells me I look too young to be a grandmother, but be that as it may, I've got three beautiful grandchildren and, oh, they used to love it out here."

Yes, but what about my wish? Had this been a trick question designed to test my character? What was she talking about her grandchildren for, and where were my clothes?

"The first time I brought them out here they saw Cliff Shirley standing over by the pool and said, 'Grandma,' they said, 'how come that man doesn't have any clothes on?' And I told them, 'That man is Grandma's special, special friend and he's naked because that's the way God brought him into this world. It's all right to be naked here, just don't mention it to your friends at school and, whatever you do, don't say anything about this to your mother and father.'" She frowned down at her breasts. "I should have known they couldn't keep a secret. My daughter's just like the rest of them, thinks we're some kind of sex fiends having orgies in the parking lot. And my son, forget it. I just tell him I'm going camping for the summer."

I felt I should offer her some kind of sympathy but wasn't sure where to start. Instead, I wound up asking her to explain the rule concerning body jewelry and intimate attire.

"Clothingwise, they're talking about thongs and negligees, anything that might be showy or suggestive. And the jewelry, it's all right to wear rings and necklaces and so forth, they just don't want any . . . Oh, Lord, how can I put this . . . If you have earrings, they should be in your ears — get it? It's against the rules to have any pierced . . . thingies, you know, either up top or down . . . there."

It struck me as odd that the subject had made her so uncomfortable. With sweat pooling just south of her shaved vagina, this grandmother could sit naked with a strange man but not for the life of her use the words *breast* or *penis*. We all just had "thingies," mine simmering in my lap like a boiled shrimp. It was acceptable to be naked but improper to acknowledge the details. This drastically reduced the number

naked

272

of conversational topics. The absence of clothing made it very hard to describe people. You couldn't say, "Who's the uncircumcised gentleman with all the hair on his ass?" What made it even harder was that most of the men were bald, which meant you couldn't even describe them by their hairstyle. I asked Jacki about a man I'd seen down by the fully stocked pond. "He was a tallish man with a . . . friendly face and a blue towel."

"Work with me," she said. "A lot of men have blue towels."

"He didn't have a mustache or a hat, or any hair. He was maybe in his seventies."

"Big scar across his stomach and another one running down his leg? Oh, that's Dan Champion from Lot Sixteen. Nice man, used to be quite a dancer."

I was relieved to know that it was socially acceptable to describe people by their scars. It was much easier than trying to identify them by their sandals.

Every few minutes Jacki would lean forward to shoot another stream of eucalyptus-laced water into the cauldron, and I found myself too weak to stop her. Sweat had blurred my vision, and the room had grown so unbearably hot that I could practically hear the blood bubbling in my veins. It occurred to me that I was going to die — not at some advanced, hypothetical stage in my life, but right now. My heart had been steamed, and I'd released so many gallons of sweat that my towel now weighed more than I did.

"Out with you," Jacki said. "Go on now, quick. Scoot."

I left the sauna, spread out my towel, and lay on the concrete patio beside the pool. It was a clear evening, chilly, but the air felt good. I heard a door slam and watched as Jacki waddled back to the clubhouse. She didn't see me lying there, and I saw no point in calling out to her. I'd be fine on my own, lying naked on the ground and thinking things over. From off in the distance came a mournful, lowing sound I couldn't quite identify. Neither quite natural nor manmade, it sounded like a combination of a sick cow and a foghorn. I'd heard it last night at around the same time and now came to think of it has the trailer park's version of "Taps."

Because of the pleasant weather, the tarp has been taken from the swimming pool, which is surrounded by comfortable reclining chairs, several of them positioned beneath a sign reading HANDICAPPED PARKING. It is a posted rule that you must be naked not only in the pool but also in the area surrounding it. This struck me as harsh. All I had on were sneakers and a T-shirt, but these things meant the world to me since, without them, I would be a freak. "The doctor will be right with you," I told myself. "Just lay your towel here on the recliner, remove your shoes and shirt, and he'll be here with the sedative as soon as he's finished with the other patients."

I stripped off my T-shirt and there I was, naked, easy prey for low-flying surveillance planes. Naked in broad daylight, surrounded by strangers who rolled from their backs to their stomachs, leafing through the pages of their books and magazines. The upswing was that I didn't have to look at myself. There were no mirrors or plate-glass windows, and as long as I looked straight ahead, I thought I'd be able to slowly ease into my public nudity. I had just gotten used to this idea when I was approached by a man named Dusty who had clothespinned a sheet of shirt cardboard to the brim of his sun visor in order to extend its shading capacities. The man was doubled over, stooped with osteoporosis, his back and shoulders burnished like fine Italian leather and his belly white from lack of sun. He wore his thick gray hair shaved

naked

274

close to his scalp and, to my horror, a pair of mirrored sunglasses that reflected with great clarity the sight of my pale, fidgety nakedness. I asked him a question about the hot tub, and twenty minutes later he was reflecting on the zoning ordinances of his hometown. "I don't think that legally they're allowed to build a grocery store in the neighborhood because it's not zoned for that. Oh, there used to be a little mom-and-pop operation where you could buy bread and soda and so forth, but that's been closed and turned into a little church for the snake handlers. You might could put up an apartment building, but first you'd have to check with the city council and see if they have some kind of restriction on occupancy. I suppose if it was a big enough complex, they might let you build some kind of grocery but not a big one because the neighborhood's not zoned for that."

Had I mistakenly introduced myself as a real estate speculator? Why couldn't he look away when he talked to me?

"Course, down in the city I guess you can build yourself an eight-story concrete beehive just so long as you have the money to pay everyone off. That's the way it goes where you come from, anything for a dollar. Then you come up here thinking we're all just a bunch of stupid hicks!" He mugged, widening his face into a spooky, exaggerated grin and running the tip of his tongue around the track of his lips. "We just a group of bumpkins, are we?"

Well, Dusty, now that you mention it . . .

He waved his hands as if he were casting a spell. "Oh, you're all just so sophisticated sitting in your little cafes and looking up at the Empire State Building while the rest of us lie around in haystacks smoking our corncob pipes. Is that it?"

His attitude was both hostile and playful and was shared by many of the people I had met so far. I might have arrived from a militant Muslim nation with no problem, but something about New York seemed to rub people the wrong way. This was a family campground and New York was, to many of them, the place where wholesome families were regularly shot for sport. I'd go out of my way to admire someone's trailer or praise the local countryside, but it was never enough. Dusty's mobile home was parked nearby, and I complimented him on keeping such a nice yard. "Pretty nice, isn't it?" he said.

"Very nice."

"What do you think of that toilet I use as a planter?"

"It's a cute idea, Dusty, and the flowers are beautiful."

"You're darn right they're beautiful. You know, back where you come from a person probably couldn't put a toilet in his front yard."

"No, Dusty, that probably wouldn't be a very good idea."

"It'd be filled with crap, that's what would happen! You'd have those New Yorkers lined up around the block waiting to shit in your front yard, but not here."

"No, not here."

"It's nice and quiet out here, isn't it? A person can hear himself think!"

I agreed with him, saying "Yes, it's wonderful. No car alarms or sirens. The only thing that gets to me is that loud farty sound I hear every night at sunset."

"You like that?" he said. "That's me! I've got a tube yea long and usually try to practice every night. Oh, it's not a trumpet, nothing fancy like that, just a length of plastic. Old Pete Manchester up to Lot Thirty-Seven, he's got what you call a conch shell that he holds up to his mouth and we kind of call back and forth to each other to pass the time. Most people, come nightfall, are inside their houses washing dishes, but not me. I have no dishes to wash because all I eat are raw vegetables. Yes, sir, I try to eat right and swim half a mile a day. If it's cloudy and the pool is covered, I just slip un-

naked

276

der the tarp when no one's looking! Of course, that won't be a problem today, will it?"

Dusty raised his leg, planting his foot on the edge of my lounge chair. "Yes, indeed, we've got ourselves some beautiful weather this afternoon. You're not likely to find a day like this where you come from."

I agreed with him.

"Sunshine, blue skies, and just a touch of breeze — it doesn't get any better than this." He adjusted his sunglasses and worried a bunion on his toe. There were maybe a dozen nudists taking in the sun. People came and went, walking clear around the pool in order to avoid Dusty, who would turn at the sound of the gate. "Phyllis!" he'd call. "When are you going to come by and see my turtles?"

"Cody and I have been meaning to do that, Dusty, it's just that we've been so busy building our new deck."

"Oh, I get it. What with your brand-new sundeck you're too high and mighty to be seen with me, is that it?"

On the other side of the pool, a stocky, handsome young man moved from his lounge chair to the sauna, to the hot tub, into the pool, and back to his chair. He was someone who had come in just for the day and seemed determined to get his twenty dollars' worth. Beside him sat the couple I'd seen on the tennis court, and next to them a wiry gray-haired woman leafed through a copy of *Sports Illustrated*. The two o'clock *pétanque* game had started, and I could hear the faint click of metal balls along with the familiar cry, "Great shot. High five, high five." The young man was on his fifth rotation, and I admired his ass, which was plump and unblemished, high and firm enough to support the first-prize trophy I'd mentally awarded him for Outstanding Physical Achievement.

"Have you ever seen a compost heap?" Dusty asked. "I've got one going in my backyard, and you'd be amazed at all the

naked

activity. All kinds of creatures show up to take a nibble or two: skunks, birds, itty-bitty chipmunks. Then, of course, you've got your flies and maggots, who like to burrow in once things gets nice and mushy."

I could feel myself burning, the flesh growing tight and dry. Reflected in Dusty's glasses I saw that my face had moved past its pink period and settled into a deep, fiery red.

"I'm sorry, Dusty, but I think I need to go back to my trailer and put on some lotion."

"Oh," he said, "is that your way of telling me I'm boring? What, I'm not exciting enough compared to all your friends back in the city?"

He continued to harass me as I put on my T-shirt and folded my towel. "Is that what they do back where you come from, walk away from people while they're talking to you?"

"Yes, Dusty, it is."

The initial excitement I'd felt had worn off, and it no longer seemed novel to walk around my trailer naked. My household nudity was becoming routine, and this for some reason frightened me. After barricading the door, I lay on my bed and tried to masturbate, just to remind my penis that it wasn't as free as it thought it was. Usually I have no problem completing this exercise, but suddenly I was having a hard time concentrating. I tried thinking of the young man beside the pool, but his body was repeatedly pushed off the stage, replaced by vivid images of Dusty, whose enormous testicles hung like a wasp's nest between his shriveled legs. I had never before experienced a sunburned penis and worried that my incessant tugging might have the same effect as rubbing together two dry sticks, the wisp of smoke leading to a sudden, violent flame. It became obvious that my penis had no intention of cooperating. I thought of forcing it but worried that the struggle might result in a blister that would drive me into hiding for the remainder of my stay. For the time being, my penis had the upper hand and lay upon its nest, gloating. "All right," I whispered. "You won this round. Enjoy it while you can because once we get back home I'm going to beat the living daylights out of you."

Returning naked from the sauna this evening, I passed a group of senior citizens who had gathered to watch a game show on the clubhouse TV.

"Ask for an *e!*" someone shouted at the screen. "I mean a *c*, ask for a *c*." The speaker was a rowdy white-haired woman with wrinkled, sun-cured skin the color and texture of a blond raisin. She wore nothing but a pair of bedroom slippers and a cardigan sweater she'd draped over her shoulders. "I meant a *b*, that's it, a *b*."

It's an odd sensation watching TV this way. Because they are dressed, the people on television seem even more remote than usual. It's as if they inhabit another world, something familiar but also closed off by high fences and aggressive border patrols.

"I wish this show was naked." The woman absentmindedly ran her fingers over the tabletop. "It would be so much better that way, don't you think? They could take all the money the hosts spend on clothes and make the prizes even bigger. I could play the nude version and make enough to — I don't know, maybe I'd have someone dredge me a lake and fill it with boats. I like boats, always did. There's nothing like a boat." She scratched at her arm, leaving white tracks that quickly faded, the skin resuming its natural color.

I like the idea of that, filming two separate versions of any given program, one clothed and the other tailored to capture what the network saw as its vast nudist audience.

"Do I have to?" Peter Jennings would ask.

naked

279

This is Friday and I awoke to a loud, grinding noise that turned out to be the owner's grandson circling my trailer on a riding lawn mower. He made several rotations before his mother ran up shouting, "What are you, an idiot out here mowing the grass this way? For God's sake, boy, lay a towel down on that seat!"

I went to the pool this morning and watched as a man removed his colostomy bag and taped a sheet of plastic over the hole before entering the water. I was thinking of how uncomfortable he must feel and turned to see a very old man who walked with a crutch and had no penis. It hadn't been shriveled by the water; he just didn't have one. His testicles were large and hairless, but where the penis should have been, there was only a small cavity. He noticed my staring and said only, "Hot enough for you?"

I'm trying not to aggravate my sunburn, so I spent my early afternoon in a T-shirt, wandering the grounds and noticing the great number of people who rarely visit the clubhouse or recreation areas. Here were men and women kneeling in their gardens and operating Weed Eaters, doing the same things other homeowners do but without the benefit of clothing. Sitting on the grass beside a concrete mermaid, a father and daughter strummed "Muskrat Love" on their guitars while a middle-aged woman hummed along, washing her hair and rinsing off the lather with a garden hose. On the playground a freckle-faced child stood alone in the plywood tower, lifting a plastic bucket filled with stones. A man lit a charcoal fire in his backyard grill. He had protected his chest with an apron reading "World's Greatest Chef" and used his spatula to startle a fly off his ass. Nudist life was just as mundane as any other, perhaps even more so as its practice demands that you never leave the grounds. The clothed world was out there, just beyond the front gate. They had restaurants there, and movie theaters, a wide variety of distractions my neighbors had surrendered in exchange for the opportunity to grill chicken breasts in the nude. Obviously, I was missing something. I had washed dishes naked and eaten in the clubhouse, picking potato-chip crumbs out of my pubic hair and wondering what all the fuss was about. I have played games naked and watched TV naked and afterward I have yawned naked, finding my sigh no different than any previous expression of boredom. I hear people say, "Why go into town for lunch when we can stay here and be naked?" A person might enjoy golf or fishing, but that doesn't stop them from visiting a department store or Chinese restaurant. I suppose if you're a die-hard nudist, you can't really *go* anywhere except for the few parks and isolated beaches that will have you.

Everyone's very excited about the coming weekend, which brings a large, reportedly younger crowd of day visitors and trailer owners who haven't yet retired. I went late this afternoon to the sundeck overlooking the pool, where I met a fun couple in their late thirties. Duke and Roberta own a lawn-maintenance company and were just beginning their week-long vacation. At thirty-six, Roberta is already a three-time grandmother. Duke, her third husband, is tattooed with sports cars, top hats, and beautiful women. Everything he can't have in real life is pictured on his arms, back, and chest. The nudist park management frowns upon drinking, but the couple sat defiantly working their way through their third six-pack, the empty cans stacked in a bee-covered pyramid on one of the surrounding tables.

"Duke here is the big nudist," she said. "It took him two

years to get me down here, and then, last summer, we finally bought our own trailer. It's been great except for all the god-damned snobs. Some of these snoots have got their noses so high in the air, they're choking on their own snot. They're up there on Snob Hill with their eighty-thousand-dollar trailers and jazzed-up golf carts, thinking their shit smells better than ours. Some of these bitches . . ."

Duke patted her arm and nodded at the white-haired woman staring in our direction.

"What?" she said. "I can say the word *bitch*. It's a female dog. Look it up in the dictionary, fuck face." She beckoned me close. "They don't allow cursing here, so you really have to watch what you say. Some of these old fuckers will turn you in, just like that." She tried to snap her fingers but they were coated with suntan oil and produced only a weak, slapping sound. Roberta filled me in on everyone, moving from anger to a drunk, sloppy sentimentality I would have found repellent had I not liked her so much. "Look at me," she said, blinking back a tear. "My goddamned tits sagging halfway down to my knees, rolls of fat hanging off the sides of my chair, but what the fuck, I'm happy, right?" Without warn-ing, she grabbed my sunburned face and hugged it to her breast. A thimble-sized nipple poked me in the eye, and she held me tight, rocking my head as though it were a baby.

I've noticed that when forced to go into town, the costumed nudists appear ornery and uncomfortable, like cats stuffed into little outfits for the sake of a wacky photograph. They claw at their buttons and zippers, their eyes wild and desper-ate. Because clothing doesn't interest them, most of these people are liable to wear anything: stripes with checks, pants three sizes too large or small — it simply doesn't matter to them. This morning I saw a woman wear her sweatshirt toga-style, the neck stretched beneath her arm in order to re-

naked

veal a single breast. I've seen a lot of warm-up suits, which many of the couples tend to view as two separate outfits. On the cooler mornings the wife wears the bottoms while her husband takes the top. I'm wondering if it isn't the complete inability to throw together an outfit that turned these people nudist in the first place. Coming here from New York, it is heartening to walk into a room and know you're not being judged by your clothes. Still, though, as bad a dresser as I am, anything beats being judged by my character.

Tonight is the scheduled Hobo Slumgullion, and we were instructed to bring a canned vegetable to the pavilion no later than noon. I took the only canned good I'd bought at the grocery store and carried it down the hill, where I found two naked women wearing chef's hats and stirring a kettle of ground beef and water.

"Just pray nobody brings any more corn," the heavier woman said. "We got corn coming out the yin yang."

I set down my can of corn and asked what they meant by "hobo slumgullion."

"It's a stew. This here is the base, and we add whatever people bring, which in your case, is corn. Come five o'clock everyone will dress like a hobo and we'll eat out of tin cans. There's even a prize for the best costume. It's fun. You'll see."

When I returned that evening for the slumgullion, close to a hundred people sat eating out of cans. One man had smeared some charcoal on his cheeks. He wore a tie and tattered sports coat and carried a stick onto which he had fastened a plastic grocery bag. Everyone else was naked, so he won the prize for best costume.

While eating my dinner I spoke to a small, topless mother of four grown children who said, "Oh, you should have been here for last year's pudding toss."

naked

283

"I beg your pardon?" *Pudding toss.* I thought it must be some nudist term for a potluck supper. Pudding isn't conducive to being tossed, is it? "Oh no, you can toss it, you just can't catch it!" She chuckled, mopping the inside of her can with a slice of bread. "What we do is make the pudding in five-gallon tubs and carry it out to the field, where we have the chocolate team against the vanillas. Then we just dig in and start pitching it at one another and, oh, what a time we had. Some good times! Bees and flies pretty much occupied the field for the next few weeks. A lot of people got stung, so we won't be doing it this year." She studied her crust of bread for a moment or two. "I keep thinking that maybe if we'd used diet pudding, this wouldn't have happened but no, no, I just have to put it out of my mind and move on. Let it go, I have to let it go."

Her husband gently patted her hand. So real was her grief that you'd think she had lost a child rather than an opportunity to sling a fistful of pudding.

This is Sunday and looking out my bedroom window, I've noticed that a lot of today's visitors have spent the morning in church. Men, women, and children stand beside their cars stripping off their sober costumes. The suit jackets and dresses are carefully folded and placed into backseats. This would be a terrible place to get locked out of your car, as the nearest coat hanger is probably a good fifteen miles away. It's probably not a good place to find an iron either, but if you're searching for a Bible you'll have no problem. The clubhouse shelves are lined with religious books and pamphlets, and several of the campers attended the recent Christian Nudists Conference held at a resort in eastern North Carolina. One of today's visitors was a Presbyterian minister, a plump, freckle-faced man with Daffy Duck tattooed on his ass. He wore it with a swagger, calling attention to a body part the Lord had clearly not blessed with muscle tone or unblemished skin. The duck's beak was distended and he appeared to be picking at a rash of strawberries.

There were quite a few new faces today. A black man arrived in the company of two enormous white women whose bodies were dual masses of rolling, dimpled flesh. Fat spilled over their knees, and their stomachs fell like heavy sacks of birdseed, covering their vaginas and hanging halfway down their thighs. Legs like tree trunks led straight into sandals with no mention of ankle or discernible calf. The women went unnoticed, but not the man. "Who's the colored guy?" everyone asked. It was as though he carried a spear and wore a necklace fashioned from shrunken heads. There was speculation that he was a pimp or white slaver who'd come from the city in search of naive nudist girls. I was beside the pool when the black man, speaking to Dusty, mentioned that he had two sons at Penn State.

"That's tough," Dusty said. "I've got a nephew in prison myself and I know just what you're going through. When are your boys getting out?"

This was the first day I'd left the house completely naked without even thinking of wearing a T-shirt. Suddenly it felt normal to tuck my cigarettes into my socks and head out the door carrying nothing but a towel. We'd had an overcast day, the sky a flat, mustard color. Just when I'd surrendered any hope of refreshing my tan, the sun came out and hundreds of people flocked to the pool area. The air filled with the scent of tanning lotion, and from the playground to the *pétanque* court, there was a genuine outpouring of goodwill. The deck and sunning corral were filled to capacity, and I wandered around, searching for a place to lay down my towel. Duke and Roberta had a table near the hot tub, and I joined them as they sat listening to a slim woman in her early fifties. The woman spoke about a nudist resort in Arizona that charges only five dollars a night for camping privileges. "And," she said, "get this, they'll even pick you up at the airport and drive you to the grounds free of charge! It's a marvelous place, and the people? I mean to say there are some *great* naked people out in Arizona, and don't let anyone tell you any different."

I listened to her for a good ten minutes before realizing that she was missing her left nipple. Not the breast, just the nipple. The surgeons had done an excellent job, and the scar was slight, resembling a short length of fishing wire. It was like discovering that someone had six fingers instead of five. Had she been the first nudist I'd met, I would have noticed it immediately, but part of feeling at ease with my own nudity involved not noticing it in others.

"Betsy's real people," Roberta said after the woman had left. "And I like what she's done with her cunt. It's a cute look. Wouldn't work for me, but than again I'm bigger-boned."

I hadn't noticed anything out of the ordinary and I looked over the edge of the deck, where the woman stood speaking to the visiting minister.

"There are some sweet naked people out in Arizona, and they'll drive you to camp grounds free of charge," she said. I saw then that she had shaved all her pubic hair except for a brief, Hitler-style mustache. The exposed, lotion-coated vagina resembled one of those shiny plastic coin purses given away by banks and car dealers and carried only by the very young or very old. The phrase, *keep the change*, came to mind. I've been here for almost a week and still haven't figured out this shaving business. It is common to see men with five o'clock shadows on their faces but fresh, bleeding razor

naked

nicks on their bald testicles. Is it done to expedite the search for ticks, or are these men and women shaving away the gray in the hope that they might appear younger?

"It's to keep the hairs off the furniture," Roberta said. "Personally, I'd just as soon suck it up with a Dustbuster, but what the fuck. To each his own. You might save a little time on the cleaning, but when you consider all those hours spent shaving, I don't know that it's really all that efficient. Maybe it's better to just buy a sofa that matches your hair color, that way you can forget about both the shaving *and* the cleaning. That's what I've done and I ain't hearing no complaints, right, Duke?"

This was my last morning at the nudist park. Returning from the sauna last night, I saw a naked woman run from my trailer and jump into a waiting car. It had been Roberta, and she'd left a note, inviting me to join her and Duke for breakfast. Before arriving here, I tried to imagine what it might be like to go to someone's house for a meal. According to my mother, it was fine to use your plate as an ashtray but under no circumstances should you ever enter anyone's home barefoot. With this in mind, I wore sneakers and, on the off chance they dressed for meals, carried a canvas bag I'd packed with a towel, shirt, and a pair of shorts. I arrived to find my hosts seated naked in their kitchenette playing SuperNintendo and listening to one of those early-morning wise guys on the radio. Unlike my trailer, which was grounded to the earth, theirs was designed to be pulled behind a car, and it sat parked upon a tiny lawn, its wheels blocked with bricks so that it wouldn't roll down the hill.

"Why so formal?" Duke asked. "Take off your shoes and stay awhile."

We wedged ourselves around a tiny, built-in table, and Roberta presented a pillow-size omelette, filled, she said,

naked

287

"with all kinds of shit. There might even be some cat litter in here, for all I know. We left the fuckers back at our apartment in town but that stuff has a way of working itself into the damnedest places. Oh well, eat up everybody."

Every now and then someone will offer some little bit of information that suddenly changes everything. I asked how many cats they had, and Roberta pulled out a pencil and notepad. "Let's see, seventeen plus twelve minus two plus the one that asshole gave back after it shit on his rug." She squinted at the paper, struggling with the figures. "Twenty-eight. We had twenty-eight cats the last time I checked, but that was a few days ago. Coppertone dropped eight kittens last month, and I was trying to deal with those fuckers when what's-her-name, the crippled one, had four babies right there on the goddamned bed while Duke and I were getting it on."

She shrugged, mystified. "I don't know where the damn things come from. Got ourselves a bunch of horny cats, I guess. Duke here drove one of the mothers out into the country and booted her out once he came to a nice-looking farmhouse. Thirty miles he took her, but one week later the little bitch was back shredding up the furniture as if nothing had ever happened. What can you do?"

A blackened mushroom dropped from my hostess's mouth and settled onto her breast.

There was with Roberta, and with everyone else I'd met, something larger and more definitive than her nudity. People were stamp collectors and gardeners, ham radio operators, registered nurses, and big-time pet owners. It was no different than anywhere else, except that while describing their passions, these people just happened to be naked. They lived in cans rather than houses and considered themselves fortunate when a warm, sunny day allowed them to leave

naked

their homes and walk among people who shared at least one of their interests. It's not too much to ask for, and if they've accidentally dropped some cat litter into the omelette, then so be it.

Nudism didn't cause me to love my body, it simply allowed me to accept my position in what is clearly the scheme of things. Take a seat beside an eighty-year-old man and you can see the sagging, age-spotted body that awaits you. Rather than inciting panic, this truth seems to have a calming effect. Marching toward the clubhouse with a multitude of naked strangers, I felt the proceedings should be narrated by one of those hushed, scholarly voices commonly used for television nature programs.

I'd planned to take a cab to the bus station but was offered a ride by Jacki and Millie. This was the first time in a week that I had to get dressed. Clothing was no longer optional. Now it was mandatory, and I found myself resenting it. Turn your back on a pair of pants and things can get nasty. We rode into town, each of us tugging at our clothing. Jacki had a bumper sticker on her car that read, "Nudist on board!" and I noticed other motorists follow closely before pulling up beside us, their faces registering profound disappointment. Had we been naked, they probably would have vomited blood. It is ironic that nudists are just about the last people you'd ever want to see naked.

During the ride into town Millie reflected upon the upcoming sunbathers' convention set to take place next week in Massachusetts. "That's where I married Phil," she said, referring to her second husband. "My four sons gave me away, just as nude and beautiful as they could be. They used to be so much fun, my children. We'd go to all kinds of nude parks and beaches, but then they got older and married clothes-minded girls who won't have anything to do with my way of life." She shook her head and scowled at the passing land-scape. "Why did they have to go and marry girls like that? You try to raise them right and look what happens."

This was the lament of any parent. You try to raise your children right, and look what happens. Jacki had the same problem: the children she had raised naked now spent all their money on clothes. They'd never even seen her new trailer. How had it happened? When had they decided it was wrong to see their mother naked, standing beside the sink or kneeling to wipe out the inside of a garbage can? Was it a specific event that had set them off?

"Beats me," Millie said. "Maybe I'll ask them that question the next time they call asking for money."

The women dropped me off at the bus station with twenty minutes to spare, and I raced up and down the street, passing college students in baggy, knee-length shorts and bank tellers wearing navy blue suits. For the first time in what felt like years, I saw stockings and handbags. Bodies, fat and thin, were packed into slacks and pleated skirts. Every outfit re-sembled a costume designed to reveal the aspirations of the wearer. The young man on the curb would like to make the first Olympic skateboarding team. The girl in the plastic skirt longs to live in a larger town. I found myself looking at these people and thinking, *I know what you look like naked. I can tell by your ankles and the tightness of your belt. The flush of your face, the hair sprouting from your collar, the way your shirts hang off those bony hips: you can't hide it from me.*

It was as though I'd received the true version of the X-ray specs I'd ordered as a child. The glasses were advertised in the back pages of comic books and promised the ability to see through clothing. I'd counted the days until they arrived and was clinically disappointed to discover that I'd been cheated. These were black plastic frames supporting cardboard lenses. The eyeballs were rendered to appear bloodshot, and the

naked

pupils were tiny peepholes backed by plain red acetate. The glasses, when worn, gave me the look of someone both enthused and exhausted by what he saw. They suggested the manic weariness inherent in their promise, capturing the moment when the sheen wears off and your newfound gift becomes something more closely resembling a burden.